MOVING AHEAD WITH ISO 14000

WILEY SERIES IN ENVIRONMENTAL QUALITY MANAGEMENT

John T. Willig, Series Editor

AUDITING FOR ENVIRONMENTAL QUALITY LEADERSHIP: BEYOND COMPLIANCE TO ENVIRONMENTAL EXCELLENCE

John T. Willig, Editor

STRATEGIC ENVIRONMENTAL MANAGEMENT: USING TQEM AND ISO 14000 FOR COMPETITIVE ADVANTAGE

Grace Wever, Ph.D.

THE ISO 14000 IMPLEMENTATION GUIDE: CREATING AN INTEGRATED MANAGEMENT SYSTEM

Suzan L. Jackson

MOVING AHEAD WITH ISO 14000: IMPROVING ENVIRONMENTAL MANAGEMENT AND ADVANCING SUSTAINABLE DEVELOPMENT

Philip Marcus and John T. Willig

MOVING AHEAD WITH ISO 14000

Improving Environmental Management and Advancing Sustainable Development

Edited by
Philip A. Marcus
and
John T. Willig

JOHN WILEY & SONS, INC.
New York • Chichester • Weinheim • Brisbane • Singapore • Toronto

Copyright © 1997 by John Wiley & Sons, Inc.

Library of Congress Cataloging in Publication Data:

Marcus, Philip A.
    Moving ahead with ISO 14000 : improving environmental management
and advancing sustainable development / Philip A. Marcus, John T.
Willig.
        p.   cm.—(Wiley series in environmental quality management)
    Includes index.
    ISBN 0-471-16877-7 (cloth : alk. paper)
    1. ISO 14000 Series Standards.   2. Manufactures—Environmental
aspects.   3. Sustainable development.   I. Willig, John T.
II. Title.   III. Series.
TS155.7.M3339   1997
658.4'08—dc20   96-41848

Printed in the United States of America

10 9 8 7 6 5 4 3 2 1

Contents

SECTION TWO

Gaining Support Throughout Your Company—Improving Environmental and Business Performance

SECTION THREE

Registration, Certification, and Implementation Issues

SECTION FOUR

Implementation and Integration Issues, Impacts, and Tools

SECTION FIVE

Advancing Sustainable Development and Creating Competitive Advantage

PART I: STRATEGIES AND TOOLS

Contributors

Braden R. Allenby
AT&T, Engineering Research Center
Princeton, NJ 08542

Thomas P. Ambrose
125 Grey Fox Run
Chagrin Fall, OH 44022

Howard N. Apsan
Clayton Environmental Consultants, Inc.
160 Fieldcrest Avenue
Edison, NJ 08837

Paul E. Bailey
ICF Kaiser
9300 Lee Highway
Fairfax, VA 22031-1207

Henry R. Balikov
Environmental Management &
   Compliance Assurance Services
TLI Systems, Inc.
Centre Square East
1500 Market Street, 12th Floor
Philadelphia, PA 19102

Dr. Pamela J. Bridgen
10334 48th Ave., N.E.
Seattle, WA 98125-8130

Linda G. Brown
Scientific Certification Systems
The Ordway Building
One Kaiser Plaza Suite 901
Oakland, CA 94612

David Burdick
37925 NE Vernon Road
Washougal, WA 98671

Lawrence B. Cahill
Environmental Resources Management,
   Inc.
855 Springdale Dr.
Exton, PA 19341

Judith A. Cichowicz
Compliance Systems, Inc.
2701 California Avenue, Suite 209
Seattle, WA 98116

Barry F. Dambach
Global Manufacturing and Engineering
Lucent Technologies
Basking Ridge, NJ 07920

Craig P. Diamond
NSF International
3475 Plymouth Road
Ann Arbor, MI 48113

Jim Dray
RPM Systems
50 Elm Street
New Haven, CT 06510

John R. Ehrenfeld
MIT-CTPID
1 Amherst Street
Bldg E 40-207
Cambridge, MA 02139

Bob Ferrone
87 Lura Lane
Waltham, MA 02154

Scott Foster
Wiggin & Dana Counsellors at Law
One Century Tower
New Haven, CT 06508-1832

Ellen A. Huang
Associate Research Engineer
United Technologies Research Center
411 Silver Lane
East Hartford, CT 06108

David J. Hunkeler
US-Japan Center for Technology
    Management
Vanderbilt University
Nashville, TN 37235

Lynn Johannson
E2 Management Corp.
113 Mountainview Road South
Georgetown, Ontario
CANADA L7G 4K2

Rodger A. Jump
Proforma West Limited
7475 Dakin Street Suite 600
Denver, CO 80221-6926

Robert J. Kainz
Chrysler Corporation
800 Chrysler Drive
Auburn Hills, MI 48326-2757

Michael Lenox
MIT-CTPID
1 Amherst Street
Bldg E 40-207
Cambridge, MA 02139

Philip A. Marcus
ICF Incorporated
9300 Lee Highway
Fairfax, VA 22031

Monica H. Prokopyshen
Chrysler Corporation
800 Chrysler Drive
Auburn Hills, MI 48326-2757

Stanley P. Rhodes, Ph.D.
President and CEO
Scientific Certification Systems
The Ordway Building
One Kaiser Plaza Suite 901
Oakland, CA 94612

James E. Rogers
Cinergy Corp
139 East Fourth Street
Cincinnati, OH 45201-0960

Dawne P. Schomer
Texas Instruments
8330 LBJ Freeway
MS 8363
Dallas, TX 75243

Peter A. Soyka
ICF Kaiser
9300 Lee Highway
Fairfax, VA 22031-1207

Cynthia A. Unger
Coopers & Lybrand
370 17th Street Suite 3300
Denver, CO 80202-5633

Stephen A. Watson, III, Esq.
Foster Wheeler Environmental
1290 Wall Street W.
Lyndhurst, NJ 07071

John T. Willig
920 Riverview Drive
Brielle, NJ 08730

Susan A. Yester
Chrysler Corporation
800 Chrysler Drive
Auburn Hills, MI 48326-2757

Introduction

The release of the new ISO 14000 standards on environmental management is a watershed event for environmental professionals and their companies. Businesses of all sizes will need to face what is expected to become the de facto international standard for proactive environmental practices and a requirement for conducting business overseas.

In the United States, at least, there have been two major drivers forcing companies to consider adopting the ISO 14000 standards: first, continued access to markets and customers who require conformance to the standard as a condition of business, and second, the interest of regulators in adopting the ISO 14001 environmental management systems standard in regulatory reform initiatives at the federal and state levels.

ISO 14000 has been described as the new global passport for international trade. A prime motivation for seeking conformance with the ISO 14001 environmental management systems specification is concern that companies not willing to move ahead with ISO 14000 may do so at their own peril.

The extent of worldwide participation in the development of the ISO environmental standards under the auspices of Technical Committee 207 is ample evidence of this. Hundreds of delegates and technical experts from over 50 nations have been engaged in the drafting and approval of the standards. These delegates and experts represent the entire cross-section of stakeholders with environmental concerns, including government, standards bodies, business and environmental groups.

Since 1995, as a result of the drafting and approval of the ISO 14001 environmental management systems (EMS) specification, countries and organizations from every continent have been performing assessments and conducting pilots to prepare to conform to the specification. Their motivations vary. In some regions, the ISO 14001 standard is seen as putting up a potential barrier to trade. For others, the adherence to the EMS specification offers an opportunity to develop an effective EMS that can demonstrate a reasonable standard of environmental care. For governments, and not only those in developing countries, the ISO 14001 standard offers an alternative approach to the command-and-control regulatory model increasingly seen by critics as expensive, awkward, and outmoded.

At the same time, certain groups are skeptical about the benefits of the ISO 14000 standards. Companies wonder if adhering to these voluntary standards will bring them regulatory relief and credit from various stakeholder groups. Depending on the government agency, this issue is far from decided. The recent and continuing debate in the United States over auditing privileges and disclosure highlights how, in the environmental field, good intentions can always lead to rancor.

Environmental organizations are, for the most part, reserving support for the standards. They want to see actual environmental performance improvements that are to accrue from the adoption of ISO standards. These groups are also concerned that ISO 14000 may roll back the environmental gains won over the past several decades through regulation and enforcement.

Many experts predict that the impact of these standards will surpass the extensive adoption of the ISO 9000 quality standards. More than 75,000 companies worldwide have achieved official ISO 9000 registration. The results of a recent A.D. Little survey shows that the interest in ISO 14000 will be equally high. Eighty-five percent of the respondents said it was critical for their environmental management systems to meet the standards, even if they did not seek actual certification. Some leading companies have already announced they are applying the standards to their business practices and benchmarking operations. In some regions of the world, tax incentives for ISO 14001-certified companies have already been proposed and are being discussed.

To help managers and companies meet these ISO 14000 challenges, 30 environmental authorities have joined together to put together this new book. In it, you will find expert guidance on a wide array of topics and pressing issues needed to successfully understand, initiate, and implement an ISO 14000 program.

The chapters have been prepared with a keen eye on how these potentially costly efforts will help companies improve their business performance through the enhanced eco-efficiency of their operations. Eco-efficiency refers to the concept developed by Stephen Schmidheiny and others of increasing value added at the enterprise level while decreasing pollution and resource use.[1] The collective consequence of widespread adoption of the concept of eco-efficiency may be to advance the ill-defined but imperative demand for global sustainable development. If the adoption of ISO 14000 worldwide can provide a platform for initiatives to define and incorporate eco-efficiency into business operations, then the international effort to develop the standards may well be justified.

In fact, we may be seeing the evolution of a new framework for the contribution of environmental management into organization's operations. The figures below present a three-stage model of ISO 14000 leading to eco-efficiency. In stage I, ISO 14001 registration provides for contractual and business relations on a two-party basis. Registration, self-declaration, and the like assure the contracting party that their supplier is operating its environmental activities in conformance with the EMS standard. Similarly to ISO 9000, stage I represents a purely voluntary private relationship. The benefits include continued access to markets and retention of preferred supplier status, among others.

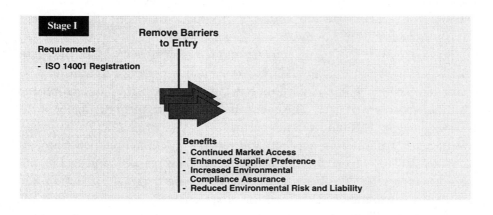

Stage I

Requirements

- ISO 14001 Registration

Remove Barriers to Entry

Benefits
- Continued Market Access
- Enhanced Supplier Preference
- Increased Environmental Compliance Assurance
- Reduced Environmental Risk and Liability

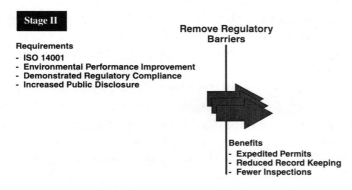

Stage II

Requirements

- ISO 14001
- Environmental Performance Improvement
- Demonstrated Regulatory Compliance
- Increased Public Disclosure

Remove Regulatory Barriers

Benefits
- Expedited Permits
- Reduced Record Keeping
- Fewer Inspections

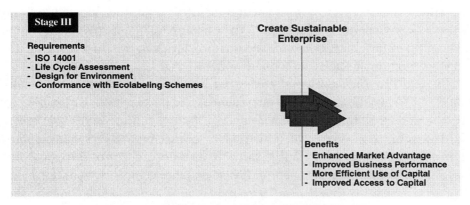

Stage III

Requirements

- ISO 14001
- Life Cycle Assessment
- Design for Environment
- Conformance with Ecolabeling Schemes

Create Sustainable Enterprise

Benefits
- Enhanced Market Advantage
- Improved Business Performance
- More Efficient Use of Capital
- Improved Access to Capital

Figure 1.1 Path to Eco-efficiency Through ISO 14000

In stage II, ISO 14001 registration may be accompanied by other requirements, including demonstration and publication of improved environmental performance beyond that demanded by regulations. Organizations may gain a number of benefits from government in exchange for this greater level of environmental commitment, including fewer audits or inspections, less burdensome recordkeeping, and expedited permitting. This outline of the use of ISO 14000 in the regulatory relationship is not confined to the United States alone, but is being considered worldwide.

Stage III represents a significant transition to eco-efficiency. Here, the enterprise or organization uses the ISO 14000 standards not only to transform its relationship with clients and government, but also to transform its relationship with the environment itself. The enterprise adopts and integrates many of the ISO standards into its fundamental business processes of product design, operations, and distribution of products and services. The potential benefit to the company may be enhanced customer preference, new markets, and greater production efficiencies. The benefit to society may be decreased pollution and improved conservation of energy and natural resources.

ISO 14000 will involve many critical investment and implementation decisions. Integrating environmental factors into broader business management systems and decision making will be, for many companies, a long process of change and improvement. We have, therefore, developed this book from the perspective of managers needing support throughout their companies to maximize the benefits of moving ahead with ISO 14000. Our experts have provided timely insights, case studies, assessment checklists, and essential guidelines to help companies take advantage of ISO 14000 in improving their environmental performance and enhancing global trade opportunities.

Section One: A New Global Challenge—Voluntary Management Standards looks at why companies need to respond to the new standards from a global business perspective. A country-by-country guide to specific government and industry initiatives is a compelling call to action for firms beginning to analyze ISO's impact. Many company studies from the ongoing NSF implementation initiative of voluntary management standards provides valuable insights into the implementation obstacles and opportunities.

Section Two: Gaining Support Throughout Your Company examines how managers can "make the case" to top management and other critical groups affected by the standards. Integrating environmental factors and investment decisions into other functional areas will initiate a long change process for many corporations. These chapters show managers what to consider in their cost/benefit analyses and highlight other ISO opportunities to enhance competitive positions.

Section Three: Registration and Implementation Strategies details the how and why of implementing ISO 14000 and provides a first course on the registration process. Leading experts offer valuable guidelines to help companies optimize all of their resources to make this initiative cost effective. Most companies spend more time doing over what they could have successfully planned. These chapters show what needs to be discussed before and after taking the critical ISO path.

Section Four: Implementation and Integration Issues, Impacts, and Tools gives vital information on how various groups will be affected by the new efforts and shows how companies can leverage their present resources and systems to make the most out of the ISO investment. It shows what needs to be done to link current policies and systems effectively. Given the cost of quality programs and other management initiatives such as reengineering, managers will want to know how ISO will impact their operations. These chapters offer companies many ways to implement and integrate without imploding.

Section Five: Advancing Sustainable Development and Creating Competitive Advantage presents many timely contributions from industry experts that show what needs to be done to continue the ISO momentum by using new tools for environmental and business decision making. How companies can rethink and enhance their accounting, design, and manufacturing practices to improve their environmental report card and contribute to the ISO 14000 goal increased sustainability is thoroughly covered. Life-cycle assessment tools bring together many key players within organizations and have been embraced by many global companies as a means to create greater competitive advantage. These chapters show managers what they need to know to continue moving ahead of their global competitors.

The editors would like to take this opportunity to thank all of the contributors who have generously given their time to prepare these chapters for their colleagues in the environmental and business community. Our numerous discussions have helped bring forward the most useful information firms will need to make the most of their ISO 14000 efforts and navigate to new shores. We would also like to thank the staff of professionals at John Wiley & Sons—in particular, Dan Sayre, Diana Cisek, and Donna Conte—for all of their enthusiasm, patience, and thoughtful guidance.

Notes

1. Stephen Schmidheiny and Frederico J.L. Zorraquin, *Financing Change, The Financial Community, Eco-efficiency and Sustainable Development,* (Cambridge, MA: MIT Press, 1996).

MOVING AHEAD WITH ISO 14000

A New Global Challenge—
Voluntary Management Standards

In this section, we look at why companies need to respond to the new standards from a global business perspective. With international trade ramifications, companies should now be assessing their strategies. Jim Rogers and Henry Balikov present compelling arguments for companies to take a proactive position. Pam Bridgen shows how governments and industries from around the world have responded and who has taken the lead. Lynn Johannson and Craig Diamond detail how companies have piloted the new guidelines and are proving there is much to gain from moving ahead.

1

ISO 14000: The Worldwide Response from Industry and Governments

Pamela J. Bridgen

The overall response around the world to the ISO 14000 series of standards for environmental management systems, eco-labeling and life-cycle analysis appears to be generally positive. There is, however, a range of reactions based on the degree of awareness of the ISO 14000 standards and the process for their development. Many developing countries have little or nothing in the way of environmental legislation and regulations. These countries, generally, are the least familiar with ISO 14000 and have had minimal involvement in the development of the standards, which may lead to concerns regarding their applicability. Recently, however, awareness of ISO 14000 has increased dramatically, and in the ISO 14000 meeting in Rio in June 1996, an ad hoc group on implementation in developing countries was being initiated.

There appears to be more movement toward the implementation of these standards in countries where industry perceives that the relative importance of the global marketplace is high compared to that of the domestic market. However, there is ubiquitous interest on the part of both governments and industry in moving from command-and-control environmental regulation, which is very inefficient and costly, to voluntary environmental management systems that can be more flexible and result in improved environmental protection.

In Europe, a complex situation has arisen due to a perceived conflict between ISO 14001 and the Eco-Management and Audit Scheme (EMAS), which is a European Union regulation that became effective in July 1993. Currently, the program is voluntary, but companies are concerned that it may become mandatory. Hundreds of companies in Europe are already certified under EMAS, and it is being implemented widely. The debate is fueled by the need to limit the number of different standards to a minimum—indeed, a single global standard is the ideal. Currently, the European Commission is considering whether ISO 14000 could be accepted as a part of EMAS. The expectation is that EMAS and ISO 14000 standards will ultimately merge, with the most useful aspects of each being incorporated into the surviving global standard.

North and South American Responses

In the United States, the government is experimenting with the applicability and usefulness of ISO 14000. There is considerable pressure to cut down on the bureaucracy within the government and a desire to move in that direction. Thus, government agencies are considering alternate regulatory schemes that are voluntary on the part of industry and do not rely on command-and-control. The government recognizes that there needs to be some quid pro quo in terms of regulatory relief—for example, fewer audits and inspections for ISO 14000-compliant companies. A dual-track approach is being considered, which would impose command-and-control where it appears to be required and have a separate, voluntary track for companies that appear to have the right attitude to environmental management systems (EMS). This may lead to new legislation.

There is concern, however, regarding the reaction of environmentalists and the general public and their degree of comfort with such an approach. U.S. industry currently is evaluating whether the ISO 14000 standards will provide it with any tangible benefits, particularly in the areas of regulation and trade. The approach at this time is cautious. Also there is considerable interest, there is also a reluctance on the part of most companies to make an investment in the process until customers start to demand participation or they can see a direct commercial advantage. Some companies are moving ahead to position themselves for ISO 14001 certification in order to be at the forefront and to meet the requirements before they develop to a greater degree of complexity.

The Canadian government, at both the federal and provincial levels, has been looking at better environmental protection management; there have been discussions about the need to find innovative approaches to this issue. The government considers ISO 14000 to be a good indication of change in the corporate culture. There has been some consideration given to the government's relaxation of enforcement and inspections for companies that have acquired certification. There is a broad spectrum of views on ISO 14000 in Canadian industry, which has learned the hard way by waiting for the government to provide controls in the past (which have proven to be very expensive to implement). Industry in Canada is starting to realize that the ISO 14001 auditing standards will soon become international standards and that certification will be essential to operate successfully in the global marketplace. In Canada, a significant number of customers are starting to demand that the standards be met, so companies are looking ahead to position themselves for certification.

In South America, awareness of ISO 14000 has increased significantly of late. Brazil has been most involved in the ISO 14000 process, as evidenced by the hosting of the ISO 14000 meeting in Rio de Janeiro in June 1996 and the support from the Ministry of the Environment. The Brazilian government recognizes that the standards will help to improve the relationship between environmental regulations and economic activities, and expects benefits from the proactive approach of ISO 14000. It will, however, maintain the command-and-control approach, at least in the near future. Large companies in Brazil can see a competitive advantage from certification. Thirty-three companies and a number of other entities have formed the Environmental Standardization Supporting Group (GANA). Industry expects that certification will assist in increasing global market share, improve access to credit with a low interest rate, improve government and public relations, present a positive environmental image, and provide a rationalization of environmental costs. There is, however, some concern regarding the costs of implementation and the potential for the ISO 14000 standards to be formulated in such a way as to promote trade barriers. Other countries in South America do not seem to be as aware of the potential importance of ISO 14000 and have had only limited involvement in the process prior to the meeting in Rio.

The Pacific Rim Reaction

Pacific Rim countries also appear to have a broad range of involvement in the ISO 14000 process. The Japanese government supports the process; the Ministry of Trade and Industry (MITI), in particular, is very proactive in incorporating ISO 14000 as part of the Japanese industrial standards and establishing a scheme of assessment and registration, even though it is concerned about how to measure the effectiveness of EMS. Industry in Japan recognizes the importance of the international standardization provided by the ISO 14000 series. Industry foresees that the standards will result in a decrease in environmental risks and costs. There is concern that some companies will merely give lip service to the standards. A recent survey by a Japanese newspaper indicated that 75 percent of Japanese companies perceive the ISO 14000 standards as helpful toward solving environmental problems.

Korea is another Asian country at the forefront with regard to ISO 14000. The Korean government recently passed a law titled "Act for the Transformation to Environmentally Friendly Enterprise," which took effect in July 1996. The purpose of the act is to encourage industry to implement the ISO 14000 series. The government believes that implementation of ISO 14000 could provide Korean industry with a competitive edge in worldwide markets, as well as translate to environmental benefits, such as pollution prevention and EMS. As a result, the Ministry of Trade and Industry has taken an active role to foster implementation of ISO 14000 and is in charge of ISO 14000 certification in the country. Although the Korean government is embracing the ISO 14000 approach, industry, with cost concerns in mind, has been a reluctant suitor. Korean industry is enticed by the potential benefits of ISO 14000, but also sobered by the possible consequences of failure to adopt ISO 14000. Industry is concerned that failure to adopt ISO 14000 will effectively shut it out of the worldwide marketplace. Despite the general enthusiasm for ISO 14000, concerns still remain that ISO 14000 focuses too much on paper, with no emphasis on objective measures to ensure that the paper translates to real environmental gains.

In Australia, the roles of government and industry are reversed from those in Korea, with industry bullish on ISO 14000 and government bearish. Industry has been quick to realize that ISO 14000 may well be the ticket to worldwide markets, and both Australia and New Zealand embraced the draft standards in November 1995. In addition, based on their experience with ISO 9000, they believe that ISO 14000 can be used as a marketing tool to attract consumers to "environmentally friendly" companies. Industry would like to get credit for sound environmental policies by translating positive consumer reaction into increases in domestic and international market share. Government, on the other hand, has been very slow to realize the benefits of ISO 14000. The federal environmental protection agency has been criticized for not keeping track of ISO 14000 developments. Recently, Australians elected a more conservative government, which is considering abandoning the environmental protection agency. Those watching government have said that it is still too early to predict whether the new government will be more proactive with respect to the adoption of ISO 14000. There is some concern, particularly on the part of environmental groups, that companies may become certified but still have poor environmental practices.

The European Reaction

Halfway around the globe, European nations are divided in their attitude toward ISO 14000. Although there is not a problem with the ISO 14000 standards per se, there is some concern regarding the applicability of ISO 14000 in the context of EMAS. Germany and the United Kingdom, among others, are cautious about how the two standards will be integrated. Some feel that EMAS is more comprehensive than ISO 14000, and that ISO 14000 could undermine EMAS's objectives. In spite of these concerns, German government and industry regard ISO 14000 as a useful tool to protect the environment and manage environmental issues. Both the government and industry, however, are concerned that accreditation procedures be equal for certification entities and that there be harmonization on an international level.

Some European nations are embracing ISO 14000 despite the existence of the EMAS. In the Netherlands, for example, influential members of the government have declared that publication of ISO 14000 is "an important milestone." The Dutch government anticipates that ISO 14000 will provide the basis for an important industry and government partnership to lead the nation and the world to sustainability. The government is considering providing benefits, such as streamlined licensing processes, for companies with ISO 14000 certification. Industry in the Netherlands is equally positive about ISO 14000, and even prefers it to the EMAS and the British standard, BS 7750. Industry would like to see the relationship between ISO 14000 and EMAS clarified, and would like to see ISO 14000 accepted as a major part of the EMAS requirements.

The story in Norway is similar to that in the Netherlands. Both industry and government are supportive of ISO 14000. A number of companies in Norway are ready for ISO 14000 certification. The level of industry readiness in Norway may partly be the result of the fact that Norway already has laws that require internal company controls for compliance with existing laws and regulations dealing with environmental protection and worker exposures. Despite the general acceptance of ISO 14000 by industry in Norway, some smaller companies with only European markets may opt to comply with EMAS, as it is perceived as being less expensive to implement. In addition, some harbor concerns that ISO 14000 will become a paper chase rather than an effective tool to achieve sustainability. These concerns, however, are balanced by practical realities. Norway is relatively a small country, and the relationship between industry and the community is close. As a result, in such tight quarters, it becomes more difficult for Norwegian industry to become certified under ISO 14000 without also implementing the standards in good faith.

In Turkey, the reaction is more mixed, although the EMAS regulations are not a factor. The general attitude of the Ministry of the Environment toward ISO 14000 is positive, but there is some concern regarding acceptance of the standards in the marketplace. In addition, there are many issues that need to be clarified between existing legislation and the ISO 14000 standards. Large companies in Turkey are very interested in the standards and are moving toward certification; small and medium-sized companies, however, have a much lower level of awareness. Industry's concerns are directed toward training of key personnel and market acceptance of the standards.

Middle Europe (Czech Republic, Slovakia, Hungary, and Poland) is ahead of Eastern Europe in its awareness of ISO 14000, but far behind Western Europe. Middle Europe is a group of industrialized countries with heavy pollution and limited environmental regulatory infrastructure. In the Czech Republic, in particular, the Ministry of the Environment has set up a committee to look at ISO 14000 as the basic structure for environmental regulation. Industry in the Czech Republic is aware of the ISO 14000 process, but there is no perceived benefit from participating in the process or implementing the standards until market pressures are felt from outside the country. In summary, there is cautious acceptance in developed countries of the ISO 14000 process as an essential tool in the development of a consistent international standard for EMS, eco-labeling and life-cycle analysis. It is generally recognized that such standards are needed to promote environmental protection and international trade. There are, however, still concerns that the standards need to be developed in a way that does not institute trade barriers. In developing countries, the level of awareness of ISO 14000 is still low, but the ad hoc group on implementation in developing countries initiated in Rio should help to address this issue.

Pamela J. Bridgen is a vice president in the Seattle office of ICF Kaiser International. Dr. Bridgen manages ICF Kaiser's west coast environmental and pollution prevention support to major clients such as the U.S. Postal Service. Her areas of expertise include pollution prevention, waste management and reduction, human health and environmental risk assessment, assessment of environmental and regulatory issues for industrial operations, environmental audits, and risk communication.

Acknowledgments: Dr. Bridgen would like to thank, among others, the following for their input: Sergio Amaral, Einar Bache, Cengiz Batigun, Joe Casio, Troy Davis, Frank Frantisak, John Henry, Dick Hortensius, Kun Lee, Dr. Manfred Marsman, Y. H. Moon, Mauricio Reis, and Dr. Yoshizawa.

2

Environmental Leadership in a Boundary-less World

James E. Rogers

More than ever before, we live in a boundary-less world. The environmental movement has helped develop this perspective; after all, environmental issues and problems don't respect political boundaries.

To describe our world as "boundary-less" also reflects the fall of political and economic boundaries to create open markets for the exchange of goods and ideas. We can see this in the instantaneous flow of information around the world, and in global communications networks, such as CNN. And we can see, in one country after another, economic forces breaking down the walls around regulated, protected markets.

Living in this time of rapid change gives us a unique opportunity to reinvent how we order our lives, the way we do business, and our relationship with the environment. We have not only an opportunity, but also a responsibility, to consider the issue of environmental leadership in this changing world.

Reordering the relationship between human activity and the environment is not an easy task. One quickly becomes aware of the complexity and interrelatedness of the environment, and how much we don't know about how our actions affect the environment.

In fact, this is not a task that any of us can hope to accomplish in our lifetimes. We must adopt what one author calls "cathedral thinking." This concept explains the heroic efforts that built the great cathedrals of Europe, and the generations of planners and builders who had no hope of seeing the finished product of their life's work. Our mission is to envision a better future, and to leave the next generation one step closer to its realization.

Why Free Markets Are Good for the Environment

Clearly, we want our country and our organizations to be on the leading edge of environmental excellence. The boundary-less world of open markets leaves no protection for poor performance—and that includes environmental performance. Environmental leadership goes hand in hand with success in global competition.

There is some concern, however, that economic battles will force competitors to cut costs at the expense of the environment. I believe that the environment will be a winner, not a loser, in a more competitive world, for three reasons:

1. *Competitive markets mandate efficiency, forcing producers to reduce waste.* The effects range from focused pollution prevention efforts by individual companies—for example, 3M's 3P (Pollution Prevention Pays) program—to the efficient restructuring of entire industries.

   Perhaps the best example is the electric utility industry, an industry with a direct and extensive impact on the environment, and one that is moving from a regulated to a competitive model.

   There is no doubt that the move toward a competitive market in the United States is going to lead to more efficient use of electricity-generating assets. Only a protected monopoly can get away with using more expensive generating capacity when cheaper capacity is available. With competitive markets for electricity, we will see economic dispatch of generating units across all utilities in a region, increasing the use of more efficient units.

2. *Competitive markets are customer-driven, and customers are demanding environmental responsibility.* This is true in the electricity business, where a "dirty" environmental record will be a competitive disadvantage. And it is true around the world, where growing prosperity and growing awareness are raising environmental demands from consumers and voters. As more countries adopt market economies, the resulting rise in incomes will inevitably lead to higher environmental standards as a key ingredient in a better quality of life.

3. *Competitive markets provide both a model and a basis for cost-effective environmental regulation.* As we have seen in the U.S. electric utility industry, command-and-control regulation often creates zero-sum games that pit shareholders against the public and economic goals against environmental goals. In contrast, free markets are based on mutually beneficial transactions that align private interests with the interests of society, and serve both.

   The spread of competition, in our industry and around the world, will not replace environmental regulation. With the spread of free markets, we can develop regulation that is compatible with markets and harnesses market forces to achieve environmental goals. The United States has a successful prototype in the sulfur dioxide emission allowance market created by the Clean Air Act Amendments of 1990.

If the advent of the boundary-less world is indeed an opportunity to reorder our relationship with the environment, how should we pursue environmental leadership and excellence? Let me address this question from the standpoint of public policy and corporate policy.

Beyond Command-and-Control and Compliance

From a public policy standpoint, the key is going beyond command-and-control. That means developing environmental regulations that reflect the best thinking to date but, more importantly, allow and encourage further innovation.

Some voices in industry have expressed concern that environmental regulation will hurt competitiveness, but Michael Porter of the Harvard Business School says it is a source of competitiveness. Porter says that lax environmental standards have the same effect as protective trade barriers—they allow domestic firms to lag behind in innovation and efficiency. He argues that the ability to meet tough environmental standards becomes an exportable product—and U.S. electric utilities are proving him right as they build and operate state-of-the-art generating facilities to meet the rapidly growing demand for power in industrializing countries.

To be most effective, environmental regulation should focus on performance rather than specific hardware requirements. Regulation should

- Allow companies to meet standards through pollution prevention rather than end-of-pipe controls;
- Utilize market-based mechanisms that motivate companies to meet environmental goals at the least cost; and
- Establish goals and give companies a chance to achieve those goals through voluntary efforts.

From a corporate standpoint, the key is going beyond compliance. State-of-the-art environmental design is a matter of self-interest when companies recognize the potential cost of retrofitting to meet higher standards in the future.

There is concern that multinational companies will establish operations in countries with the most lenient environmental regulations. But that would be a short-sighted approach for capital investments with useful lives of 30 years or more. The economics of any project should make sense without having to avoid environmental responsibilities.

Going beyond compliance also is a way for companies to demonstrate solutions as a guide for future regulation. No longer can companies simply wait until they are required to act, as under command-and-control regulation. Industry has argued for market approaches, for the right incentives, and for flexibility in meeting environmental standards—and rightly so, in my judgment. But we must demonstrate that "flexibility" is not another word for "loophole"—that we can accomplish more when we are given greater latitude to produce solutions on our own.

What is a prescription for going beyond compliance? Let me suggest five points based on principles in the Policy on Environmental Excellence of the Edison Electric Institute, an association of U.S. investor-owned electric utilities. While this list is by no means comprehensive, I believe that these issues are critical to any discussion of corporate environmental leadership:

1. *Corporate commitment.* The key element is an environmental charter that goes beyond platitudes and is tied to the strategic plan. The charter at PSI Energy was developed with the involvement of an advisory board that included the state's environmental leaders. We did not publicize their participation, because we wanted their ideas and reactions, not their public relations value.

2. *Environmental performance measurement and reporting.* One essential element is a good system for internal monitoring and reporting. Environmental audits should go beyond what is required to provide direction for future improvement. Companies should also move toward an environmental annual report; although it may start out as merely a public relations piece, it must evolve into a presentation of hard facts, in the same way that we submit financial data to shareholders.

3. *Pollution prevention and waste minimization.* This is one of the most promising areas of environmental performance and a focus of the electric utility industry, through demand-side management and integrated resource planning. With the spread of competition and the development of regional power markets in the United States, what we are really seeing is a trend toward regional, market-driven resource planning and load management.

4. *Employee training and responsibility.* Adequate training is an issue for both corporate and public policy, to ensure that we have enough talented, trained people to handle expanding environmental tasks and commitments.

5. *Environmental stewardship.* Stewardship must flow from the top down and from the bottom up, if the entire organization is really going to function as an environmental steward. The focus must always be on continuous improvement.

Cinergy supports the concept of voluntary international environmental standards that promote free trade. To that end, Cinergy is evaluating its environmental management systems against ISO 14000, and will be conforming its systems to the ISO 14000 principles.

Conclusion

We have a mission, one that is personal, corporate, national, and global. It is a mission as inspiring and energizing as the great cathedrals of Europe—to reshape the relationship of human activity with the environment. We need to unleash the energy of individuals and organizations around the world and apply the entrepreneurial spirit to new environmental solutions.

It has been said that "the best way to predict the future is to invent it." We live in an exciting time, when free markets offer new opportunities for innovation that advances both economic and environmental goals, when an increasingly boundary-less world offers new opportunities for the spread of ideas and a new level of cooperation and collaboration, and when rapid change offers us the opportunity to reinvent our role in the environment.

James E. Rogers is vice chairman, president, and chief executive officer of Cinergy Corp., a holding company for PSI Energy, Inc., and The Cincinnati Gas & Electric Company. Prior to the October 1994 merger that created Cinergy, Rogers was chairman, president, and chief executive officer of PSI Energy, Indiana's largest electric utility, and chairman and CEO of its parent company, PSI Resources, Inc. His career also includes experience as a natural gas company executive; a federal energy regulator; a partner in a Washington, D.C. law firm; and a state consumer advocate.

3

Developing Global Environmental Management Standards: Progress and Implications of the New Wave

Henry R. Balikov

We are witnessing a watershed event in the history of environmental governance. The inevitable trend to globalization of standards will be well ensconced before the end of this decade. It will include management of an organization's activities, products and services. These nongovernmental standards may elevate the standards of care and duty far beyond those enacted by legislatures and administrative agencies. They will not only fuel official enforcement efforts, but will also carry forward citizen and public interest group efforts to change the way organizations manage their shares of the environment. Those willing to commit resources to the standard-setting process on a continuous basis will have some input to those eventual standards.

There was a time, not so long ago, when the measure of any business environmental system's success was simply whether it deserved notice. If things were running smoothly, went this philosophy, there would be nothing to notice and, conversely, if attention was drawn to the environmental aspects of the business, something must be amiss.

Times have changed, and the advantages of viewing environmental management systems as part of the total quality management universe have driven a number of initiatives to better measure and, thus, better manage environmental efforts. For those who want to be in the front lines, or want to know what is going on there, this chapter will discuss several key initiatives: proliferating standards, such as ISO 14000, U.S. initiatives, and the nexus with environmental enforcement.

The Marketplace for Environmental Management Standards

The private sector in the United States has frequently complained that U.S. companies are some of the most highly regulated in the world and that, in world markets, they often compete at a disadvantage. They have sought more "common sense" by environmental regulators and flexibility for improvements in environmental performance. Congress has been a battleground for competing environmental philosophies. At the same time, the U.S. Environmental Protection Agency has stepped up its encouragement of "beyond compliance" efforts with initiatives such as Project XL and other "leadership" programs. The appearance of ISO 14001 ("environmental management systems") has been seized upon as an approach that would achieve greater compliance while fostering ethics of continual improvement and pollution prevention. It has drawn so much attention that this may have distracted many from the other attempts at international standard setting for environmental management and reporting. The BSI, ICC, EC-ECO Audit, PERI and CERES efforts, among others, need to be studied closely, if for no other reason than to understand their individual implications for the way in which business will be conducted in the global forum.

Only certain sectors of U.S. industry initially perceived the implications of such standard-setting efforts. It is not surprising that among those were some of the major petroleum and organic and inorganic chemical companies and trade associations, such as the Chemical Manufacturers Association. From their participation, it has become clear that trade in various jurisdictions throughout the world will be won, or lost, by the ability to "live with" or adapt to the evolving standards. These and other "voluntary" standards reflect a variety of value systems (and philosophies) about the purpose and goals of environmental management. Their existence should be read more for their direction, toward distribution of more control away from traditional headquarters environmental staffs, than should the individual elements be seen as having achieved ultimate shape. For those who aim merely to maintain compliance, the bar may be about to be moved higher. For those who have established a more proactive program, there will be a buffet of elements from which to choose. However, there is no free lunch. The selection or non-selection of an element will have some significant consequences, because the process has become, by that choice, institutionalized.

The U.S. Presence

As stated above, many companies in the United States who have participated in the process have done so because of their desire to remain competitive in the global marketplace. As such standards are adopted, those who cannot conform to the standards are often shut out completely. Prudence demands monitoring such initiatives closely, analyzing potential impacts on current practices, and, where there are choices to be made, using the opportunities available to lobby for choices most compatible with their practices and philosophical principles.

The process of developing new standards may seem slow, but, like von Logau's observation about the mills of God, "they grind exceeding small."

Richard Wells, of Abt Associates, has been an active member of the groups involved in development of management standards. At conferences, he has offered some observations about the role and value of standards-setting efforts. He notes that recent efforts by the U.S. EPA are headed in the direction of creating flexible opportunities, rather than attempting to achieve a "better" balance between social costs and private costs. The ability to define and initiate projects addressing such standards should be sufficiently open at the corporate level that the cost of each project is rational. Too many companies have not examined their actual environmental costs/performance and ended up endorsing a "blank check" because they are told such projects are "required." Where regulations create opportunities for initiative and the information is sufficient for decision making, Wells observes that company-driven initiatives can be at least two or three times as cost-effective as those that are government-mandated.

NSF International has led an effort to assess how well the ISO 14001 management standard works in real-world situations. As part of its tradition of thorough testing and evaluation, NSF, with EPA support, is now completing an 18-month assessment of how over a dozen organizations moved through the implementation of 14001. (See chapter 5, Industry Cases and Practices.) Each one determined its own baseline so that all changes could be measured and documented. Each of the organizations received training on the standard's requirements and also on effective approaches to implementation within the organization. All organizations initially in the project have continued to participate.

Enforcement and Voluntary Standards

The essence of a voluntary standard is that the choice is with the participant. Over time, the participation of others may convert a voluntary standard to a de facto standard; this can have implications for the participant in everything from customer expectation to liability for personal injuries related to some act that allegedly failed to meet such a standard. In a less easily traced process, regulatory authorities may plan inspections and exercise prosecutorial discretion based on their perceptions of an entity's compliance record.

At a recent conference sponsored by the American Bar Association, several federal and state officials offered observations on these points. The head of U.S. EPA's Criminal Enforcement Office indicated that the agency's growing computerized database of environmental violations will allow him to pull together all information on a given permittee from around the country. He views this as a valuable enforcement tool. The information that the agency has goes far beyond violations, and U.S. EPA's Office of Regulatory Enforcement is not planning to use the results of audits to target either inspections or enforcement.

A state prosecutor takes a different view. This member of the New York State Attorney General's office responded to the issue of voluntary standards by indicating that, because environmental audits were a "reasonable standard of care," the failure to conduct audits could result in state criminal prosecution. He was recently asked whether state prosecutors would turn ISO 14000 into an enforcement tool. Without hesitation, the reply was that "since these standards already are in use, such an enforcement tool already exists. Prosecutors will determine whether a company consciously avoided use of these standards as they decide what penalty to pursue against [them]" (as reported in *Daily Environment Reporter*, Bureau of National Affairs, September 9, 1994). Although this has yet to happen in the United States, a Canadian case has resulted in a violation after having committed to implementing ISO 14001 (even before it was put into final form).

Recent initiatives by U.S. EPA have facilitated further implementation of management standards within the context of Project XL and Region I's "Startrack Program." Recently, the agency has made major changes in its policy toward encouraging organizations to audit themselves. Although it is too complex to discuss here, a significant change has been the recognition of the value of compliance management systems. A key remaining issue will be how to resolve the need for wide internal distribution of assessment information. Such information might be attractive for use in enforcement by regulators and also might increase both toxic tort litigation and citizen suits under the federal environmental laws.

Henry R. Balikov directs the environmental management and compliance assurance practice for TLI Systems, Inc., a subsidiary of TechLaw, Inc., in Chantilly, Virginia. He has been representing a major diversified corporation in both national and international efforts to establish standards for environmental management systems and environmental performance evaluation.

4

ISO 14000: What's In It for You?

Lynn Johannson

*The impact of ISO 14000 will be swift and significant. For businesses export-
ing to global markets, and their suppliers, preparing for ISO 14000 today is
not an option—it's a matter of survival. . . .*

Dr. Frank Frantisak, Senior Vice President, Environment, Noranda Inc.;
Chair, Canadian Advisory Committee to ISO TC207

Dateline: Oslo, June 1995. Five hundred forty delegates arrived at Oslo City
Hall to hear Norwegian Prime Minister Gro Harlem Brundtland's address on ISO
14000. "Your contribution is crucial for securing the necessary changes among
industry and market operators. While industry used to be a main reason for
environmental degradation, it is increasingly becoming part of the solution to
environmental problems. . . . Your efforts must aim at real progress, not at pet-
rifying an idea whose time has passed. Our common concern must be to constantly improve industry's environmental performance, and industry must lead
that way unless it wants to be led."

Is ISO 14000 just window dressing by governments of developed countries
and multinational corporations?

Sixty nations participated in the discussions in Oslo, with more than a third
designated as "developing nations." These countries are becoming more influential players in the merging global economy. European and North American
countries and Japan (which experienced major change through industrializa-
tion earlier this century) still must evolve at a revolutionary rate to move
beyond their polluted past. Heightened expectations exist globally for development that occurs in an environmentally responsible manner. Whether the
transformation is from an "underdeveloped" economy or an industrialized
economy, the global marketplace is demanding sustainability (Figure 4.1).

ISO 14000 sets out an internationally harmonized approach, a common
pathway preparing companies and countries for the transformation to sustainability. Proof of the global interest in ISO 14000 and Environmental Management Systems has been evidenced by the increasing number and frequency of
articles, books, and conferences on this subject.

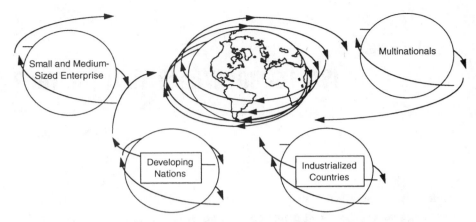

Figure 4.1 Transforming the Global Marketplace to Sustainable Development

In June 1995, draft international standards (DIS) were agreed to (Table 4.1). Perhaps even more than for ISO 9000, companies and their managers are lining up at the starting gate for ISO 14000. Some are there because they have every intention of being world leaders and have positioned themselves to take a competitive position. Just behind are those who watch the leaders and mirror their activity in order to be in sync with their customers.

Just what is the value of an EMS aligned to ISO 14000? What are the costs involved in taking on this challenge? Who really benefits? And what will happen to those that don't participate? Our company asked our environmental professionals to answer the question, "What's in it for you?" in an effort to target the benefits and barriers to environmental management systems aligned to ISO 14000.

Table 4.1 International Standards

The ISO 14000 series includes:

14000, Environmental Management Systems—General Guidelines on Environmental Management Principles, Systems, and Supporting Techniques (slated to be renumbered as 14004 to coincide with ISO 9000 series)

14001, Environmental Management Systems—Specification with Guidance for Use

14010, Guidelines for Environmental Auditing—General Principles

14011.1, Guidelines for Environmental Auditing—Audit Procedures—Part 1: Auditing of Environmental Management Systems

14012, Guidelines for Environmental Auditing—Qualification Criteria for Environmental Auditors

14060, Guide for the Inclusion of Environmental Aspects in Product Standards

The Case for Voluntary Initiatives

Ron Harper, Director, Environmental Regulatory Affairs Directorate, Industry Canada, presented a case for an environmental policy regime promoting voluntary initiatives. Voluntary environmental initiatives—and, in particular, ISO 14000—are becoming increasingly important to both government and industry.

"A brief discussion of the evolution of environmental policy will provide the context for the current environmental policy regime promoting voluntary initiatives such as ISO 14000. The command-and-control regulations introduced to respond to the plethora of environmental problems brought on by industrial pollution were prescriptive and intrusive. The regulations dictated when, and to what level, industry should clean up, and they sometimes went so far as to prescribe the actual technology. More often, industry was told to use the best available control technology, which meant that less expensive ways to abate pollution were not pursued. Almost no attention was paid to the roles of economic instruments and voluntary action by industry in environmental protection.

"The traditional command-and-control measures have led to very real and quantifiable results in addressing a variety of environmental problems. The air is getting cleaner (Table 4.2). Water quality has improved dramatically. In fact, tremendous progress has been made in reducing industrial pollution in first-world countries. However, the problems that remain (habitat destruction, biodiversity, climate change) are of a different nature. They are more complex. The solutions require a shift in focus from a relatively easy task—the further targeting of large point sources—to the more difficult task of changing the behavior of people controlling diffuse, nonpoint sources. A paradigm shift in the approach to the current more complex environmental problems requires new remedies and the use of more sophisticated techniques (Table 4.3).

Table 4.2   The Air Is Getting Cleaner

	Canada % Change 1974–1992	United States % Change 1970–1990
Particulate Matter	−54	−60.5
Sulfur Oxides	−61	25.1
Nitrogen Oxides	−38	5.9
VOCs	na	−25.2
Carbon Monoxide	−70	−40.7
Lead	na	−96.5
Total Emissions	na	−33.8

Table 4.3   Change in Paradigms

OLD	NEW
Environmental protection and economic growth seen as opposed	Sustainable development links environment/ economy decision making
Focus is on local problems	Focus is on regional, global problems
Agenda driven by domestic consideration	Agenda responsive to international trade and climate for investment
Public looks to government to prioritize problems, find solutions	Public participation in identifying problems and developing solutions
Jurisdictional fragmentation leads to duplication and overlap	Jurisdictional cooperation strives to eliminate duplication and overlap
Mind-set is react and cure	Mind-set is anticipate and prevent
Command-and-control is instrument of choice	Broad array of instruments, including voluntary action and economic instruments, are utilized
Regulations prescribe technical solutions, inhibit innovation	Performance standards give industry flexibility, encourage innovation
Addresses large, easy-to-identify and manage point sources of pollution	Addresses diffused and difficult to manage nonpoint sources of pollution

"Under this new paradigm, innovation has been identified as the key to economic growth and renewal. The question for policy makers then becomes, how can we provide a regulatory environment that promotes environmental improvement while at the same time provides the flexibility to be innovative?

"The answer, in many circumstances, is to promote the use of voluntary initiatives. Voluntary initiatives build on existing regulation while still allowing industry the flexibility to be innovative. Industry is able to select the most cost-effective approaches to complex environmental problems and to time capital investment to fit into business investment cycles. The result is an approach that is compatible and consistent with the maintenance of a favorable climate of investment.

"The spectrum of voluntary initiatives in effect in Canada today is very broad. However, the majority of these initiatives fit into one of four categories.

"The first category of voluntary initiatives includes environmental performance improvement by industry sectors through memoranda of understanding (MOU). An example is the MOU among the representatives of the Motor Vehicle Manufacturers Association, Chrysler, Ford, and GM and the Ontario Ministry of the Environment and Energy and Environment Canada to reduce persistent toxic substances, as well as other environmental contaminants of concern. Other industry sectors have signed similar MOUs, including the Canadian Association of Metal Finishers, the Canadian Automobile Parts Manufacturers Association, Ontario Fabricare Association, and the Korean Dry Cleaners Association.

"The second type of voluntary initiative is where the industry association takes the lead and 'encourages' its members to improve their environmental performance. Two examples include the Responsible Care Program of the Canadian Chemical Producers Association and the Warehousing Standards written by the Crop Protection Institute of Canada.

"The third type focuses on environmental performance improvements made by individual companies. It is becoming increasingly important for companies to use their resources more efficiently and to generate less waste. Both practices improve a company's bottom line. As more and more companies become motivated through self-interest to improve their environmental performance, both the environment and the economy will benefit. An example of the joint benefits is highlighted in some case studies provided to Industry Canada by DuPont Canada.

"The final initiative is the ISO 14000 series. Companies that choose to comply with the requirements of ISO 14001 are doing so for a number of reasons. First, although most formal barriers to trade have disappeared in recent years, differing standards on environmental codes of practice can still create nontariff barriers. Companies that want to successfully compete in today's global marketplace are seriously considering the implementation of an EMS benchmarked against the ISO standard. Second, and more often, customers or clients are requiring verification that their suppliers are taking their environmental responsibility seriously. A supplier that is responsive to customer concerns regarding environmental performance will implement an EMS benchmarked against the ISO standard.

"Canadian companies planning to undertake a voluntary environmental initiative are confronted with many obstacles. A significant obstacle is the cynical attitude of some stakeholders toward voluntary initiatives and, in particular, the environmental improvements brought about by voluntary initiatives. However, if properly structured, voluntary initiatives can enable industry, government, and the public to work together to identify and address areas of greatest environmental concern. Some issues that must be addressed to provide increased comfort to all stakeholders include the issues of accountability, the reporting of results, and minimizing the incidence of 'free riders.'[1] We should recognize that, as the use of these voluntary initiatives increases, a significant partnership becomes available to government in seeking to improve the environmental performance of industry. For Canadian industry, operating leaner, keener, and greener will facilitate trade in the global marketplace and, in many circumstances, it can improve their competitive position."

"Greening" the Suppliers

May F. Chiu, a managing principal with IBM Environmental, Health, and Safety Technology Services in Allentown, Pennsylvania, focused on the benefits of preventing problems from entering IBM by "greening" its suppliers.

"To compete in the global marketplace, businesses must become more proactive in managing the environmental aspects of their operations. It makes good business sense to adopt the standards being established by ISO 14000, starting with the Environmental Management System (ISO 14001).

"ISO 14001 establishes a framework for an organization to evaluate its impact on the environment and to begin understanding the aspects to consider in enhancing environmental performance, thereby enhancing business performance. The answer to the question, 'ISO 14000, what's in it for me?' is, 'It will enhance business performance and provide for continuous improvement.' This benefit will be the overwhelming driver to adopt ISO 14000 as part of a business core management system. ISO 14001 also establishes a framework to achieve total quality management across business operations to improve profitability, customer satisfaction, productivity, and company image.

"One environmental aspect to consider is the use of materials in a business prior to authorizing purchasing and use of the material, and, once purchased, tracking the material from its receipt to disposal. Materials include chemicals, equipment, and energy. Whether the chemical is used as a raw material or cleaning agent, the environmental impact could produce significant costs or savings for the business. For example, one type of chemical may be less expensive to purchase but more costly to dispose. Another may be very effective in a cleaning operation, but if it is a hazardous material, it would require more procedures to ensure the safety and health of workers and the environment. A proactive approach to materials management would be to put practices in place to ensure that appropriate materials are purchased and used in a business. This would reduce costs in inventory, manufacturing operations, compliance reporting and generate benefits including reducing or minimizing waste disposal, maximizing inventory, reducing product costs, minimizing risks, and reducing worker compensation.

"By adopting ISO 14001, a business demonstrates its commitment to continuous improvement for its customers, shareholders, community, and regulatory agencies. It positions a business to compete more effectively in the global market and to ensure continuous improvement in environmental performance, and it creates cost savings and opportunities for pollution prevention. All these benefits are aimed at one core issue—enhancing business performance and competitiveness. Meeting the standards makes good business sense."

The Challenge to SMEs

The last respondent was Ted Mallett, senior economist with the Canadian Federation of Independent Business (CFIB). CFIB is Canada's largest political action group for small and medium-sized businesses, representing 85,000 members from all sectors across Canada.

"The mention of small and medium-sized enterprises (SMEs) and the environment in the same sentence conjures up a wide range of descriptions and opinions. SMEs have been described as willful environmental offenders that are unsophisticated and ignorant with respect to environmental practices, conscientious citizens doing their small part to help, and entrepreneurial innovators at the forefront of green technologies and processes. With this range of opinions about small firms, it is no wonder why it has been a challenge to fit the EMS concept into the small business context, because SMEs defy convenient categorization. Rather than trying to pick one description that best describes the SME sector as a whole, one has to settle for 'all of the above.'

"Once this step is made, one quickly concludes that small businesses, as a group, are not a unique case to be pasted into an EMS model. In fact, what is 'special' about small businesses is that they are not special at all. Their awareness, attitudes, and behavior with respect to environmental practices are no different from those of society as a whole. Because most small firms do not have formal operating procedures, they more resemble households than they do larger, more formalized businesses.

"This becomes a challenge to one of the primary goals of EMS models—that they can be seamlessly integrated into any business's operations. Informal business contexts have difficulty incorporating any formalized concepts, no matter how flexible. This is not to say that this results in a failure of small firms to meet the objectives of EMSs and ISO 14000. In fact, the lack of structural rigidities may make it easier and faster for small firms to make changes to the way they do business. The chief difficulty is in the apparent lack of signs of small business adherence to green principles because no ISO 14000 committees exist for these groups, nor are there detailed work plans. For those used to observing and evaluating formal operating procedures, the fact that a small firm did not stop to leave a paper trail may lead them to believe that the business was not addressing the issue: 'If an EMS file is not at least two inches thick, how can it be serious?' The effort required to satisfy these types of standards, therefore, tends to be proportionately more difficult for small businesses than for larger firms. Based on observations of SME and ISO 9000, it is not unreasonable to suggest that achieving standards designation is often more difficult than meeting the quality goals themselves.

"None of these concerns, however, should dilute the importance of the concept of ISO 14000 and the development of consistent standards of environmental management practices. Expectations, however, have to be reasonable for an EMS to reach as broad a base as possible. Approaches followed by multi-national manufacturers are not the same as those of small business, just as small electronic components firms are not comparable to neighborhood dry cleaners. If ISO 14000 can achieve true consistency in allowing businesses large and small to take part, it will be a worthy accomplishment."

Conclusion

Why should you tune into ISO 14000? Because it will make a good business better, enabling more efficient use of resources (e.g., knowledge, skills, capital/financial, time) and helping to establish credibility through verifiable processes. Very shortly, customers will be asking about a company's EMS as part of their vendor evaluation process.

ISO 14004 (the guidance document, renamed to coincide with the 9000 series numbering) has articulated a number of benefits, which include:

- Assuring customers of commitment to demonstrable environmental management;
- Maintaining good public/community relations;
- Satisfying investor criteria and improving access to capital;
- Obtaining insurance at reasonable cost;
- Enhancing image and market share;
- Meeting vendor certification criteria;
- Improving cost control;
- Reducing incidents that result in liability;
- Demonstrating reasonable care;
- Conserving input materials and energy;
- Facilitating the receipt of permits and authorizations;
- Fostering development and sharing environmental solutions; and
- Improving industry-government relations.

What specific benefits should you expect? It depends on your organization's specific needs and goals and those of your customers. However, just like the lottery, in which you cannot expect to win unless you play, with ISO 14000, real benefits will come to those who buy into the core spirit of EMS, not just the specifications outlined in ISO 14001. Not all benefits are predictable either. May Chiu's focus for IBM on cost savings and opportunities for pollution prevention can produce significant bottom line and customer/community results. The training costs estimated by Dow Chemical Texas for ISO 14001 ran around $80,000 to $180,000 for 100 employees based on 180 to 360 labor days. These costs could drop by 30 percent to 60 percent for facilities already 9000-registered. Of course, the cost will vary depending on what the company's training goals are. It is very important to assess the needs of the people to be trained and benchmark their initial knowledge, skills, and attitude. If this is not done, it will be difficult to ascertain all the benefits gleaned from training.

What barriers lie ahead? Poor implementation or interpretations that are too rigid are perhaps the greatest potential barriers. I agree with Ron Harper's comment about the skeptical stakeholder. The biggest barrier I repeatedly encounter stems from a mind-set resistant to change. The mind that remains closed to progress is typified by those who, when presented with opportunity, state, "We can't do that." What these people are really saying is, "I won't make a change." In today's business climate, flexibility—the ability to adapt to a global marketplace—is a basic requirement for survival.

Ted Mallet's comments regarding rigidity in viewing the paper trail are valid if a limited mind-set lingers. A "two-inch-thick" manual does not constitute a quality or effective document. Typically, SMEs are under-resourced for time, money, and people, but not for brains. We should continue to encourage the tens of thousands of small and medium-sized enterprises in North America to conquer this challenge through innovation and creativity. Japan, while quiet and unassuming at the ISO table, has already come out with early action steps based on a competitive strategy based on 50- and 100-year plans. At least now we know who's leading the charge with which Prime Minister Brundtland challenged us with at the country level. Additionally, a number of companies are reportedly readying themselves to be certified against ISO 14001 by meeting the specifications in DIS 14001.

Special thanks to Ron Harper and Nada Vrany of Industry Canada, May Chiu of IBM, and Ted Mallett of CFIB for taking the time to share their concerns and support for ISO 14000.

Note

1. A "free rider" is a company that avoids implementing a voluntary program and the costs involved, yet benefits from the efforts of other firms and the ensuing improvement in the industry's public image and its relationship with regulators. The incidence of free riders can be reduced by monitoring participants' activities, reporting the programs' results, and helping smaller firms that want to participate. The Canadian Chemical Producers Association has effectively dealt with the "free rider" issue by requiring member companies to fully comply with all the responsible care practices and guidelines. If a company is unable to follow the code of practice in any or all areas of its operations, it must discontinue that activity or face expulsion from the association.

Lynn Johannson is president of E2 Management Corporation (E2M), an environmental management consulting firm specializing in assisting clients to integrate environmental issues into their organization's business activities using environmental quality management systems. She is also vice-chair of the technical committee in Canada responsible for the development of environmental management systems with alignment to the ISO 14000 series.

5

Industry Cases and Practices: Voluntary Environmental Management System Standards

Craig P. Diamond

The ISO 14000 series of environmental management standards has been officially under development in the International Organization for Standardization (ISO) since the summer of 1993. One question often asked about the ISO 14000 standards is, how will EPA and state regulatory agencies incorporate them into decision making? Of particular interest is how the draft environmental management system (EMS) standard, ISO 14001, will be used in regulatory development, compliance, and enforcement.

There is a growing hope in industry that regulatory agencies will provide preferential treatment to companies that are registered to an EMS standard. One possibility is that regulators will be less likely to focus compliance and enforcement efforts on companies that have a recognized EMS in place. The EMS might assure agencies that those companies were in compliance with regulations, allowing regulators to concentrate their limited resources on companies with significant compliance problems.

How this will unfold remains to be seen. ISO 14001 will likely play an important role in federal and state environmental policy, but regulatory agencies will need to develop a much greater understanding of how an EMS will influence environmental management and performance before they can determine what the role of an EMS standard should be. For example, a critical issue for government is the extent to which small and medium-sized companies will be able to implement and/or become registered to EMS standards. A concern is that smaller companies may lack the resources to develop an EMS. And even if EMS implementation is cost-effective, the cost of registration could be prohibitive. Small and medium-sized companies may need government incentives to implement EMS standards.

To learn more about EMS implementation issues, EPA awarded a grant to NSF International, a not-for-profit company specializing in environmental and public health standards and certification, to manage a two-year pilot project to demonstrate the application of EMS standards in a variety of U.S. organizations. The project is a cooperative effort between EPA and NSF. Its purpose is to help government and industry learn more about the potential benefits of, and barriers to, implementing EMS standards and to determine what guidance and resources companies—particularly small and medium-sized firms—will need to successfully develop an EMS.

NSF International was chosen to manage the project because it had already developed an EMS standard (NSF 110: Environmental Management Systems: Guiding Principles and Generic Requirements) very similar to ISO 14001, and because it had been an active participant in the ISO 14000 development process. The standard, was released in the fall of 1994 and published in April 1995. Although some of the individual requirements differ, the two standards contain the same basic elements of an EMS (including policy development, environmental effects evaluation, objective setting, implementation, emergency preparedness, monitoring and measurement, auditing, corrective action, documentation, and communication). ISO 14001 will become the U.S. national standard for EMS when it is completed.

EMS Implementation in a Variety of Organizations

The 18 organizations participating in the demonstration project represent a variety of products and services. They range from Fortune 100 corporations to small manufacturers to government agencies. The organizations also vary significantly in their approaches to environmental management: Some have well-established, complex environmental, health, and safety (EH&S) systems; others have more traditional environmental programs, which, until recently, have focused primarily on regulatory compliance. The seven companies included in this article were chosen to represent the diversity of organizations in the project. Two of the companies have fewer than 250 employees (K.J. Quinn & Co., Milan Screw Products); two have between 250 and 1,000 employees (Globe Metallurgical Inc., Hach Company); and three have more than 1,000 employees (Allergan, Inc., NIBCO, Inc., Pacific Gas & Electric Company).

The project consists of two major activities: (1) EMS self-assessment and implementation and (2) group training and discussion. Each organization in the project performed an initial self-assessment of its EMS in the spring of 1995 using NSF 110 and the ISO 14001 draft as benchmarks. Based on the initial assessment, participants developed an implementation action plan. They did a second self-assessment in the spring of 1996 to determine the progress made over the project period. In addition to the self-assessment and implementation, the organizations met in four two-day meetings at NSF over the course of the project to receive training on specific EMS issues and to share practical, "real-world" implementation strategies.

All the organizations in the EMS demonstration project are participating because they believe, for a variety of reasons, that a comprehensive EMS will be a source of competitive advantage. Many are planning to become ISO 14001 registered soon, which would likely place them among the first group of companies in the United States to become registered. Others, who may not be specifically aiming for registration at this time, still recognize the potential environmental *and* financial benefits of adopting a proactive approach to environmental management—one that is based on self-established objectives and targets that fully integrate, but that are not driven solely by, environmental regulation. While many common themes emerge, each company faces issues unique to its organization and to its industry.

K.J. Quinn & Co.

K.J. Quinn & Co. is a privately owned specialty chemical company involved in the research, development, and manufacture of high-performance liquid resins, coatings, and adhesives worldwide. Quinn consists of three divisions: the Coatings and Adhesive (C&A) Division, which manufactures solvent-based, water-based and 100-percent solid urethane products; the QureTech® Division, which manufactures UV and E-Beam curable products; and the Shoe Finish Division, which manufactures shoe-related products.

Presently, Quinn is working on ISO 9001 certification for both its C&A and QureTech® Divisions with plans to obtain certification. Both divisions are located in one facility and were certified together. During the certification process, the managers involved with quality, safety, and environmental issues became aware of the developing ISO 14000 Environmental Management System (EMS) standards and began investigating whether Quinn should also pursue EMS certification.

As a chemical manufacturer and formulator, Quinn has significant environmental obligations, including an ever-expanding set of regulations with which to comply, a need to develop more environmentally friendly products, and increased demand from customers for assistance in complying with their requirements. It concluded that implementation of an EMS would improve and properly focus the resources of the company in meeting its environmental responsibilities. Similar to other businesses today, Quinn operates with a lean workforce in all areas, including its environmental and safety department, and needs to be more efficient with the limited resources currently available. It views the establishment of an EMS as a process that forces it to better organize its priorities and projects and to identify problems, exposures, and even responses before they occur, as preventing an incident is much more efficient than responding to one.

Quinn also concluded that, eventually, it would have to be ISO 14000 certified to compete internationally, as companies now need ISO 9000 certification to compete in these markets. Additionally, implementing the EMS while working toward ISO 9000 certification made sense because all Quinn employees were already knowledgeable about the certification process.

In early 1995, Quinn became involved in the NSF pilot EMS program to learn more about the EMS certification process and to assist in establishing an EMS for the QureTech® and C&A Divisions. As a first step in the program, Quinn performed a self-audit of its current environmental and safety programs. It was decided to include safety in Quinn's EMS because of the close relationship and common overlapping of both safety and environmental concerns in this type of industry. The director of safety and environmental affairs (DS&E) completed the preliminary self-assessment, which was reviewed and commented on by the company's officers. The assessment process followed an outline developed by NSF and was surprisingly not as time-consuming as was expected, taking approximately 20 to 25 hours to perform a comprehensive review.

The assessment showed the need to concentrate efforts toward developing more formal environmental and safety policies and establishing better communication of environmental issues with Quinn's neighbors, customers, and other stakeholders. The company's efforts toward ISO 9000 certification showed positively in work policies and procedures, documentation, document control, and training. Its compliance with the OSHA process safety management (PSM) regulation and related regulations reflected positively in the evaluation of problems and managing change, and identified that procedures developed for the PSM could be extended to include environmental actions not currently included.

With the assessment completed, the next step obviously was to implement the changes and additions necessary to bring the program into step with the requirements of the EMS. The biggest hurdle in the implementation process continued to be devoting the time and resources necessary to develop the missing components of the system, to improve on the existing components, and to remain current once the system is in place. With all employees operating at a significant pace, this became a trying situation, especially in the final days toward ISO 9000 certification.

There are still some issues that need to be addressed, particularly legal and regulatory access to audit records. This will be a challenging task, but a necessary one that should be very rewarding both in savings and in protection of our employees and the environment.

Milan Screw Products

Milan Screw Products is a small manufacturing firm of 35 people. Its products are precision fittings machined from steel bars for the fluid power, auto, and refrigeration industries.

Generally, few hazardous materials are used in metal turning operations. The most frequent environmental issues in the screw machine industry include the containment of cutting oils and coolants, the replacement of chlorinated solvents, and the disposal of waste oils. A persistent challenge is the containment of cutting oil within production machines, many of which were manufactured in the 1940s and 1950s, and are often found operating with inadequate oil splash guards and leaky gearbox covers. Many shops have simply accepted the oily floors and the oil mist that soon coats everything from light fixtures to lunch boxes. Oil escapes the building in many ways (e.g., trash bins are filled with saturated oil absorbents swept from the floor, carpets are stained by the oily shoes of workers, and liquid wastes are generated from the solvents and soaps used to remove the oil film). Changing this environment requires a clear management policy, written procedures, documentation, training, and corrective action—elements similar to those of the company's ISO 9000 quality program.

An environmental task group of five people was appointed with representatives from production, support, and management. They were assigned the tasks of preparing and submitting the reporting forms required by federal, state, and county regulators, assuring regulatory compliance and improving environmental performance. The task group began by reviewing the reporting forms and instructions. They assumed the responsibility of completing the forms and submitting them in a timely manner. The need for training both existing and new employees was mentioned, but a source for training material was not known. It was a relief to observe the growing environmental awareness of the task group members as they assumed duties that had previously been the realm of management. Although progress was made, Milan had no vision to guide its goal setting, no structure for a program, and no means to measure progress. At this critical point, the company joined the EMS Demonstration Program at NSF International.

Milan began its participation in the program with an environmental self-assessment. The checklist and instructions prepared by NSF as self-assessment tools were particularly helpful in evaluating the company's environmental performance. The initial assessment score was very low because the company had no formal EMS in place. But the self-evaluation process, by questioning present conditions, forced Milan to consider the many potential benefits of implementation. Specifically, it determined an EMS could improve employee retention, new hire selection, working conditions, and the perceptions of the company's customers, suppliers, lenders, neighbors, and regulators. It would also ease management fears of inadvertent environmental problems that could arise from simple ignorance or lack of training.

We are committed to full EMS implementation. The environmental task group has been the key to Milan's progress. The task group has examined the company's purchases, processes, and waste streams; identified stakeholders; listed potential emergencies; and gathered training materials. The participation of shop-floor people in designing an EMS is essential to its successful implementation because it encourages their ownership of the process and provides an opportunity for deeper involvement in a global issue.

The greatest challenge to a small company such as Milan is the allocation of human resources to the project while production demands are high. It seemed to have the manpower and money for new projects, but never both at the same time. Training sessions were scheduled where some workers clocked in a half hour early or a half hour late for training. During the shift, some training was repeated several times to small groups while production continued. The company's best success occurred with "brown bag" sessions, where the trainees brought their lunches, listened to a training presentation while they ate, and remained "on the clock" for the lunch period.

It must be accepted that most training time in a busy company will be paid at overtime rates. Nevertheless, opportunities exist for reducing EMS implementation costs for those companies that have earned ISO 9000 certification. Not only is the implementation process similar, but also they have similar program elements—such as document control, management review and internal audits—that may be shared.

A cost/benefit analysis of Milan's EMS is difficult because several of the important benefits cannot be assigned monetary value. These intangible benefits involve the perceptions of all those with whom the company does business or communicates. For example, Milan's proactive environmental approach has improved its stature and assisted in communications with regulatory agencies. Being one of the first in the industry to successfully implement an EMS may encourage customers to perceive Milan as innovative, and perhaps more capable than its competitors. An EMS may provide lending institutions and insurance companies a perception of lower risk, which can lead to lower interest rates or premiums. Similarly, it is impossible to tally the citations that are not written, the lawsuits not filed, and the fines not levied because an accident does not happen. If an accident does happen, an EMS would potentially influence stakeholders to perceive the problem as an understandable mistake by a company that is otherwise environmentally competent.

Globe Metallurgical Inc.

Globe Metallurgical Inc. is a privately owned producer of silicon metal and specialty ferrosilicon products. It operates 10 submerged-arc furnaces located in four manufacturing facilities in Beverly, Ohio; Selma, Alabama; Springfield, Oregon; and Niagara Falls, New York. Globe is the oldest ferroalloy company in the United States and the largest U.S. producer of silicon metal and specialty ferroalloys. Silicon metal is marketed to the primary aluminum and the chemical industries, and the specialty ferroalloys are used in the foundry industry. Globe has been recognized by its customers as a quality leader in the industry, winning the first Malcolm Baldrige Quality Award for small business in 1988, The Shigeo Shingo Prize for Manufacturing Excellence in 1989, General Motors' Targets for Excellence, and Ford's Total Quality Excellence award.

Globe decided to participate in NSF's EMS demonstration project after receiving a survey requesting information on its environmental management program from a customer. Another customer had included environmental commitment in its current Supplier Excellence Agreement. Finally, Globe sells about 25 percent of its specialty ferroalloys overseas, and as is the case with ISO 9000, some early indications are that ISO 14001 registration will be a prerequisite for doing business internationally, especially in Europe. The demonstration project is helping establish an EMS that will satisfy Globe's requirement for continuous improvement while meeting any future requirements requested by customers or regulatory agencies.

At the beginning of the demonstration project, Globe did not have a formal EMS program in place. Its focus was to satisfy the federal, state, and local environmental regulations. The EMS consisted of a corporate environmental policy and various programs established at each of the manufacturing plants. Each plant had implemented parts of an EMS, without knowing it at the time, based on requirements of the local regulatory agencies, rather than as a result of corporate directives.

Globe decided to perform a self-assessment of its EMS for all four plants, to identify what was in place by looking at records, talking with individuals at each plant, and comparing this information with the requirements of NSF 110. The results indicated that Globe had partially implemented some of the elements of NSF 110, but with very few elements complete.

To continue to make progress in this area, Globe must tackle the fact that people are resistant to change. New procedures and programs must demonstrate some actual benefits before they are ever fully accepted, as was the case during the initial phases of Globe's ISO 9000 implementation. What the company learned during the ISO 9000 certification process should make establishing an effective EMS less stressful. Employee training and clear internal communications are the critical elements of a successful program.

Globe expects that once the EMS is in place and effectively implemented, the firm will be able to demonstrate continuous improvement in the environmental arena. As with the quality system, it expects some financial rewards. The 1990 amendments to the Clean Air Act require monitoring of emissions limits and paying fees based on tons of pollutants emitted. For this reason, reducing emissions saves money by reducing waste and by limiting air pollution fees. In addition, with the interest shown by customers, ISO 14001 registration will also be a valuable marketing tool.

Globe has also recently started on the road to ISO 9000 registration. Two of the four plants have been ISO 9002 certified, with the remaining two scheduled for review. Where it is appropriate, the ISO 14001 requirements will be included in the existing management system. Some of the elements, such as training, documentation, and management review, have obvious opportunities for ISO 9002/14001 integration. Employees do not want to be responsible for learning and maintaining several sets of procedures; therefore, where it is appropriate, quality, environmental, and safety concerns have been integrated into work instructions and training sessions. Environmental, quality, and safety concerns have always been included in Globe's Quality, Efficiency, Cost (QEC) monthly meeting. The QEC is a committee composed of management members from all four plants and the corporate office. It is logical that the new EMS would be integrated into the existing management system along with quality and safety.

Hach Company

Hach Company is an international manufacturer and distributor of instruments for analysis and reagents for colorimetric testing, with fiscal year 1995 sales of more than $105 million. Instruments include spectrophotometers for field and laboratory use, turbidimeters, electrochemical meters, and chemical process monitoring equipment. The company is headquartered in Loveland, Colorado, where instruments are manufactured and assembled, and maintains a chemical manufacturing plant in Ames, Iowa. The Ames facility was the participating site for this study.

Hach decided to participate in this study for several reasons. A properly structured and implemented EMS (1) provides assurances to the officers, board of directors, and company stockholders that the company is equipped to meet regulatory compliance issues and handle environmental issues facing the company through adequate staffing and other resources; (2) provides a logical framework to maintain support from senior management and a commitment of resources to meet the environmental objectives and targets of the organization; (3) can help create market opportunities for the company, and can bring to the fore issues facing customers that the company may want to address; (4) can be a mechanism used to gauge environmental performance (i.e., "Are we doing the right things right at the right times?"); and (5) may help the company define its responsibilities beyond the regulatory and statutory requirements for all stakeholders in the company (which includes stockholders, employees, the community, neighbors, customers, vendors, and suppliers).

Hach Company is registered to ISO 9001 and is a member of the Chemical Manufacturers Association (CMA) and CMA's Responsible Care® program. Responsible Care® requires Hach Company to fully implement CMA's six Codes of Management Practices over a five-year time period, with elements that share some requirements with the EMS standards.

Hach decided to study the Ames facility because its chemical production processes are most heavily affected by environmental issues. In addition, it is the only Hach facility currently participating in the Responsible Care® program.

Before signing onto the project, Hach reviewed the NSF 110 and ISO 14001 standards for similarities and found the two standards to be in very close agreement. Next, it looked at its own internal environmental strengths and weaknesses and compared them to the elements of the NSF 110 EMS standard.

The self-assessment was conducted by the company's internal quality director. He familiarized himself with the standard and interviewed the environmental safety and health department staff at length. Throughout the self-assessment audit, the quality director gathered information to support implementation of given elements of the standard. The internal auditor determined that the firm currently complied with roughly 33 percent of the standard, which was about the average for the entire NSF study group and about where Hach anticipated to be at this initial stage.

In order to fully implement an EMS, some of the key areas the company needed to address were related to documentation and document control and communications. Other elements were either already implemented or in progress. Hach believed that its ISO 9001 system for quality control provided it with good models for documentation, document control, records retention, and communications.

One particularly important environmental issue for the company is the impact of Hach's chemical products on its international customer base. What environmental effects and issues did customers face? How could the company simultaneously meet the needs of the Fortune 500 company and the "mom and pop" shop or the wastewater treatment plant? How did the needs of a customer in Singapore differ from those of a customer in Germany? Were customers capable of meeting their legal and regulatory requirements with regard to the products Hach supplied to them? Should customers be assisted with their environmental concerns, even when they purchased the problem chemicals elsewhere? What additional liabilities, if any, extend to the company?

An important aspect of an EMS involves examining a business by defining key stakeholders, such as raw material suppliers, manufacturing equipment suppliers, and others. This is a perspective that, until now, Hach hadn't fully considered. What if a supplier's plant is shut down due to a chemical release or fire? Could Hach benefit from defining the company's stakeholders and the issues they face?

While the implementation of an EMS and its associated costs were not exceptionally burdensome, Hach recognized that it does take time and requires a strong commitment from management. Hach Company will proceed with its plans to meet the objectives outlined in the Responsible Care™ Codes of Management Practice, and will simultaneously meet similar goals outlined in the EMS. As an added advantage, Hach feels the lessons it has learned through ISO 9001 registration will aid it in the implementation of an EMS.

Hach Company has not yet determined whether registration to ISO 14001 is a viable or valuable pursuit. It has many issues to consider, and the ISO 14001 standard seems to raise many questions that must be answered before committing the resources necessary for its implementation. What is the full cost of implementation, and what benefits accrue to the company? Would it lose customers by not registering? Will there be a market demand for it? Does an EMS fit the company culture? How does an EMS fit it with auditing policies and procedures? Will ISO 14001 become a de facto standard that must be implemented in order to remain in compliance with regulations? These and many more questions have to be answered before Hach Company can determine the most appropriate and beneficial approach to the implementation of an EMS. Regardless of the ultimate direction it takes, it believes it will have benefited greatly from participating in this study. At minimum, an honest assessment of the company's EMS (or lack thereof) has provided Hach with some wonderful insights into its strengths and weaknesses and may provide some opportunities for the company.

Allergan, Inc.

Allergan, Inc., a manufacturer of eye care and skin care products, is headquartered in Irvine, California, with operations worldwide. The Allergan, Inc., facility in Waco, Texas, participated in the NSF International EMS Demonstration Project.

The following represent some of the reasons Allergan is pursuing the development of a formal EMS, as well as independent certification under various worldwide standards:

- Compliance should be ensured if a formal EMS is in place.
- A high environmental standard is already in place at Allergan.
- Allergan's competitors are preparing for these standards and intend to become certified.
- Required participation in formal EMS development is anticipated if the voluntary efforts are not effective.

- Obtaining permits and approvals from government agencies and communities is expected to be streamlined if a facility has an ISO 14000 or Eco-Management and Auditing Scheme (EMAS) certification.
- Regulatory audits and inspections should be reduced.
- Ministry of Health/FDA new drug approvals and other required approvals should be streamlined.
- EH&S operations at the facility will operate better over time because a formal plan and actions associated with attaining and maintaining certification are in place.
- There are perceived marketing opportunities by easing the entrance into new markets.

The Waco facility already had a very well developed and formalized environmental standard in place. Allergan wanted to test this program against the NSF 110 standard and determine where improvements could be made. This facility also had attained ISO 9002 certification and had a formalized quality process in operation. The facility is routinely inspected by the FDA, as well as other agencies, and thus was ready to be evaluated by an external independent third party with a focus on the EMS.

NSF provided a self-assessment tool along with training and workshops providing guidance on how to use the assessment tool and how to interpret the status of the items listed in the NSF 110 Standard. Allergan's Facility Management Team and Corporate EH&S Team supported the pilot project. An internal assessment was conducted by Allergan prior to the independent third-party assessment. Some minor deficiencies in the EMS were discovered, and corrective actions were implemented. Next, Allergan contracted with one of the assessors who had been working with the NSF standard development team to conduct an independent self-assessment three months later at the Waco facility. The independent assessor was provided with an environmental manual, which covered the nine items contained in the NSF 110 standard, and was given one day to complete the assessment.

By bringing together various efforts and parties, such as the EH&S effects and policy, business and legal requirements, stakeholder interests, and the objectives and targets at the facility level, this pilot project proved to be very beneficial. Allergan also benefited from the development of written EMS implementation action plans based on the desired targets and objectives of the project.

Some EMS standards interpretation issues the company is addressing include the following:

1. It is not clear within the EMS standards whether certification at a particular facility belonging to an organization must stand alone on all

items, or if some of the items can be corporate-driven and others facility-driven. One example is product design. Allergan's Waco manufacturing facility has very little control over product design, including packaging. It may be several years after research and development of a product before the manufacturing facility is aware of the product.

2. It is not clear what the threshold criteria are for certification. Can a facility achieve certification if all items within the EMS standards are not complete? Guidance is needed to allow internal judgment as to whether a facility is ready for the certification process or not.

3. A one-day on-site review of the EMS was not adequate to cover all items and show evidence of achievement. Two days would be adequate. It would be better to have two assessors evaluate a facility, thereby ensuring a more objective view of the EMS, as well as allowing "reality checks" between the assessors.

NIBCO, Inc.

NIBCO, Inc., is a worldwide manufacturer of fluid handling (plumbing) products for the residential, commercial, and industrial markets. Founded in 1904, NIBCO is a family-owned Fortune 1000 and Forbes 500 company. NIBCO has 13 manufacturing facilities, 11 of which are ISO 9002 certified, and employs approximately 3,200 associates worldwide. NIBCO is committed to continued excellence, leadership, and stewardship in protecting the environment and conserving natural resources. Environmental protection, including compliance with applicable laws and regulations, is a primary management responsibility and the responsibility of every NIBCO associate.

In light of constantly and rapidly changing public expectations, community concerns, customer expectations, and federal, state, and local legislative and regulatory activities, it is recognized that successful companies can no longer merely respond to these changes. NIBCO realized that it had to learn how to anticipate these changes and adopt new ways of providing for continuous improvement in its efforts to manage environmental compliance and environmental performance. The fundamental driving force behind developing and implementing an EMS was the desire and need to formally define the structure, practices, procedures, processes, and resources necessary to ensure regulatory compliance and continual environmental improvement.

NIBCO's EMS is focused around two distinct, yet intimately connected, concepts: total quality environmental management (TQEM) and waste minimization and pollution prevention (WM/PP). The key objective was to expand on the concepts, tools, and experiences of NIBCO's ISO 9002 quality system and apply them to environmental compliance and environmental management. This allowed NIBCO to integrate the control, monitoring, and management aspects of the quality management system with the cost-saving benefits of WM/PP. The process of developing the EMS involved an in-depth evaluation of the existing ISO 9002 quality system, the development of national and international EMS standards (e.g., ISO 14000, NSF 110, BS 7750, CSA Z750), and a review of the company's environmental policy and environmental objectives. This evaluation resulted in the development of an internal environmental management standard unique to NIBCO. This internal standard outlined the minimum requirements for the development and implementation of a formalized, systematic environmental management program at each of the manufacturing facilities. The development, implementation, and auditing of the program are directed and supported internally by the corporate environmental department. The brunt of the work, however, is accomplished at the facility level by cross-functional environmental management teams. These teams generally include the plant manager, the plant environmental professional, the plant quality manager, and representatives from other departments within the facility, such as production, accounting, maintenance, and safety. The combination of these strategies and the involvement of cross-functional teams have been the catalysts for NIBCO's early success in its attempt to manage environmental activities.

Because the environmental management program emphasizes cross-functional team building and problem solving, it has enabled NIBCO to begin realizing some of the benefits of an EMS. The most significant results have been improvements in communication, environmental awareness throughout the company, employee involvement and interest in EMS efforts at the manufacturing facilities, and cost-savings benefits of initial WM/PP projects. Other benefits that NIBCO expects to realize in the future include reduced environmental risk and liability, marketplace advantage, improved compliance posture and relations with regulators, improved public acceptance, the ability to benchmark and measure progress against consistent methods, and strategic environmental planning and budgeting. It is also expected that continued EMS efforts will result not only in WM/PP cost savings, but also in an actual reduction in operating cost.

The process of developing and implementing an EMS has not been without its challenges. Initial barriers that had to be overcome in order to sell the concept of EMS to senior management and the manufacturing facilities included overcoming the fear of increased liability as a result of auditing, the cost of technology required to meet NIBCO's policy and objectives, and the fear of compromising production. The implementation process has presented, and continues to present, some significant hurdles and challenges, including limited time resources, lack of data required to support continual improvement, performance measurement (how and at what cost), lack of definition of best management practices, and the degree to which the EMS and ISO 9002 quality system can and should be integrated.

Despite the drawbacks and potential hurdles of implementing an EMS, doing so has provided NIBCO with a mechanism for the control of operational and waste management activities, an effective strategy for monitoring and measuring compliance status and continuously improving environmental performance, and a link to the ISO 9002 quality system and other management standards and initiatives. The combination of the concepts of EMS and TQEM has allowed the company to move toward the development of a single cohesive management system designed to meet and exceed customer expectations.

Pacific Gas and Electric Company

Pacific Gas and Electric Company (PG&E) is a public utility supplying electric and natural gas service throughout most of northern and central California. Its service territory covers 94,000 square miles with a population of about 13 million. In 1994, utility assets were about $27.3 billion, and operating revenues were $10.2 billion. PG&E has about 21,000 employees and more than 1,500 facilities subject to environmental regulations.

PG&E's electricity production comes primarily from seven natural gas-fueled power plants, two nuclear units, 70 hydroelectric powerhouses, and a geothermal energy complex. PG&E also purchases power from a wide array of resources, including hydroelectric, wind, solar, biomass, and cogeneration. Its gas supply comes primarily from Canada (54 percent) and the U.S. Southwest (42 percent), with the remainder from California fields.

PG&E's participation in this project was driven primarily by its desire to benchmark its existing EMS against the developing international standard and against the other participants in the project. PG&E's goal was to use the project to identify areas for potential improvements. Participation had the additional benefit of providing a realistic assessment of what would be required to achieve ISO 14001 certification, should a business need for certification develop. While PG&E does not market its products in international markets, many of its customers do, so ISO 14001 certification may provide a competitive advantage in a California energy market that is rapidly approaching deregulation.

The electric and gas services PG&E provides to its customers cannot be associated with specific production facilities. Even the routes of transmission can vary, as loads within the system change. PG&E therefore determined that its self-assessment should cover the EMS for the entire company and include all aspects of production and distribution. The self-assessment was conducted by senior managers in the environmental and law departments. Because many of the ISO 14001 requirements were already covered by the existing EMS, the principal focus was on the success of its implementation throughout the company.

From the self-assessment, PG&E created a prioritized action plan for desired improvements. In developing the action plan, the utility recognized that while some improvements have existing environmental or business justifications, others should not proceed without a business decision to seek ISO 14001 certification.

PG&E foresees two major challenges to achieving certification. The first is that the standard's strong emphasis on documentation runs counter to an ingrained corporate bias to minimize paperwork. Given that current environmental regulations already mandate extensive recordkeeping systems, establishing new voluntary documentation requirements may be a hard sell, particularly if existing systems have functioned adequately to protect the environment. As regulatory agencies themselves are moving to reduce mandatory paperwork, why levy new requirements?

The second challenge will be common to most utilities. Under ISO 9000, certification has pertained to individual production facilities, not entire companies. Because PG&E cannot tell a customer the exact source of the electrons or gas molecules it provides, certification of individual facilities is meaningless. However, if the utility must certify all (or even most) of its 1,500 facilities, the costs and administrative burden would be unacceptable. PG&E will work with the certifying bodies in an attempt to find an acceptable documentation process for the industry.

PG&E believes that participation in this demonstration project will help meet a corporate policy to continuously improve its EMS, as well as possibly position the utility for eventual ISO 14001 certification, if that is deemed a valid business need.

Conclusion

Several themes emerge from the case studies presented here. Among them are the following:

- Many of the companies had an EMS in place before they began participating in the demonstration project. They were driven to benchmark their EMS against standards by the perception that customers are, or will be, requesting that they become registered to an EMS standard.
- An ISO 9000 system, or other type of formal management system, provides a strong foundation for EMS implementation. Management systems, whether for quality, environment, or health and safety, share common elements, including policies, procedures, documentation, auditing, and corrective action. Companies that have attained, or are pursuing, ISO 9000 registration are probably at an advantage because they have many of the elements of an EMS already in place.

- EMS implementation is associated with many benefits, but most of them are difficult to quantify. This was very clear in the case of Milan Screw Products. The company recognized the potential of an EMS to reduce environmental risk (including the possibility of noncompliance), but acknowledged that these benefits are difficult to quantify because they are preventive. Despite this uncertainty, all the companies, including Milan Screw Products, have faith that an EMS will bring financial and environmental benefits in the long run. The challenge for environmental managers will be demonstrating these benefits to others within their companies; this applies to top management, as well as to individuals on the operational level who will be required to take on additional responsibilities as part of the EMS.

Craig P. Diamond manages a variety of projects at NSF International to pilot EMS standards in industry. His background is building multistakeholder partnerships to help companies improve their environmental management and performance. He wishes to thank the following individuals for their contributions to this chapter: Douglas Baggett (Hach Company), Victor Furtado (Pacific Gas & Electric Company), Steve Hall (NIBCO, Inc.), Steven Kopp (Globe Metallurgical Inc.), Charles Tellas (Milan Screw Products), Michael Whaley (Allergan, Inc.), and Bryant Winterholer (K.J. Quinn & Co.). The case studies were written by the companies featured in them. Although NSF offered general guidelines for preparing the case studies, they were developed, aside from minor editorial suggestions, without input from NSF or EPA.

SECTION TWO

Gaining Support Throughout Your Company— Improving Environmental and Business Performance

For many organizations that seem to be managed by the "fad of the month" syndrome, showing how ISO 14000 will benefit the bottom line will be a tough assignment. Expert guidance from Judith Cichowicz and Philip Marcus details the critical considerations and paybacks to bringing environmental factors into mainstream business strategy and decision making. Their positions are further supported by Howard Apsan and Bob Ferrone in chapters that highlight the opportunities for improving business processes with ISO 14000 and how these efforts will, in turn, help drive new technology initiatives.

6

Using EH&S Management Systems to Improve Corporate Profits

Philip A. Marcus

This chapter will demonstrate how an environmental management system (EMS) approach can contribute to enhanced overall corporate performance and illustrate the importance of a financial management approach to justify investments in environmental, health, and safety (EH&S) excellence beyond those required for regulatory compliance.

The case study for this chapter will be of a diversified, global company with a major stake in the following industries:

- Electronics and defense systems
- Energy systems and power generation
- Diversified manufacturing and communications

The company's situation was as follows: First, it was reducing corporate staff and needed to reorganize the environmental, health, and safety function across the company. In other words, there was a need to reduce and eliminate redundant corporate staff and to move corporate functions down to the business unit level. This included not only EH&S, but also the legal, financial, and marketing functions, among others.

Second, the company had been receiving significant pressure from its key stakeholders, including stockholders, insurance companies, banks, clients, and environmental groups, to better document its EH&S performance and to demonstrate its degree of conformance to a number of emerging national standards, including the U.S. Department of Justice Prosecution Factors, the Occupational Safety and Health Administration Voluntary Protection Program, and other emerging international standards, including the ISO 14000 series.

Finally, there was a need to better demonstrate and document the contribution of the EH&S function to overall corporate performance and profits.

The consultant's role in supporting the EH&S function in responding to these key internal and external driving forces was:

1. To assess the current performance of the existing EH&S management systems against key national and international, and external and internal, standards of practice.
2. To evaluate the EH&S function's overall contribution to corporate profitability now and in the future.
3. To identify sound EH&S-related capital projects and operations and maintenance opportunities with a favorable return on investment (ROI) to the corporation.
4. To suggest an implementation plan to support the above-mentioned improvements.
5. To assist in drafting global standards of practice to guide performance in their business subsidiaries throughout the world in accordance with the findings of the review and plans in items 1 through 4 above.

To accomplish this assignment, a six-step process was developed, as presented in Figure 6.1.

Developing the Assessment Protocol

At the request of the client, an assessment protocol was created to assist the evaluation of the EH&S management system against current and emerging national and international standards. Among the standards considered were the following:

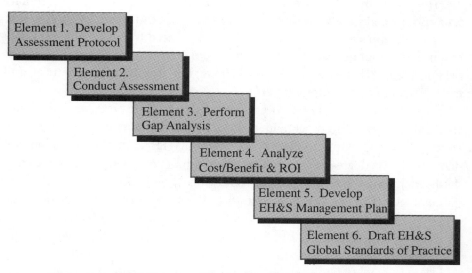

Figure 6.1 EH&S Management Assessment and Improvement Process

ISO 14001—Environmental Management Systems Specification

The elements of the 14001 EMS specification include environmental policy, planning systems, a system to ensure that implementation and operations are conducted in accordance with objectives and targets, checking and corrective action programs to respond where necessary to match performance to plan, and a top management review requirement.

Specific elements include the following:

- Environmental policy, which must be defined by top management, includes a commitment to continual improvement and prevention of pollution, and a commitment to comply with relevant environmental legislation and regulations. It will provide the framework for setting and reviewing the environmental objectives and targets and must be documented, implemented, maintained, and communicated to all employees, and be made available to the public.
- ISO 14001 planning elements require that the organization identify the environmental aspects of its activities, products, and services and determine which of those can have a significant impact on the environment. These significant environmental impacts must be accommodated in the development of the organization's environmental objectives and targets. The organization also should have developed a procedure to identify, and have access to, legal and other requirements to which the organization subscribes. The objectives and targets, along with legal and other requirements, will greatly influence the establishment and maintenance of an environmental management program that designates responsibilities and assigns means and a time frame for its achievement.
- Implementation and operation elements include developing the organizational structure and establishing accountabilities that need to be defined, documented, and communicated in order to implement the environmental management program.
- Training, awareness, and competence programs must be established to assure that all personnel whose work can have a significant impact on the environment receive appropriate training to perform their job assignments.
- Communications programs shall be established to ensure effective internal and external communication regarding environmental aspects and environmental management systems.
- Documentation systems are necessary, in paper or electronic form, to describe the core elements of the environmental management system and provide direction for document control activity.

- Operational controls must be established, as well as emergency preparedness and response controls.
- Checking and corrective action, including monitoring and measuring of systems and equipment, is necessary, as well as a well defined, documented, and implemented corrective and preventive action system to eliminate the causes of actual or potential nonconformance and to meet objectives and targets. Records and environmental management systems audits must be established and maintained to assure that the EMS conforms to planned arrangements for environmental management and has been properly implemented and maintained.
- Management review is necessary to provide top management with information on the performance of the environmental management systems and for top management to judge their continued suitability, adequacy, and effectiveness.

Department of Justice Prosecution Factors

A second standard considered was the U.S. Department of Justice (DOJ) "Factors in Decisions on Criminal Prosecution to Environmental Violations in the Context of Significant Voluntary Compliance or Disclosure Efforts by the Violator." This 1991 document identified a number of factors to be considered by the DOJ in deciding whether it should prosecute violators of environmental standards. The factors include voluntary disclosure to the DOJ, cooperation with the DOJ, the establishment of preventive measures and compliance programs to protect and correct potential violations, and the establishment of strong institutional policies to comply with all environmental requirements, including the conduct of an audit program. Additional factors include pervasiveness of noncompliance, internal disciplinary actions, and subsequent compliance efforts.

OSHA Voluntary Protection Program (VPP)

Membership in the Occupational Safety and Health Administration (OSHA) VPP program provides organizations in the United States with some exemption from reporting and inspection by OSHA. Among the requirements of the VPP program are the development of a health and safety program with objectives and goals, priorities, practices and responsibilities, concurrence of the employee representative, development of management responsibility, and provision of resources. The program also includes assigning of accountability, informing employees of their EH&S responsibilities, establishing disciplinary approaches, developing written corporate standards, and involving employees in health and safety programs. Also required are a job process hazards analysis, a management of change process, required commitment of contractors to health and safety, prior assessment of new or updated facility processes and materials, correct placement of hazard controls, implementation of emergency prevention and response programs, communication and awareness programs, and recordkeeping systems. Finally, it includes development of auditing and monitoring systems, prompt corrective action, annual self-assessment, and regular performance evaluation.

The requirements of each of these standards were organized into an assessment protocol, using a 0–3 scale to measure conformance, as follows:

0—EMS element not developed
1—EMS element developed and documented
2—EMS element communicated and implemented
3—EMS element audited, assessed, and verified

Conducting the Assessment

There are three major aspects to conducting an assessment or gap analysis. These include, first, conducting interviews with key personnel at corporate, business unit, and facility locations; confirming their level of awareness, and the degree of implementation of the EH&S system; and observing and verifying the effectiveness of each major EH&S management system element.

Second, a document and document systems review is necessary. Since many of these standards require explicit documentation, documents must be reviewed to determine the extent of documentation, the dissemination of documents, and the completeness of EH&S documentation.

Finally, it is essential to verify EH&S systems implementation. The verification stage looks for demonstration of EH&S management systems implementation and any corrective action program established to address nonconformance, as well as the effectiveness of any corrective actions taken.

Performing the EMS Gap Analysis

The gap analysis, illustrated in Figure 6.2, essentially compares the current level of implementation of the EH&S management system against the requirements of a given set of standards. Figure 6.2 illustrates a hypothetical gap analysis of the EMS against the ISO 14001 specification, as portrayed on a bar chart. EMS implementation lies on a scale of 0 to 100; any score less than 100 represents a gap that should be closed to attain full conformance with the standard.

The causes of the gap are illustrated in Figure 6.3, which portrays the results of the gap analysis. This provides the basis for developing specific action items to reduce the gap and conform to the standard desired.

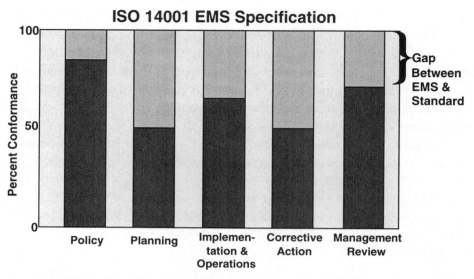

Figure 6.2   Element Three: EMS Gap Analysis Against Standards

Cost/Benefit and Return on Investment Analysis

Element 4—Cost/Benefit and Return on Investment (ROI) Analysis examines the benefits and costs of potential EH&S improvements to identify changes that are financially viable. It also identifies the contribution of specific EH&S improvements to the conduct of the business, including areas of regulatory relief, cost reduction, profitability enhancement, reduction of risks and liabili-

	Not Developed (0)	Developed/ Documented (1)	Communicated/ Implemented (2)	Assessed/ Verified (3)
Policy	Does not contain all ISO required elements.			
Planning	No formalized method for setting objectives at every level			
Implementation & Operations		Not all procedures developed	Certain procedures trained and implemented	
Checking and Corrective Action		Audit program developed	Incomplete audits at sites	Corrective action program not verified
Management Review		Process for review and improvement documented	Not implemented	

Figure 6.3   Element Three: Perform EMS Assessment (example)

ties, provision of competitive advantage, trade enhancement and provision of marketing advantage for products and services. This analysis defined three major categories for conducting the cost/benefit and ROI review to close the gaps identified in Element 3 above, and to meet the requirements of national and international standards.

Category One—Capital Cost and Investment

This included pollution control, pollution prevention, and resource conservation investments and accident prevention opportunities.

Category Two—Expenses

This category included reductions or increases in operation and maintenance costs, including use of raw materials and energy and requirements for external assistance.

Category Three—Human Resources

This category evaluated requirements for additional employees, reallocated employee hours, training needs, and time required to implement new standards.

Based on this assessment, the following environmental opportunities were identified with potential for benefiting the overall financial performance of the corporation:

- Pollution prevention
- Resource conservation
- Reducing capital project and process changes mistakes
- Eliminating accidental releases
- Eliminating fines and penalties
- Reducing site remediation reserves
- Disposing of previously unsaleable properties

With regard to major safety cost and opportunities, the following were found to be economically viable:

- Capital project and process change mistakes
- Workers' compensation allowance
- Lost time incidents and accidents

The potential EH&S-related savings is substantial. Improvements in pollution prevention can result in avoiding capital expenditures for pollution control equipment that are not valuable and productive uses of capital. The company found that about 5 percent of capital budgets represented redesign and rework required because EH&S considerations were not addressed early enough in the capital planning process. It discovered that resource conservation, including energy conservation, but also effective capture and reuse of raw materials, can result in a major reduction of raw material costs in resource-intensive industries. The capital required to design and build such systems can be recovered within two to three years of the investment.

The company found that the cost of responding to releases of pollutants or hazardous substances is often greatly underestimated. The full cost of response is often five to ten times the amount of any fine levied, when cleanup costs, outside engineering and legal assistance, damages payments, downtime, and managerial oversight costs are evaluated.

U.S.-based, publicly traded companies have to set aside substantial reserves to cover actual or potential environmental liabilities or workers' compensation costs. Reduction of the need for these investments can free considerable capital for more productive investment. All in all, the savings generated by EH&S activities was the equivalent of almost one billion dollars in revenue, and translated to several cents per share in profits.

Figure 6.4 demonstrates the projected annual cost and after-tax savings in millions of dollars (US) over a five-year period for another company. The last bar shows net program savings of over $4 million. This also represented an ROI well beyond the "hurdle rate" required for corporate approval.

However, the problem is very often how to gain approval to make early expenditures that will eventually lead to savings. Figure 6.5 illustrates the cost/benefit relationship of EH&S program investment over time. The problem

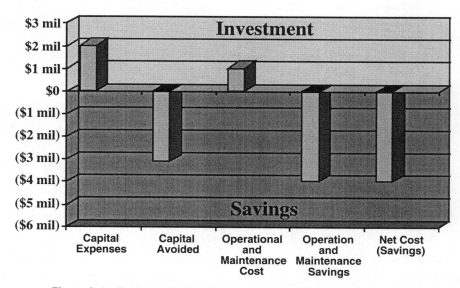

Figure 6.4   Projected Annual Costs and After-Tax Savings (projected)

in many companies is almost always how to justify near-term expenditures that will result in longer-term profits.

Developing an EH&S Management Plan

Once the improvements with positive effects on corporate financial performance were identified, a revised EH&S management program was required for implementation. This essentially followed the ISO 14001 EMS requirements for development of a focused program for achieving policy, objectives, and targets. Essential elements of this program include:

1. Defining responsibilities;
2. Setting defined, objective, quantitative performance measures;
3. Identifying the means and the time frame to implement the performance measures; and
4. Assuring that management of change procedures are developed for new activities, products, and services.

Before the plan could be finalized, overall program dimensions needed to be defined. The dimensions related to the major EH&S management priorities are indicated in Figure 6.6. The organization identified three categories of management priorities to which a plan needed to respond. The three areas include, first, preventive processes to assure that no errors were made in new activities that could generate an environmental, health, or safety problem. These program elements included capital project and process change guidance, property management and due diligence standards, guidance to those involved in designing products and packaging, and, finally, development of material and energy usage guidelines for pollution prevention and resource conservation programs.

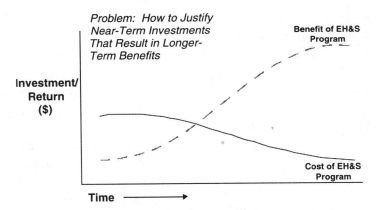

Figure 6.5   Cost/Benefit Relationship of EH&S Program Investment

Figure 6.6   Major EH&S Management Priorities

Second, daily or routine management processes, especially at operating locations, must assure regulatory compliance and continual improvement, including reduction of costs and risks. While the corporate level itself cannot ensure effective daily management, it can develop the tools and means to assist facilities to perform EH&S management in a manner consistent with the corporate worldwide standards and regulatory requirements.

Finally, strategic management processes help the organization anticipate, track, and respond to emerging issues and to integrate EH&S into the business at appropriate levels.

The organization decided that a management system approach would be necessary not only to assure compliance, but also to meet its overall EH&S priorities. Figure 6.7 illustrates the relationship of management systems to compliance. The only sustainable way to meet compliance is through a management system. At that point, efficiency improves and cost and risk can decrease, thus permitting pollution prevention and resource conservation benefits to be obtained.

Figure 6.8 illustrates the EH&S management program that was developed.

Drafting Global Standards of Practice

The corporation determined that global standards of practice were needed that would translate its policies, objectives, and targets into program requirements and responsibilities at the corporate, business unit, and facility levels. A standard states the basic requirements to be met and establishes minimum actions to meet the requirements, but is flexible in that it allows operating units

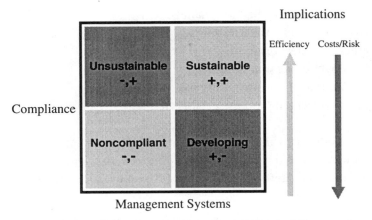

Figure 6.7   Relationship of Management Systems to 100 percent EH&S Compliance

latitude in how they meet the basic requirements and their performance standards. The following standards were identified by this corporation:

1. Accountability
2. EH&S management systems
3. Acquisitions, divestitures, and real property transactions

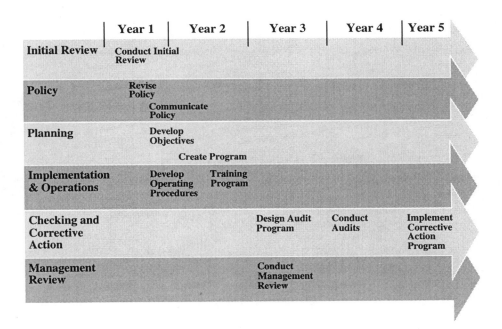

Figure 6.8   EH&S Management Program

4. Environmental protection management
5. Occupational health and safety
6. Emergency response
7. Employee education training
8. Communications and awareness
9. EH&S aspects of products and services

The next steps for this program are to gain internal commitment, to test, evaluate, and analyze the results of applying the standards at pilot facilities throughout the organization, and then to roll out the program globally.

Conclusions

In summary, an EMS approach, including a financial analysis, can demonstrate overall performance improvement to the corporation's top management in "dollars and cents" language. Today's company must justify any EH&S investments beyond the simple commitment to compliance. The justification can be based on the following elements:

- A favorable cost/benefit and ROI analysis;
- Improved liability and risk management;
- Continued access to markets for products and services; and
- Enhanced EH&S performance of products and services.

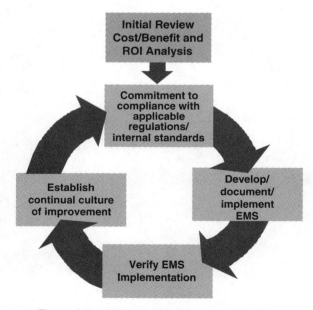

Figure 6.9   EH&S Implementation Framework

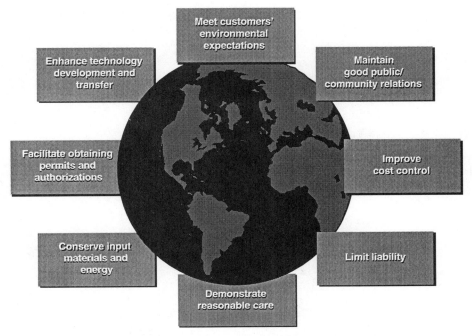

Figure 6.10   Benefits of Integrated EH&S Management System

The basic framework for implementing a full functioning EMS is illustrated in Figure 6.9. This includes (1) an initial review of performance against standards, including cost/benefit and ROI analysis; (2) a commitment by top management to compliance and conformance to applicable regulations and internal standards; (3) the development, documentation, and implementation of an EMS; and (4) the verification of EMS implementation and performance and the establishment of a culture of continual improvement. If these are accomplished, we can expect the benefits illustrated in Figure 6.10 to be gained.

Philip A. Marcus is a Vice President with ICF Kaiser at their Fairfax, VA headquarters. Mr. Marcus has over 20 years experience in environmental management and performance enhancement. For the past ten years he has developed environmental, health, and safety (EHS) management systems which improve compliance and competitive advantage for Fortune 500 companies, including benchmarking, strategic EHS plans, worldwide standards of EHS practice, TQM-based systems, and reporting measurement and improvement systems.

Mr. Marcus is a US Delegate to ISO Technical Committee 207 and serves as ANSI's technical expert on Subcommittee 1, Environmental Management Systems. He negotiated the ISO 14004 Environmental Management Systems Guidance Standard on behalf of the US. He is a member of the US Panel which interprets the ISO 14001 EMS standards.

7

Standardizing Environmental Management beyond ASTM

Howard N. Apsan

Just as nature abhors a vacuum, environmental managers hate uncertainty and inconsistency. Bosses have differing expectations, companies have differing policies, states have differing regulations; and international regulations are all sui generis. If that were not bad enough, environmental management is an inherently tricky business, because absolute truths and conclusive scientific data are in short supply. The fact that so many environmental professionals are engineers and scientists, yet so little of their work is quantifiable or absolute, simply adds to the frustration. It is enough to make environmental managers throw up their hands in dismay.

Historically, as practitioners of total quality environmental management (TQEM) are well aware, standardizing products or equipment tends to be much more straightforward than standardizing processes or services. Nevertheless, environmental professionals have taken up the challenge with great vigor, first by attempting to standardize the environmental assessment process (largely under the rubric of the American Society for Testing and Materials (ASTM)) and, more recently, by attempting to establish standards for environmental management under the aegis of the International Standards Organization (ISO).

Today, the environmental profession is abuzz with ISO 14000, the benchmarking system for a wide range of environmental activities. The promise of a standardizing scheme that is broad in scope and global in perspective is quite tantalizing and should be embraced with optimism. It is the latest effort in what appears to be an ongoing attempt to control and rationalize some complex and cumbersome environmental processes. This chapter will attempt to provide some comparative perspective, and, it is hoped, give us a clearer sense of what to expect.

Environmental Assessment Standards

Few processes in the environmental field engendered more conflict and frustration than environmental site assessment. How much diligence is due diligence? How far beyond the site is beyond concern? How many historical documents are needed, and how far back should they go? These and related questions began to test the efficiency of the assessment process. As the demand for environmental assessments proliferated, the lack of standardization posed an ever greater problem.

Just as things started to look bleak, along came several standard-setting and professional associations that started to create order out of the chaos. Better known for its standards on mechanical equipment and child-safe toys, the ASTM, through its Environmental (E-50) Committee, began to carry the banner for environmental standardization.

Probably the crowning achievement of the E-50 committee was the Phase I Environmental Site Assessment Standard Practice (E1527-93), promulgated in 1993. Although this standard was established with a fairly narrow focus (relative to lender liability under CERCLA), it evolved into something much more. One can still hear occasional griping from environmental purists, but to most, the ASTM has all but revolutionized the environmental assessment process by creating the (virtually) universally recognized standard for conducting a Phase I assessment. (Although it is clearly a U.S. standard, some lenders or purchasers rely on ASTM protocols for multisite assessments, even when some of those properties are outside the United States.)

Prior to the issuance of ASTM E1527-93, every consultant had a preferred Phase I checklist, every bank had unique sets of protocols, and every environmental attorney had to protect clients from ever-changing scopes of work and limitations of liability. Now, just about everyone recognizes the ASTM standard as the site assessment benchmark. If individuals decide to vary from the standard, they will generally first cite the standard and then address the "out-of-scope considerations" that they feel need to be added.

The success of E1527-93 led to the drafting of additional standardization documents by ASTM and by others. In addition to E1527-93, ASTM's E-50 committee began to generate documents on a wide array of environmental concerns, ranging from asbestos to underground storage tanks and covering issues as complex and diverse as regulatory compliance auditing and subsurface investigations. Now, looming on the horizon, is possibly the ultimate in environmental standardization schemes: ISO 14000.

Why ISO 14000?

As an environmental standardization scheme, ISO 14000 has the potential to outstrip the impact of even the most successful ASTM standards. The broad reach and long arm of the various ISO 14000 standards present a difference in kind from existing environmental standards. Whereas ASTM has revolutionized environmental due diligence, primarily in the transactional arena, ISO 14000 standards will likely affect the much broader arena of environmental management. This includes environmental management systems, environmental auditing, environmental labeling, environmental performance evaluation, and life-cycle assessments. ISO 14000 has no less an ambitious goal than to standardize these environmental activities on a global basis. While that might sound like overreaching, the same was said about the ISO 9000 quality management standards that have since become the sine qua non for doing business in Europe and beyond.

As a result, it is time to start taking a harder look at some of the potential implications of ISO 14000 while there is still sufficient time to influence its ultimate form. This assessment should address at least two key questions. First, how is ISO 14000 different from the plethora of existing and emerging environmental management and auditing systems? Second, what are the potential implications of living under an ISO 14000 regime?

How Is ISO 14000 Different?

The International Standards Organization, headquartered in Geneva, Switzerland, is the parent organization of the ISO family of standards. Its U.S. affiliate is the American National Standards Institute (ANSI). And, although they are occasionally rivals in the standardization game, ANSI, ASTM, and the American Society for Quality Control (ASQC) are teamed together to administer the ISO 14000 process, with ANSI serving as the lead organization of the U.S. Technical Advisory Group (TAG) to ISO Technical Committee (TC) 207, and ASTM and ASQC administering the TAG and the sub-TAGs. Based on this lineup, it is safe to assume that any ISO 14000 standards will at least address some of the ongoing efforts at standardization, including ASTM standards currently in progress. On the other hand, care must be taken to avoid duplication of effort, not to mention the potential for stepping on some delicate toes.

The focus of ISO 14000 is where the key difference lies. Where the ASTM standards focus largely on specific environmental concerns—a property transfer, an underground storage tank closure—ISO 14000 addresses broader environmental issues—management systems, life-cycle analysis, eco-labeling. Where existing standards focus largely on legal and regulatory liability—lender liability, state transfer acts, regulatory disclosure—ISO 14000 focuses largely on business concerns—effective and efficient management systems, profit maximization through pollution prevention, recycling and reuse, and truth in labeling—to ensure a level playing field.

Environmental Management under ISO 14000

If one wants to venture a guess as to what environmental life will be like under ISO 14000, a good place to start would be with ISO 9000. Although ISO standards are all voluntary, it should be remembered that they came into existence to fill a gap. Therefore, although compliance is voluntary, one declines to comply at one's peril. On the other hand, the scope of ISO 9000 is quite limited, relative to ISO 14000, and ISO 9000 does not potentially conflict with existing and upcoming local, state, national, and international regulatory obligations.

Cutting through all the hype surrounding ISO 14000, the promulgation of several new guidelines is not likely to generate earth-shattering results. Before the ASTM environmental site assessment standard was issued, people were still conducting environmental due diligence; they just did not have the benefit of a neat, well-organized, and widely accepted benchmark. ASTM E1527-93 provided that benchmark. Of course, establishing a benchmark has pluses and minuses. The pluses, obviously, are the benefits of uniformity and consistency. The minuses include the forced obsolescence of other schemes, some of which may have been quite effective.

The same will likely be said of ISO 14000, if it lives up to its promise and becomes the environmental management benchmark. Remember countless environmental management systems, life-cycle assessment programs, and green-labeling schemes have existed and are thriving, and their impact is measurable and material. What ISO 14000 adds to the mix is the potential to integrate all the disparate components on a worldwide basis and, yes, add some uniformity and consistency.

The effort to standardize environmental management under ISO 14000 or any other systemic approach is still in its nascent stages. Most business people welcome standardization because it minimizes the confusion, complexity, and controversy associated with environmental quality. On the other hand, they have learned expensive lessons in the past by buying into various standardization schemes that lost their popularity and impact over time. The success and apparent longevity of ISO 9000 would suggest that it behooves business to jump on the ISO 14000 bandwagon before it leaves without them. On the other hand, if it is the wrong vehicle, it might be just as well to let it pass. The decision is a difficult one.

Howard N. Apsan is Director of Environmental Management Services, Northeastern Operations, for Clayton Environmental Consultants, Inc., in Edison, New Jersey, and also serves on the faculty at Columbia University. He advises clients on environmental management and compliance issues.

8

New Opportunities for Expanding P2

Judith A. Cichowicz

A recurring challenge for pollution prevention (P2) practitioners within corporations is to effectively communicate to their company leaders how a specific P2 project can directly contribute to the bottom line by making money or reducing operating costs, in addition to potentially reducing regulatory fines.

P2 technicians and managers who view the objective of pollution prevention solely as emissions reduction impede their companies' ability to judge their true environmental performance, because implementation of emissions reductions gives ever-diminishing returns—and eliminating all emissions can be accomplished only through closing down all production. Furthermore, when emissions reductions are attained through a regulatory enforcement action (or a threat of such action), they often are automatically perceived by senior management as a negative, a drain on limited resources.

When P2 is woven into an environmental management system, however, it gains a vocabulary and organizational structure that enables the company to better understand the monetary benefits of specific P2 projects and evaluate such projects objectively against other competing expenditures. In this way, P2 expands its mission to embrace any activity that improves overall environmental performance.

The ISO 14000 standard on environmental management systems offers an important vehicle for integrating the traditional "P2 culture" into an overall environmental management approach that can further business objectives. Meeting the requirements of the ISO 14000 standard will be achievable for many companies. Organizations that have already begun implementing the existing ISO standard on quality management (ISO 9000) will be a step ahead, since the framework they have developed for meeting that standard can be expanded to encompass ISO 14000 as well.

This chapter begins with an introduction to ISO 9000 and ISO 14000, both of which can be influential in promoting or inhibiting P2 implementation. (It also briefly discusses other approaches to environmental management that have been developed.) The chapter goes on to describe the components of an ISO 14000 environmental management system and analyzes who has a stake in

ISO 14000. Finally, the chapter notes some beginning steps that a P2 practitioner can take to integrate pollution prevention into the company's overall environmental management scheme.

ISO 9000

ISO 9000 refers to a series of standards on quality management systems (QMS). Included within the series are specification standards (ISO 9001, 9002, 9003) that define requirements, and guidance standards (ISO 9004) that assist a company in implementing a quality management system. As of late 1995, 8,026 U.S. facilities had been registered to one of the ISO 9000 specification standards.[1]

The objective of a quality management system designed to an ISO 9000 specification standard is to provide the purchaser of a product or service with confidence that the product or service provider meets a specified level of quality performance. Meeting the standard requires implementing a management system structured to verify the consistency of quality processes.

ISO 9001 and 9002 specify requirements that cover an array of functions (Figure 8.1). Depending on market forces, verification of conformance to these requirements can be achieved through:

- Self-certification;
- Customer certification; or
- Third-party certification by a registrar.

Can the ISO 9000 series influence the P2 practitioner? Yes, specifically through requirements for process control, control of nonconforming products, and storage/handling. For example, if the production of a product or service results in a spill or release of a toxic chemical, a de facto nonconformity occurs under ISO 9000. Concurrently, this presents a P2 opportunity.

ISO 14000

The ISO 14000 series is directed at requirements and guidance for environmental management systems (EMS), with environmental management divided into the two broad evaluation areas of "organization" and "product and process."

The specification standard for organization is ISO 14001. Under the ISO 14001 scheme, an EMS addresses specific functional areas. A commitment to "prevention of pollution" is mandated by the standard's policy requirements.

"Prevention of pollution" is defined within ISO 14001 as the "use of processes, practices, materials or products that avoid, reduce or control pollution, which may include recycling, treatment, process changes, control mechanisms, efficient use of resources and material substitution." It is noted that the

Clause Number	ISO 9001
4.1	Management Responsibility
4.2	Quality System
4.3	Contract Review
4.4	Design Control*
4.5	Document and Data Control
4.6	Purchasing
4.7	Control of Customer-Supplied Product
4.8	Product Identification and Traceability
4.9	Process Control
4.10	Inspection and Testing
4.11	Control of Inspection, Measuring, and Test Equipment
4.12	Inspection and Test Status
4.13	Control of Nonconforming Product
4.14	Corrective and Preventive Action
4.15	Handling, Storage, Packaging, Preservation, and Delivery
4.16	Control of Quality Records
4.17	International Quality Audits
4.18	Training
4.19	Servicing
4.20	Statistical Techniques

* Not required under ISO 9002.

Figure 8.1   ISO 9001: Elements

benefits of preventing pollution are "the reduction of adverse environmental impacts, improved efficiency and reduced costs."[2]

In contrast to the ISO 9000 series (which measures consistency in work process performance), the ISO 14000 series focuses on implementing systems that are directed toward improving environmental performance. This "continuous improvement" approach requires the identification of measurable performance goals or metrics to verify improvement, rather than maintenance of the status quo. Thus, a company has the opportunity to achieve greater productivity and cost efficiency through introduction of an EMS than it may have experienced through introduction of a quality management system (QMS).

Because ISO 14000 is an international standard, and, thus, is subject to application throughout the world in countries with varying degrees of regulatory, infrastructural, and managerial development, it offers substantial latitude for a company to define facility-specific baselines from which improvement can be measured.

The ISO 14000 standards on product and process evaluation have not advanced through the consensus approval process as far as the ISO 14001 specification on EMS. Nonetheless, familiarity with these standards offers a significant opportunity for the P2 practitioner to gain credibility within the company, while responding to stakeholder demands on environmental management. The product and process standard includes three components:

- Life-cycle assessment
- Environmental labeling
- Environmental aspects in product standards

ISO 9000/ISO 14000 Synergy

Companies that are already involved with ISO 9000 (i.e., those that have achieved, or are seriously working toward, certification under this standard) can find several affinities between ISO 9001 or 9002 and ISO 14001. The synergy between the standards can enable a company to control costs by integrating the management systems used to achieve certification to the two standards. The most synergistic functions include:

- Document and data control
- Process control
- Training
- Internal auditing

Document and Data Control

Integration of document and data control is a basic cost control device. Although the actual documents and data used for quality and environmental management may be different, the process for achieving document and data control can and should be systematized.

If a company has a formal record retention process, then integration can be a simple matter of applying that process to environmental recordkeeping. To see how this could work, consider the environmental and regulatory compliance issues involved in Superfund Amendments and Reauthorization Act (SARA) Tier 2, Chemical Inventory Reporting.

ISO 9001 requires that storage areas be designated to prevent damage or deterioration of product. SARA Tier 2 requires that storage locations be reported to regulatory authorities to assist in emergency response planning. When a storage area is defined and assigned to a product, this information becomes recorded data. These records can be used to verify that things are stored where they should be so that they do not deteriorate and require emergency response.

If the quality manager and the environmental manager/company P2 practitioner refuse to build a linkage, the company will have at least two separate systems for collecting and retrieving similar data. These will be more than just redundant systems: They will be competitive systems, fighting for perennially scarce resources.

Successful companies establish a structure for formatting documents and naming them on personal computer disks so the documents can be retrieved or can otherwise function within the document control process.

Process Control

Relative to "process control," ISO 9001 states that a controlled condition includes "suitable maintenance of equipment to ensure continuing process capability." ISO 14001, as part of "operational control," mandates planning for activities, including maintenance.

Training

The training link between quality and environmental management again involves administrative procedures. These include:

- Assigning training requirements to employees; and
- Tracking implementation of those requirements.

From an administrative standpoint, it does not matter what the actual training requirements are, or whether they are used to support QMS, EMS, or both. The idea is to use a systematic approach for documenting the requirements and tracking their implementation.

Internal Auditing

The final prime candidate for integration is internal auditing, required with both QMS and EMS. Irrespective of who conducts these audits within an organization, having common administrative systems for tasks such as data collection and retention and document control facilitates the audit process and helps a company systematically identify errors and exceptions. From there, decisions can be made about improving systems for accomplishing various quality and/or environmental objectives.

In the environmental area, it is much wiser for a company to identify its weaknesses before a regulator or an activist group does. To promote the internal audit process, EPA has issued a policy statement on "Incentives for Self-Policing: Discovery, Disclosure, Correction and Prevention of Violations." Pursuant to this policy, the agency states that it will not seek gravity-based (or "punitive") penalties for environmental violations when companies voluntarily identify, disclose, and correct the violations in accordance with the requirements set out in the policy.[3]

The internal auditor role in an environmental management system is more proactive than in a quality management system, with greater flexibility for participation in the development of corrective action strategies and P2 alternatives.

Alternative Systems for Improving Environmental Performance

The concept of improving environmental performance did not originate with ISO 14000, of course. Several compatible approaches have been developed and are currently being implemented, most notably by companies within the United States, Canada, and Great Britain. Some of the more prominent initiatives are noted below.

Chemical Industry Initiatives

On December 4, 1984, a toxic release at a pesticide production facility in Bhopal, India, resulted in more than 2,500 deaths and more than 200,000 injuries. That event has been classified as the worst industrial accident in history. In its aftermath, the Canadian Chemical Producers Association developed a voluntary industry initiative for continuous improvement in chemical manufacturing, naming it Responsible Care®. Soon after, this initiative was embraced in the United States by the Chemical Manufacturers Association. The industry-defined "Codes of Management Practices" included within Responsible Care®, especially those on pollution prevention, process safety, and community awareness and emergency response, are directly applicable to ISO 14001 implementation.

In addition, both the Canadian Association of Chemical Distributors (CACD) and the National Association of Chemical Distributors (NACD) in the United States adopted their own voluntary approach to continuous improvement in chemical distribution, the Responsible Distribution Process®. As part of Responsible Distribution®, defined "Codes and Elements" establish targets for performance improvement in environmental areas, including waste reduction, emergency response, and handling and storage.

BS 7750 and NSF 110

BS 7750 is the British standard for environmental management systems. It was adopted in 1994 and has been influential in the structuring of ISO 14001.

NSF 110, which was formalized in 1995, is the U.S. standard for environmental management systems. Although the standard is voluntary and does not have the force of regulation, EPA participated as a member of the joint committee of regulatory and public health officials, users, consumers, and industry representatives that prepared this consensus document.

EMAS

The European Union (EU) is working toward eliminating trade barriers for its member companies. Like any new governmental structure, EU has developed regulations on a variety of subjects. It has created the Eco-Management and Audit Scheme (EMAS) in an effort to protect the environment, promote free trade, and foster sustainable development.

EMAS is a voluntary process for company assessment of, and ultimate improvement in, environmental performance. While EMAS is compatible with ISO 14001, it has some additional requirements. More significantly, it has the potential to become mandatory throughout the EU as early as 1998. Companies with sites located within the EU are advised to become familiar with it.

Using Compliance as a Baseline under ISO 14000

ISO 14000 permits considerable flexibility in how a company or facility approaches EMS implementation. The prudent company will use regulatory compliance as a viable baseline from which to set objectives for continuous improvement over time.

In many parts of the world, achieving environmental compliance is a rather simple implementation process. In the United States, however, a complex "command and control" regulatory structure, coupled with the legal system of a highly industrialized representative democracy, creates additional barriers to making things work.

Some environmental managers argue that compliance is not a driver for ISO 14000. But to ignore regulatory compliance in an esoteric reach for perfection in environmental performance is a perilous decision for U.S.-based facilities. As a practical matter, regulatory compliance provides a ready-made benchmark for improving environmental performance.

The Basics of an EMS under ISO 14001

To achieve successful implementation of an environmental management system that complies with ISO 14001, a company must meet the requirements of management and organizational commitment and must codify that commitment through a written policy. Moreover, the standard requires that P2 be addressed within the policy.

Once a written policy has been developed, the next step is to prepare an EMS plan for accomplishing the policies to which the company has committed. A plan would typically identify environmental "aspects" that are subject to the ISO 14001 standard. Using some type of systematic approach for determining environmental requirements, the plan would:

- Present the actual or potential environmental impacts of the aspect;
- State objectives and targets for improvement; and
- Describe the mechanism(s) or process(es) for meeting those objectives.

If a company uses regulatory compliance as a baseline, and lists in its plan all the regulations that must be complied with, it can then state impacts, based on legislative intent. Objectives and targets for improvement would consist of either initially achieving compliance or moving past compliance by some factor the organization chooses.

To see how this would work in practice, consider the management of hazardous waste, which would be an environmental aspect under ISO 14001. One impact of improper hazardous waste management can be on-site soil contamination.

In terms of stating objectives and targets for improvements, a small-quantity generator could certify that, in implementing the RCRA process for hazardous waste management, it has made a good-faith effort to minimize waste generation. The company could then go beyond this baseline effort with a planned target for improvement that is more specific, and consistent with its environmental policy. The company's objective may be to reduce the production of some specific waste stream by a stated percentage through a process modification. This could be accomplished through a plan that would include a budget allocation, a defined schedule for accomplishing the process modification, and designation of a responsible party.

Finally, the EMS program must be implemented. This requires training employees, routinely monitoring and measuring performance against the plan, identifying nonconformance, and taking corrective action when necessary. Additionally, internal audits of the system must be conducted, with senior management participating in a systematic review of audit results.

Environmental Performance Evaluation

A simple method for evaluating environmental performance under ISO 14000 is to write a goal statement and then monitor whether the goals are being met. For instance, a small-quantity generator may set as a target reducing the volume of a specific waste stream based solely on improvements in housekeeping practices. This would be written into a performance target report.

Performance could be evaluated by comparing the actual volume of the targeted waste stream with the baseline year's volume. With the advent of easy-to-use spreadsheets for personal computers, these data can be evaluated easily throughout the year. Quarterly evaluations provide the environmental manager with data that can be shared effectively to keep senior management apprised of progress throughout the year. Figure 8.2 shows a method of dis-

Environmental Regulation	Item	Goal for 1996	1995 Volume in Gallons	1996 Target Volume in Gallons	1996 Actual Volume in Gallons, First Quarter
RCRA	Waste Stream #261	Reduce volume by 5%	524	498	118

Figure 8.2   Displaying Environmental Performance Information

playing environmental performance information. (In this figure, the baseline used is the volume of waste generated in 1995.)

Environmental cost accounting is another mechanism for communicating improvements in environmental performance. Initially, it can be used to describe projected costs associated with achieving an improvement, thus serving as a component in the decision-making process. Later on, it can facilitate a monetary comparison of actual results versus projected results.

From an implementation standpoint, environmental cost accounting does not have to be a complex mathematical algorithm. In fact, simpler approaches generally are easier to explain to the broad audience of employees who ultimately must direct the fate of implementation.

Environmental Auditing under ISO 14001

There are three potential types of environmental auditing under ISO 14001:

- Internal
- External
- Extrinsic or "third-party"

Of these, only internal auditing of the environmental management system is mandatory for compliance with the standard. This type of auditing serves an internal monitoring function, determining the status of EMS implementation and systematically presenting information to management for review. Because of the emphasis on continuous improvement in environmental management systems, the ISO 14001 internal auditor is more likely to be involved in developing corrective action plans than the ISO 9000 QMS auditor.

A functioning EMS is designed to address a variety of regulatory and technical requirements. Thus, it is essential that internal auditors have competency in the areas they are asked to audit. This includes training and experience in basic audit practices, such as objective evidence collection, communication, planning, and knowledge of the ISO 14001 standard.[4] It can also include competency skills geared to the U.S. regulatory environment. For example, because ISO 14001 has an emergency preparedness and response requirement, an auditor with an OSHA Hazardous Waste Operations and Emergency Response (HAZWOPER) certification to the 24-hour level should be expected to bring to the audit a higher level of competency than someone who is not HAZWOPER certified.

In an external audit, a customer or customer representative (such as a consultant) verifies that the company is conforming to specific EMS criteria or implementing a corrective action on schedule. For example, if a customer contracts with a warehouse company for hazardous materials storage, the customer may audit to ensure that the warehouse files SARA Tier 2 reports.

"Extrinsic" auditing refers to the practice of having an independent third party (typically an ISO 14000 registrar) audit to verify conformance with the standard. As of this writing, it has not yet been decided who will be the responsible organization in the United States, or what its process for accrediting registrars will be.

Product and Process Evaluation

ISO 14000 requires that a company have a structure to conduct product and process evaluation. As noted above, this structure involves three components: life-cycle assessment, environmental labeling, and environmental aspects in product standards.

Life-Cycle Assessment

Life-cycle assessment (LCA) is emerging as a systematic tool for assessing the environmental impacts of products and services. Using a cradle-to-grave analytical approach, LCA evaluates impacts from raw material purchase through production, use, and ultimate disposal of the product. Under ISO 14000, LCA is a guidance (rather than a specification) standard. It presents the P2 practitioner with a functional method for communicating selected issues to the boardroom.

Environmental Labeling

In response to marketing pressures created by so-called green labeling, the ISO 14000 environmental labeling scheme establishes a process for using labels to inform consumers that a product meets predetermined criteria considered to promote environmentally sound purchasing decisions. Under the standard, "green" claims are subject to third-party verification—no doubt to the chagrin of marketing gurus and advertising copywriters.

Environmental Aspects

The concept of "environmental aspects evaluation" in product standards is also presented in ISO 14000 as a guidance, rather than a specification, standard. It is targeted to those who write product standards and enables environmental effects to be addressed within such standards. Among the environmental aspect components that can be addressed are the scale, severity, probability, and permanency of the impact. When implemented, this type of evaluation will make it easier for the P2 practitioner to access accurate information on products being considered for substitution.

Who Has a Stake in ISO 14000?

Exactly how substantial a role ISO 14001 and its sister standards will play in the international marketplace remains a calculated guess. The one truism is: The stakeholders will decide.

Who are the stakeholders? While the range of potential stakeholders is very broad, among the most significant are companies that make and distribute products in highly regulated industries (such as chemicals), officers and directors of regulated companies, employees, environmental leaders (particularly those seeking "environmental justice"), regulators, financial service providers—and, of course, customers.

Companies in heavily regulated industries (particularly chemical manufacturers and distributors) clearly have a stake in ISO 14000. When environmental risk is reduced or mitigated, the costs of managing product liability and environmental impairment decrease.

The officers and directors of both publicly and privately held corporations clearly have an interest in improving their organizations' environmental performance. In addition to their financial responsibility to shareholders, they have a personal interest because of their potential to become "designated jailees" in the event of criminal environmental liability. An EMS can both improve the management of environmental costs associated with past practices and reduce future liabilities through preventive action.

Employees have a stake in preserving the financial stability of their employer while enabling the company to stay internationally competitive. They further benefit when their own workplace exposure to environmental toxins is reduced. Employees who live in or near the community where their employer is located have an even greater stake. And it is employees who determine, through daily practice, whether an EMS is successfully implemented.

If perception is reality in our society, then increasing pressure from leaders within the "environmental justice" community create a reality in which "environmental racism" must be recognized and managed. The thrust of environmental justice is that the poor, minorities, and other generally disenfranchised members of the community tend to bear a disproportionate part of the costs associated with industrial pollution. Steps taken to mitigate a perceived environmental injustice, whether through a consent order or a community agreement, should be integrated into the EMS structure.

The regulatory community certainly views itself as a stakeholder. For example, during 1995, EPA funded a portion of an EMS demonstration project run by

NSF International, a not-for-profit standard-setting organization headquartered in Ann Arbor, Michigan. EPA plans to use the results of this demonstration to learn more about the potential benefits of an EMS.

A less visible (but no less important) group of stakeholders is financial service providers, such as banks, insurers, and venture capitalists. U.S.-based companies' environmental management systems are driven by a number of powerful financial forces:

- Environmental liability insurance, if available, is expensive.
- Regulatory fines for noncompliance are high.
- The indirect costs to managers of "working with the lawyers" to respond to or reduce fines can be excessive, grueling, and personally painful.
- Environmental cleanup or remediation, in response to past practices, can drain today's capital resources.
- Lending institutions do not like risk.

When an environmental management system clearly articulates P2 goals, objectives, and accomplishments—and when this fact is understood by the company's financial spokespersons—it has the effect of creating greater flexibility for tapping capital markets.

Finally, it is the marketplace that will control the destiny of ISO 14000 and drive decisions about whether a company can or must pursue it. Do customers view themselves as stakeholders? Or do they continue to shop only for today's price without taking future costs into account? Will ISO 14000 become a cost of doing business, similar to ISO 9000? A comment frequently heard in discussions on this issue is that no one wants to be first, but no one can afford to be last.

Expanding the P2 Mandate through ISO 14000

Is there an optimal approach for the P2 practitioner to fit pollution prevention into the EMS puzzle? The process must begin with obtaining a copy of the standard. The P2 practitioner must become familiar with the standard in order to identify existing and planned pollution prevention activities that may support ISO 14000. For each activity, the P2 practitioner should identify:

- The environmental aspect it affects;
- Applicable legal and regulatory requirements supported; and
- Targets/objectives and progress toward reaching them.

The practitioner should then critique the activity in order to determine whether improvements can or should be made in any areas. For purposes of ISO 14000, the areas to consider include:

- Operational control
- Emergency preparedness and response
- Records retention
- Training

The P2 practitioner should also review any records developed by the company in response to regulatory requirements. Typical records might include:

- Confined Space Entry Permits (29 CFR 1910.146)
- Process Safety Incident Reports (29 CFR 1910.119)
- Emergency Response Plan Activation Reports (40 CFR 264.56)
- Hazardous Materials Incident Reports (49 CFR 171.16)

The practitioner should then verify the status of any P2 recommendations that may have been made in the past. Have they been implemented? Is implementation in process? It is important to identify what corrective actions have been taken to mitigate the environmental consequences of past actions and what preventive actions could have been taken to eliminate the events that gave rise to these consequences.

In addition, it is important to obtain details on costs associated with actual incidents. If these costs are not readily available, they can be estimated. In arriving at an estimate, the practitioner should address such cost items as internal labor (including management time), contract labor, materials consumed, product lost, and claims settled. This simplified version of environmental cost accounting can become a fiscal benchmark for improving performance and justifying further P2 activities.

Conclusion

This chapter has considered how a P2 practitioner can begin to integrate pollution prevention into an environmental management system that can meet the requirements of ISO 14000. Using regulatory requirements as a benchmark, and describing environmental performance in business terminology, the practitioner can successfully incorporate environmental issues and P2 ideas into overall business strategies and operations. Organizations that have implemented ISO 9000 already have an established administrative framework for implementing ISO 14000.

Because business competition is increasingly dynamic and international, there can be no such thing as a perfect, static EMS. But by applying a systematic approach such as ISO 14000 to environmental problem identification and resolution, the P2 practitioner can continually enhance corporate financial performance concurrently with improving product marketability.

Notes

1. *ISO 9000 Registered Company Directory* (Fairfax, Virginia: Irwin Professional Publishing, 1995).
2. ISO/DIS 14001, TC 207/SC1, received at ANSI August 22, 1995.
3. 60 Fed. Reg. 66706-66712 (December 22, 1995).
4. ANSI/ASQC, *Guidelines for Auditing Quality Systems,* Q 10011-1-1994.

Judith A. Cichowicz is general manager of Compliance Systems, Inc., a Seattle-based consulting firm with technical expertise in both ISO 9000 and ISO 14000.

9

ISO 14001 and Environmental Management as a Technology Driver

Bob Ferrone

At first people refuse to believe that a strange new thing can be done, and then they begin to hope it can be done, then they see it can be done—then it is done and all the world wonders why it was not done centuries ago.
—Frances Hodgson Burnett, *The Secret Garden*

As exacting environmental performance criteria for new products and processes increasingly become the norm, nations with policies and economic incentives favoring environmental innovations will gain competitive advantages. Companies that develop and apply these new technologies most effectively in the global marketplace will continue to grow and prosper, and "environmental management" will increase in importance.

Growing population pressures and increasing demands on energy and resources to fuel the global economy will focus attention on the role of technology to provide food, fuel, and environmental quality improvements in virtually all countries. Unprecedented advancements in technologies for increasing energy and resource productivity will be required just to maintain the existing "environmental quality" standard of living in developed countries, let alone provide for basic needs and environmental quality improvements in developing countries.

Today, we are in the early stages of a major environmental management technological transformation. Twenty-five years of environmental leadership through command-and-control and investment in meeting performance goals defined by compliance standards are ending with a more ambitious international approach that goes beyond compliance, as reflected in voluntary management standards such as ISO 14000.

Not long after the U.S. federal, state, and local governments took action to protect environmental quality in the early 1970s, economists began debating whether environmental regulatory requirements raised barriers to U.S. technology innovation, job creation, and competitiveness. Particularly during the

1980s, the argument was heard that increasingly complex environmental regulations raise manufacturing costs above those of foreign competitors, thereby driving jobs overseas and reducing financial incentives for creating new technologies. If the United States were the only country in the world with environmental regulations, this argument might have some force.

Thoughtful analyses of the jobs issue by Robert Reppeto of the World Resources Institute and others show persuasively that U.S. manufacturing operations, when they relocate, do so for a variety of reasons—but not, with rare exceptions, to evade U.S. environmental regulations. The opposite case—that investments by some countries create competitive advantage in selected environmental technologies—is increasingly part of the debate, supported by Professor Michael Porter and others. As the global economy continues to expand in the future, the value of environmental quality will increase. This is especially true in industrialized countries and will cause environmental managers to rethink their role.

Today, environmental managers seldom think of themselves as technology leaders in the product and process areas. But the essential challenge of any manager is to position the corporation so that it can improve, innovate, and create a product or service. Because the environment is destined to play an increasingly central role in that process, environmental managers must learn new roles.

Environmental innovation and organizational synergy include not only new technologies, but also new management systems that might be underestimated by environmental managers with traditional perspectives. Environmental innovation today is barely beginning to show up in new product design (design for the environment, efficient use of energy and materials), new manufacturing processes (environmentally conscious manufacturing), new approaches to accounting (eco-accounting) marketing products in a new way (green clean marketing) and the new management initiative ISO 14001 (environment management system).

Given these challenges, it is worth reflecting on the approach the United States is taking toward environmental quality improvements, as opposed to approaches taken by other developed countries. In the United States, the dominant focus is on compliance with end-of-pipe pollution. This does not provide a competitive basis for future technological innovation. In fact, there is a case to be made that this approach to environmental protection has peaked and now inhibits technological creativity in private sector management of environmental issues.

The U.S. approach to environmental quality improvements appears to have reached its logical conclusion. Public and private sector investments in technology innovation are also dropping relative to leading OECD countries, thereby posing further challenges to our country's leadership. During the past few years, the United States has invested about 1.9 percent of its gross domestic product (GDP) in non-defense research and development, compared with Japan's 3 percent and Germany's 2.8 percent.

An even more alarming fact is that the United States today is investing a smaller share of GDP in plant and equipment than any other Summit 7 country. In fiscal 1992, the U.S. investment level was half of Japan's 22 percent and below German's 14.5 percent.

These are warning signs that the United States can ill afford to ignore. We indeed face a loss of competitive advantage if we continue with our traditional approach toward environmental management.

While the United States is peaking with its command-and-control approach to environmental quality improvements, Japan, Germany, and a number of Northern European countries are in the vanguard with energy conservation and resource productivity policy initiatives. Japan's framework "Law for Promotion of Utilization of Recyclable Resources" (Cabinet Order No. 327 (1991))[1] requires manufacturers to design specified categories of products, designated by MITI, for ease of disassembly and recyclability.

MITI and other technologically sophisticated ministries in Japan are heavily committed to understanding the intersection of environment management and technology. MITI, in particular, regards environmental management and technology as a policy priority and continues to increase its investments in this area. MITI is apparently convinced that the connection between environmental management and environmental technology offers a significant competitive opportunity for Japanese industries.

In Europe, Germany's Ordinance on Avoidance of Packaging Waste (1991) obligates manufacturers, distributors, and retailers to collect ("take back") packaging materials for products they make, distribute, and sell. Germany, as well as the Netherlands, Denmark, Sweden, and several other Northern European countries, is pushing the "take-back" idea into the electronics, auto, and consumer durable goods sectors.

Japanese and Northern European resource productivity initiatives build on a tradition of more than 25 years of energy efficiency measures (Table 9.1). By comparison, U.S. energy efficiency and resource productivity initiatives (EPA's Energy Star, Green Lights (among others), the federal executive order promoting "environmentally preferable products," and some initiatives at the state level) are generally more recent, and are comparatively uncoordinated.

Japanese industry, working in partnership with government, has set a new energy standard. By doing so, Japanese companies were able to achieve a national competitive advantage over their competitors. Energy Star is a standard that was set by U.S. EPA and a small number of visionary electronic indus-

Table 9.1 Energy Productivity (thousand dollars 1985 GDP per ton of oil equivalent)

	W. Germany	Japan	United States
1950	2.00	3.60	1.72
1960	2.58	3.47	1.74
1970	2.47	3.05	1.69
1980	2.71	3.48	1.91
1985	2.84	4.03	2.24
1990	3.24	4.28	2.40
1991	3.31	4.35	2.36
1992	3.44	4.33	2.38

Source: WorldWatch Institute (1996).

try environmental managers who recognized the future competitive impact that Energy Star would have in their industry. This program set the energy benchmark for PCS and drove new technology to reduce energy in office equipment worldwide.

The "systems" approach to environmental management, with its emphasis on integrating environmental management into the entire value chain of the enterprise, fits very well with these energy efficiency and resource productivity policy initiatives. Perhaps this helps explain why formal environmental management systems standards arose in Europe (e.g., BS 7750 in England, EMAR, the European Union Eco-Management and Audit Scheme, and the ISO 14001 series environmental standardization). Long overlooked as a corporate function with a major role to play in a company's superior environmental performance, the engineering and R&D functions become equally (if not more) important than manufacturing in a company adopting a formal environmental management system such as ISO 14001. This is because product and process technology designs offer vastly greater opportunities for improving the energy efficiency and resource productivity of materials used by the industrial enterprise, which, in turn, improve the company's environmental performance (Figure 9.1). Continuing to insist on strict regulatory limits on environmental releases is, of course, essential. However, a systems approach to environmental management offers industrial enterprises a more powerful framework and set of tools with which to move upstream in the value chain and tackle the harder, but more promising, opportunities for environmental performance advancement.

Large Japanese multinationals are now committed to conforming their environmental management program to the new ISO 14001 standard. Zeroing in on one of these companies—one of the Japanese electronics giants—we see environmental objects and targets being set by top management that focus on

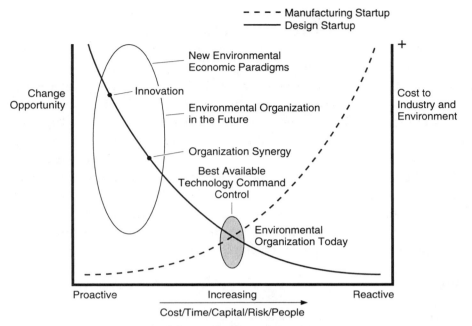

- - - - Manufacturing Startup
———— Design Startup

Change Opportunity

New Environmental Economic Paradigms

Innovation

Environmental Organization in the Future

Organization Synergy

Best Available Technology Command Control

Environmental Organization Today

Cost to Industry and Environment

+

Proactive   Increasing   Reactive

Cost/Time/Capital/Risk/People

Figure 9.1   Environmental Innovation

the engineering design side of the enterprise. The company is setting specific targets for reducing the energy of materials used. The environmental function is now being dominated by materials scientists and product and process design engineers looking for new ways to improve the environmental performance of materials. Complementary environmental objectives are being set for decreasing the energy usage requirements of its product manufactured and lowering product environmental burdens during useful life and at end-of-life.

Training is refocused toward these environmental objectives and targets. Communication of environmental objectives and targets throughout the company is a top management priority so that employees in many different areas can contribute to the effort. Building on prior successes in improving operational energy usage, the company fully expects to see comparable improvements in energy requirements of materials used in its products. Above all else, the company's top management is convinced that this approach will improve its competitiveness in the global marketplace.

One of the most important assets an environmental manager can have is the gift of early insight into trends that have not yet been widely observed but will ultimately be important nationally and internationally. For example, Japanese managers sounded the early warning to their firms about the importance energy efficiency would eventually play in the global economy. This, in turn, led to development of new, energy-efficient products and processes.

Today, many European companies, the top Japanese multinationals, and some North American firms are committed to conforming their environmental programs to the ISO 14001 environmental management system standard. It remains to be seen whether these companies will use the environmental management system to drive technology innovation and environmental performance improvements throughout their engineering design functions, or whether they will use it primarily for green marketing. At least one large Japanese electronics firm is clearly gearing up to use ISO 14001 as an opportunity to drive environmental performance improvements through engineering design.

In the United States, an argument favoring conformance to ISO 14001 is that the "systems" approach will provide increased efficiencies. It is not clear what companies mean by this. If they mean increase efficiencies in compliance management and reduction in overhead, they may be missing opportunities to increase their global standing through technology innovations.

Note

1. Japan's "Law for Promotion of Recyclable Resources" is not really aimed at recycling in the conventional context. One of its basic objects is to promote product design for ease of disassembly, enabling efficient reuse of parts, components, and materials. "A business shall make units easily disposable by using components that are easy to attach and a structure that permits easy recovery and transport of components"—in other words, a system approach to design that covers a cradle-to-grave approach. The law facilitated Japan in developing a resource productivity framework for the Eco-factory.

Bob Ferrone has 28 years of experience at both the corporate and plant level in design engineering, quality, manufacturing, and environmental sciences, as they affect product and process development. This experience has encompassed consulting to various groups and vendors such as DuPont, 3M, Motorola, and Micropolis. In addition, he has received national recognition, by both the government and industry, as one of the country's leaders in environmental technology.

10

Industry Cases and Practices: A Recent Survey of Benchmarking Corporate Perceptions of ISO 14000 Benefits

David Burdick, P.E.

In late 1995, Global Environmental Management Systems conducted a survey with top environmental executives of leading U.S. corporations, including IBM, Hewlett Packard, Procter and Gamble, 3M, Johnson and Johnson, Motorola, General Electric, Herman Miller, four of the largest international consulting firms (including ABB Environmental Services and Woodward-Clyde), and the three top registrars, BVQI, Lloyds, and SGS International Certification. The purpose of the survey was to benchmark the current perceptions and views of ISO 14001's benefits among key U.S. manufacturers, consultants, and registrars. The following questions were asked:

- What do you perceive are the strengths and weaknesses of implementing the ISO 14001 EMS within your or your client's organization?
- What do you perceive could be done to improve the acceptance of the ISO 14001 EMS by industry?
- Do you plan on implementing ISO 14001, and, if so, when?

Survey Results

Below is a summary of the responses to the survey. The answers fell into nine categories:

1. Environmental performance
2. Trade
3. Public awareness
4. Quality management
5. Regulatory compliance
6. Savings and costs
7. Liability premiums and interest rates
8. Motivation
9. Certification

The study results averaged the responses together in order to draw out the perception versus intent of ISO 14001. Actual comments are given in order to maintain objectiveness in interpreting the results (see Figure 10.1).

Environmental Performance

Although the intent of the ISO 14001 standard does not itself state specific environmental performance criteria beyond commitment to an organization's policy, it requires procedures to be established to monitor and measure the key characteristics of its operations that can have a significant impact on the environment.

Only 7 percent of comments perceived this area to be a strength of the ISO 14001. Twenty-two percent of comments perceived this area to be a weakness of ISO 14001, as there is "no guarantee of an actual and continuous improvement in reducing environmental impact." Yet only 3 percent of reactions perceived a need to emphasize continuous improvement in the standard as a means to improve the acceptance of ISO 14001.

Trade

One of the main intents of the ISO 14001 standard is to prevent the creation of non-tariff trade barriers and to increase or change an organization's legal obligations. Yet there is language to encourage contractors and suppliers to establish an EMS.

A large percentage, 31 percent of comments, noted the competitive advantage of being able to market to customers who require ISO 14001 and for leadership recognition as strengths of ISO 14001. No one perceived trade issues to be a weakness of ISO 14001. Eighteen percent of comments perceived trade issues as a means to improve the acceptance of ISO 14001, with comments such as "need for clear marketing trends" and "need for environmental groups and customer-supplier relationships to embrace and push for EMS and eco-labeling in products."

Public Awareness

The ISO 14001 standard requires that the company's environmental policy be available to the public, and that the company communicate relevant matters to external interested parties.

None of the comments viewed public awareness to be a strength of ISO 14001. In fact, 19 percent of comments perceived this area to be a weakness of ISO 14001, with comments such as "lack of public knowledge" and "lack of experience to get measurable results." Twelve percent of respondents felt improved public awareness would be a means to improve the acceptance of ISO 14001, citing comments such as "need for customer, public's and organization's awareness" and "need shifts in attitudes."

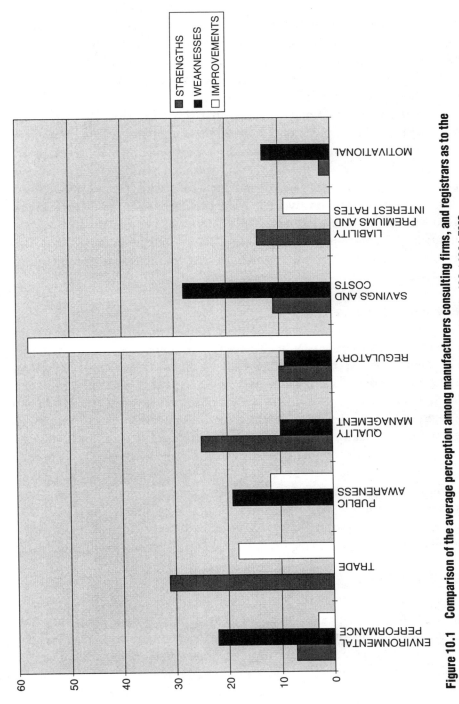

Figure 10.1 Comparison of the average perception among manufacturers consulting firms, and registrars as to the strengths, weaknesses, and suggested improvements to the acceptance of the ISO 14001 EMS

Quality Management

One of the intents of the ISO 14001 standard is to offer an effective and structured management system that will implement, maintain, and improve environmental policy and objectives. It shares management system principles with the ISO 9000 quality system standards, with the additional point that it must "address the needs of a broad range of interested parties and the evolving needs of society for environmental protection."

A good quarter of comments stated that this area was a strength of ISO 14001, with such comments as "harmonize throughout a large multinational corporation," "systematically manage and improve one's environmental management system," "gives one universally accepted standard," "is consistent environmental framework," "gain operational efficiency," "benchmark improvements," and "develop proactive management." Ten percent of comments perceived this area to be a weakness of ISO 14001, with comments such as "can potentially become a paperwork exercise." None of the comments had perceived this area in need of improvement in order to increase the acceptance of ISO 14001.

Regulatory Compliance

An objective of the ISO 14001 standard is to establish systems that require that regulations are heeded. Only 10 percent of comments perceived this area to be a strength of ISO 14001, with remarks such as "reduction in regulatory inspection," "reduced compliance exposure and costs," and "improvements from systematic compliance." Nine percent of responses noted this area to be a weakness of ISO 14001, citing "potential for loss of confidentiality" and "meeting voluntary standards will then become de facto regulations." However, a substantial 58 percent of comments felt this area to be in need of improvement in order to increase the acceptance of ISO 14001. Suggested improvements include: "Need the U.S. EPA to make more tangible incentives to industry," "reduction of inspection, monitoring, and reporting," "reduction of time required for attaining permits," "decrease in fines," "protection of audit results," and "federal requirements for ISO 14001 registration for government projects."

Savings and Costs

The ISO 14001 standard does not specifically set out to reduce cost or improve material or energy savings, but such savings could be a significant by-product of implementing the ISO 14001 environmental management system. The review and policy statement suggests addressing these impacts for organizations that have significant energy and material use.

Eleven percent of comments perceived this area as a strength of ISO 14001, with thoughts such as "reduction of material and energy usage" and "improved efficiency." A rather substantial 28 percent of comments saw this area to be a weakness of ISO 14001, reflected in the statement "Manpower costs will not be worth the savings." None of the respondents felt this area to be in need of improvement in order to increase the acceptance of ISO 14001.

Liability Premiums and Interest Rates

The ISO 14001 standard does not specifically set an objective to reduce liability premiums of insurance interest rates.

Fourteen percent of comments projected this area to be a strength of ISO 14001, with comments such as "reduction of liability" and "reduction in insurance premiums." None of the comments saw this area to be a weakness of ISO 14001. Nine percent of responses perceived this area to be in need of improvement in order to increase the acceptance of ISO 14001, with the suggestion of "a need for premium and liability reduction to drive acceptance."

Motivation

The standard does not specifically set an objective to motivate acceptance. However, top management must define and commit to the environmental policy and be involved in its review and improvement. It is also a requirement of the standard to promote environmental awareness of the company's activities.

Only 2 percent of comments stated this area to be a strength of ISO 14001, with remarks such as "improvement in company pride." Thirteen percent commented that this area is a weakness of ISO 14001, with statements such as "concern that there are no short-term benefits perceived to motivate industry." None of the responses perceived improved motivation as a factor in increasing the acceptance of ISO 14001.

Certification

The ISO/DIS 14001 standard allows for self-certification by organizations.

Eighty-five percent of the companies are making gap analysis to the standard but are not willing to publicly state when, if ever, they will gain registration. Registrars, on the other hand, are finding a large increase in requests for certification.

Conclusion

The top three perceived strengths of implementing the ISO 14001 EMS within an organization were trade (31%), quality management (25%), and liability premiums and interest rate reduction (14%) (Figure 10.2).

The top three perceived weaknesses of the ISO 14001 EMS within an organization were costs (28%), lack of environmental performance (22%), and lack of public awareness (19%) (Figure 10.3).

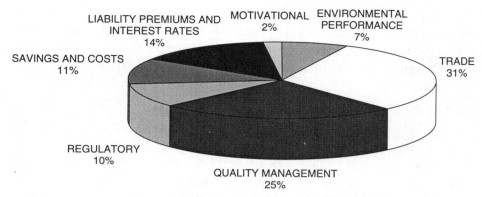

Figure 10.2 Perceived strengths of ISO 14001 EMS

The top three areas that would improve the acceptance of the ISO 14001 EMS by industry were regulatory incentives (58%), trade (18%), and public awareness (12%) (Figure 10.4).

The goals of the ISO Strategy Advisory Group (SAG) are to develop a standard that promotes a common approach to EMS (quality management), enhance an organization's ability to attain and measure improvements in environmental performance, and facilitate trade and eliminate non-tariff trade barriers (trade).

Manufacturers, consulting firms, and registrars all perceived the strengths encapsulated in quality management (i.e., harmonizing of one EMS standard) and trade (i.e., eliminate non-tariff barriers between nations) as strengths of the ISO 14001 standard.

However, contrary to the third objective of the ISO 14001 standard, environmental performance was not perceived as a strength of ISO 14001. In addition, regulatory incentives, in the form of regulatory relief and government requirements, were suggested as means to improve the acceptance of ISO 14001.

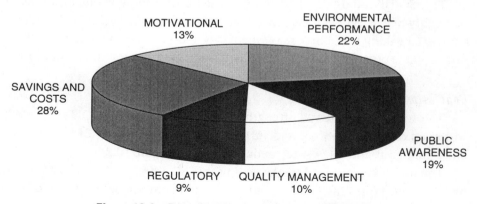

Figure 10.3 Perceived weaknesses in ISO 14001 EMS

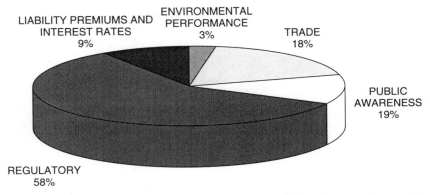

Figure 10.4   Perceived suggestions to improve ISO 14001 acceptance

There was a strong difference between the views of industry versus the registrars concerning certification. Although 85 percent of manufacturers were noncommittal and uncertain when, if ever, they will get third-party certification, the finding from registrars was that there has been a large increase in the number of companies requesting registration. This may be due to the competitive nature involved in keeping secret plans to becoming the first within an industrial sector to be registered to the ISO 14001 standard. As one registrar said, when the window of opportunity becomes clear, it's then too late, and one can only follow.

David Burdick, PE, BS-ME, BS-I.E., REM, CEA, has recently returned to the United States after several years abroad in Europe and Asia working in both the manufacturing and registrar industries. He is involved in auditing to the ISO 9000 and ISO 14001 Quality and Environmental Management Systems.

SECTION THREE

Registration, Certification, and Implementation Issues

Once the go-ahead decision has been made, companies face a myriad of issues related to registration. In chapters by Stephen Watson and Thomas Ambrose, a comprehensive course on the business implications of proceeding and how best to prepare for taking the initiative are presented. Valuable insights into the "how and why" of implementing ISO 14000 effectively are explained by Rodger Jump and Scott Foster. All of these chapters show what needs to be discussed before and after taking the ISO path.

11

The Business Implications of Implementing ISO 14000

Stephen A. Watson, III

The ISO 14000 series of standards for environmental management systems (EMSs) are voluntary standards intended to aid companies that wish to improve their environmental performance. They owe their existence, at least in part, to three widely shared views: (1) that existing environmental management systems are either inadequate or ineffective; (2) that companies will want to improve environmental performance for economic or social reasons; and (3) that governments and stakeholders will require companies to exercise greater control of the impacts to the environment through new regulations. ISO 14000 offers a solution—an "integrated" environmental management system, with components designed to affect sound management in any size organization and in any country. The standards are an embodiment of both the policy and practice of environmental management.

This chapter is a consideration of the business implications of the ISO 14000 series of standards. How will a movement toward an integrated EMS be realized? Who will be in the best position to respond? ISO 14000 is a management system and it carries with it business consequences.

There has been a great deal of discussion—indeed, confusion—about the agreed scope of work for ISO/TC 207. The Technical Committee's "Environment Management Scope" includes "standardization in the field of environmental management, tools and systems" but excludes, among other elements, "setting environmental performance levels." The dispute involves those who accept and understand the ISO mandate for a consideration of "processes" and systems and those who favor continuous improvement and performance objectives for the management systems. The proponents of the former view, a view shared by the United States, argue that ISO (private sector)-crafted performance objectives would be in conflict with the authority granted to governmental bodies and institutions that traditionally set environmental performance goals. The proponents of the latter position tend to view performance objectives as a process tool, not expressly excluded by the term "environmental performance level." In their view, "environmental performance level" seems to relate more to measurements and technology than to process tools.

The debate continues, with the dialogue focusing on "processes" versus "end-goal requirements." Lost in this debate, however, are some very important concepts. First, the ISO 14000 series of standards is founded on a rather strongly felt "policy" statement, namely, that corporations will want to improve environmental performance for social or economic reasons. In this sense, the tone of the document is clear, and we may read in the statement above the word "will" as "should." Second, the existence of the ISO 14000 series of standards is itself an evaluation or performance statement, a declaration that existing environmental management systems are inadequate and ineffective. The clear import of ISO 14000 is that environmental management systems must be integrated systems, efficient and fully an integral part of the business processes. This is a powerful, and not very flattering, assessment of current business practices.

The ISO 14000 standards call for a rather profound change in the way we manage environmental matters. There is a great deal of power in the word "integrated." Governments, industry, and stakeholders will work in concert to craft new structures and administrative procedures. Business will modify organizational structures and adjust corporate behavior to implement the standard. Governments will adjust agency authorities and modify or abandon existing regulatory schemes. The change will not be wholesale, and it certainly will not be uniformly evident in each country, but it will occur. In the United States, the self-audit components of ISO 14000 have attracted the interest of the Environmental Protection Agency (EPA) and the Justice Department. The Department of Energy (DOE), under its new General Environmental Protection Program, DOE 490, is adopting the ISO 14001 approach and developing its own EMS. In Korea, the Korean Industrial Technology Association (KITA) and Korean Institute of Science and Technology (KIST), both quasi-governmental bodies, are working in concert with the industrial sector to effect the implementation of the ISO 14001 specifications. In Taiwan, Industrial Technology Research Institute (ETRI), also a quasi-governmental body, the government, and industry are all collectively engaged in a similar exercise. A Canadian court recently ordered an offending company to achieve ISO 14001 certification, in lieu of fines and further penalties. The U.S. aversions to end-goal requirements notwithstanding, ISO 14001 may, in and of itself, be an end-goal performance objective for industries that wish to stay competitive.

The two principal components of any business or administrative system are *policy* and *practice*. The policy component is the reason why we move from point A to point B. Although policies may be expressed as goals and objectives, they tend to be reduced in actual terms to costs and benefits. Practice, the practical component of a system, is the means by which we move from point A to point B. These are the systems, structures, and procedures that are adopted to implement a policy.

ISO 14001, the specification document, identifies the elements of an environmental management system as environmental policy, environmental planning, implementing and operating the EMS, checking and corrective action, and management review. ISO 14004, the guidance document, provides a further discussion of the elements and their subtopics, adding examples to aid the implementation process. Collectively, ISO 14001 and 14004 define the "practice" of EMS, defining in broad terms the means by which we build, implement, and operate environmental management systems.

The "policy" of the ISO 14000 standards is a reflection of their existence and the arguments advanced to support the process. We build an EMS because it will allow businesses and organizations to meet regulatory demands and challenges in a more efficient and cost-effective manner. We believe that EMSs allow for better management of the environment, improving a business's or organization's environmental performance. We believe that an EMS may make an organization or business more efficient, providing a direct economic benefit that improves the profitability of the enterprise. These statements or views are more than an expression of a desire or belief; they are implicitly an end-goal performance objective.

An Attempt to Shape the "Culture" of Environmental Management

What ISO 14000 is doing is attempting a change of culture. Environment is a top management priority under the ISO 14000 model. It is not so now in many organizations. Environmental management is more often seen as being a staff function. Line functions, or operations, are reserved for the activities that advance the business purposes and revenue-generating activities of the organization.

ISO 14001 calls for the integration of environmental matters with the other business objectives of an organization. Environmental issues become a part of the decision process. For many organizations, this may require both a functional and structural change. Implementation can occur short of major institutional changes, but an EMS may require more as it grows and matures. Consider the development of environmental systems shown in Table 11.1.

Twenty years ago, if you asked a Ford plant manager what his job was, his response would be, "I make cars"; implicit within that statement was the word "profitably." Today, when you ask that same Ford plant manager what his job is, the answer is "I make quality cars (profitably)." Fifteen years from now, the

Table 11.1 Evolution of Environmental Systems

Current	Post-ISO 14000
Environmental management is a staff function.	Environmental management requires top management commitment and is everyone's responsibility
Environmental factors considered for siting issues, waste streams, and environmental consequences of operations.	Environmental factors considered for all business decisions.
ISO 9000 adds documentation and institutional controls at the point of material procurement, product manufacturing, and product distribution. Controls are added to existing institutional structure.	ISO 14000, with top management commitment and "integration," may require some institutional change.
ISO 9000 requires limited interface with government bodies.	EMS systems are fueled by and affected by new regulations and governmental initiatives EMS efforts are impacted by how government is shaped and operated. EMS is interdependent and interactive.
ISO 9000 encourages a culture of "quality."	ISO 14000 encourages a culture of sound environmental management.

answer may be, "I make quality cars in an environmentally responsible manner (profitably)." This is managing the culture of the environment, moving environmental from a staff function to a line function.

Everyone, especially line management, understands the role that profit plays in an organization—no profit, no business and no jobs. Every employee understands that the corporation is in business to make money; it is a part of the corporate culture and our understanding of business. We recognize that our cost is a function of labor and materials. Reduce the cost of labor, or the amount of time it takes to produce a product or component. This labor/materials relationship is understood, if not accepted, at virtually all levels of a business organization.

Our corporate understanding of environmental costs is inadequate and not yet fully a part of corporate culture. In many instances, environmental professionals still have to "make the connection" to demonstrate the impact that their activities will have on a product or services. The downside costs are often remote in time and the "connection" is not always readily apparent. Where there is an understanding of environmental costs, it often fails to permeate down through the organization. The relationship is not understood by all concerned.

Business decisions are not inclusive, and environmental issues do not surface because they are not a part of the corporate culture. Is there a corporation or business that would consider a new product without taking into account labor availability and costs? In these cases, the consideration of labor costs includes recruitment, placement, on-the-job training, and benefits. It is a consideration of costs on many levels, a life-cycle approach. The ISO 14000 series of standards is an attempt to establish "environment" as a part of our business culture.

Consider the case of quality control and quality assurance as a business force. Where quality has been adopted as a part of the corporate culture, everyone (particularly line managers) understands the role that quality plays in the product or service. Lower-quality service and products translate into lower sales volume, customer dissatisfaction, and lost customers. There are higher costs associated with repairs and returns. All this translates as lower profit. If everyone within a market sector plays on the same field, then quality is not an issue. But when one player makes quality a market discriminator, moving to make customer satisfaction, product usefulness, longevity, reliability, and service features of the product, they begin to capture market share and customers. Quality, as a culture, becomes a requirement of business.

Business's response to quality first manifests itself as system, management, and record-keeping requirements designed to manage the process of quality control and quality assurance. But this is only part of the process, an after-the-fact solution. When quality is adopted and believed to be a part of the job, seen as a requirement of doing business and of continued employment, quality moves from a monitor and validation function to a normative function; it is simply the way to do business.

The early efforts to "establish" a culture of quality varied. "Quality" means different things to different people. Products use components from all over the world. There was a need, or a perceived need, to give meaning to the terms used to define quality and the business systems used to measure that quality. Quality, for companies without integrated manufacturing processes, meant that vendor systems and controls had to be managed. Business systems subject to validation, accreditation, and monitoring could be relied on by producers that sought a certain measure of quality from their vendors. Yet, there needed to be some mechanisms to make the process uniform, reliable, and verifiable. ISO 9000 was the international community's response to the needs of the international marketplace.

Quality became a market discriminator; in some cases, a "trade barrier."

Quality, under the U.S. model, was managed individually by business and it was largely a response to external business or market pressures. Quality, under the Asian model, was managed as concerted effort to attract and obtain market share. Governments participated in the process; consortiums and research pools funded the projects necessary to make the better tools. Early business efforts were protected and encouraged.

An Integrated Management System—A Fundamental Change in the Way We Do Business

The ISO 14000 standard is a management system. Delete the word "environmental" from the standard and you have a treatise on sound business management. In this century, there have been at least two significant management revolutions. The ISO 14000 series of standards has the potential to be the third.

The first revolutionary management change is historically tied to Henry Ford and his assembly line production model. The United States was not the first, or perhaps even the best, manufacturer of automobiles. Automobiles were produced in a number of European nations. Europe was tied to a craft system of labor and education, with manufactured products being built from the ground up and completed as units. Mr. Ford had access to a skilled, educated labor force. Conceiving and acting on assembly line production methods, rather than unit production, Henry Ford turned his automobile and company into a U.S. success story. The assembly line production method took hold in other industries and, for 40 years, Europe and the rest of the industrialized world played catch-up.

The second major management revolution dates back to the late 1950s and the quality management practices of the Asian economies. In the 1950s, the phrases "Made in Taiwan," "Made in Japan," "Made in Hong Kong," and "Made in Korea" were identified with cheap, substandard products. Asian industries, working in concert with their governments, addressed a wide variety of quality and production issues over the course of the next 15 to 20 years. Research consortiums pooled resources to attack technology issues. Quality and attention to detail became a part of the corporate culture. Product returns were retained, analyzed, and studied to avoid repetitive problems. A great deal of attention was paid to the efficiencies of the production process. By the mid-1970s, "Made in Japan" meant quality, and higher value than the equivalent U.S. product. "Made in Korea" quickly followed suit.

The United States largely ignored this process and, by the late 1970s, several key U.S. industries had lost customers to their Asian competitors. For the next 20 years, the United States played catch-up and, although industry paid greater attention to image, quality, and production concerns, market share was still lost.

It is worth noting that the Japanese model did not work as intended. The concerted effort to address quality was more a function of competition and less a function of partnering with the government. Government-sponsored consortiums were even less successful. The Japanese Ministry of Trade and Industry (MITI) failed to sponsor a real winner in the 1960s (aluminum, aircraft manufacturing, and aerospace) and the 1970s (biomedicine, mainframe computers, and telecommunications). These failed MITI efforts, however, bore fruit in unexpected ways. The "need" for both quality improvements and technological advances was raised to the level of a priority in Japanese business. Japanese industries that were not favored by MITI adopted the priority, making it a part

100

of their corporate culture. These electronics and automotive companies, driven by a competitive fire, achieved what the MITI-sponsored industries could not.

There is, on a side note, a lesson here. The government-mandated effort under MITI met with only marginal success, but helped raise new management issues and business priorities for Japanese industry. The marginal governmental effort helped fuel a process change. The ISO 14000 standards have the same potential. Change may not be directly attributed to EMS and the efforts led by the standard, but may, in fact, come about more as a result of competition. Some industries and governments will rethink their own programs and processes. Individually, or perhaps even working together, they will build new business systems. The ISO 14000 series of standards is raising business's collective consensus about EMS and management systems in general. Change is inevitable.

A Change in Management—Responsibility and Structure

The ISO 14000 series of standards reintroduces management concepts to the environment. The intent is to give consideration to the fact that the environment is no different from any other aspect of business. We manage our business to maximize return on investment. Buy low, sell high, and keep cost down. We strive to reduce product losses. We manage the components of production. We manage energy costs, change industrial processes, and relocate plants. What ISO 14000 is really saying is that environmental matters, consequences, and costs are, and have always been, a part of business. We simply have ignored them in our planning and production processes.

ISO 14000 should force business and governments to change on at least two levels: (1) encouraging the integration of functions within companies and governments and (2) formalizing the integration of environmental issues with other decision factors in the thought processes of business.

Taking the latter point first, environmental costs, risk, and exposures were often not seen as business costs. They were incidental to business, rather than an integral part of the business effort. Environmental professionals tended to be line or staff functions. Environmental issues were not a senior or top management function, charge, or responsibility.

If we accept this institutional model, management philosophies and business systems will have to change; this is a first-order change. Take an unmanaged item, adjust philosophies, roles, and responsibilities and manage the asset—within existing structures. We would manage the asset by adjusting goals, priorities, and responsibilities, but not by changing structure and reporting lines (as a rule). This is managing the culture of the environment (or a at least a business response to managing the culture of the environment).

Consider, first, how we have managed environmental matters. In the United States, there does not seem to be a "model" structure for the handling of environmental matters. A 1991 survey of environmental managers by the

National Association of Environmental Managers (NAEM) in Washington, D.C., the Environmental Hazards Management Institute (EHMI) in Durham, New Hampshire, and Coopers & Lybrand in Boston, highlights the variety of responses. The results should displace some of the myths about just who is responsible for environmental matters in U.S. corporations.

The study involved 500 environmental managers and represented a diverse group, with the distribution of industries being as follows:

Industry	Percentage
Electronic Equipment/Instruments	16.0%
Chemicals & Refining	15.0
Metals & Fabricated Metal Products	13.0
Industrial Machinery/Equipment	7.0
Pharmaceuticals & Personal Care	6.5
Rubber, Plastics, Stone & Glass	6.5
Food Products	6.5
Wholesale & Retail Trade	6.5
Electric, Gas & Sanitary Utilities	6.0
Extractive Industries	4.0
Transportation Equipment	4.0
Miscellaneous Services	4.0
Paper & Printing	3.0
Transportation & Communication Services	3.0

The study first found that the environmental manager's position generally "evolved" as the corporation became aware of its own environmental concerns. The duties of the environmental manager were usually grafted onto existing positions or functional areas, because there was no structure in place to handle the "issue." As responsibilities evolved, the positions did, in some instances, gain an independent stature.

But contrary to an accepted belief, the study found that risk managers and safety directors generally do not handle their company's environmental matters. This new "responsibility" belongs to individuals in a number of different positions:

Functional Position	Percentage
CFO or Risk Management	2%
Field Plant Facilities	3
General Counsel	4
Human Resources Department	5
Environment or Safety & Environment	7
Administration or Regulatory Affairs	12
Engineering	15
Staff functions (reporting to President)	16
Operations	36

Environmental managers would be those individuals—whatever their official positions—who are perhaps most aware of what environmental services are required within a company.

The study also found that the duties of the environmental manager were, in large part, shaped by the functional area in which they served. For example, a functional finance environmental manager might better serve financial-driven considerations rather than the operational or technical concerns of the plants. While an individual's title may have indicated "environmental" duties, the nature of those duties varied greatly among the companies.

The survey results revealed that corporate environmental managers tended to have broad authority but little direct control over their company's environmental infrastructure (facility-level operations). Facility-level environmental managers were highly compliance-oriented and usually reported to plant managers rather than corporate management.

Environmental departments or managers seldom cover all the bases. The depth of the environmental manager's knowledge of the corporation's activity will, to some extent, be reflected by his or her duties. An environmental manager's duties, as indicate by the survey results, are largely compliance-oriented. The surveyed managers reported the following results:

Duty or Responsibility	Percentage Indicating Responsibility
Regulatory Compliance	70%
Environmental Auditing	45
Waste Minimization	45
Permitting	40
Hazardous Materials Identification	39
Waste Treatment, Storage, and Disposal Selection	39
Training	36
Safety	35
Remediation	32
Industrial Hygiene	30
Recycling	25
Risk of Discharge	19
Public & Community Relations	18
Transportation	15
Energy & Conservation	12

The "duty"-related questions are of interest. If a function or responsibility is not within the environmental manager's duties, it may be a sign of a number of problems: The nonperformance of a duty may reflect a resource need, an awareness problem, or the lack of a corporate commitment. Finally, the study found that the environmental managers generally complained that resource needs were not being met and that "management awareness" was lacking beyond their immediate area.

The environmental managers' most common complaints or concerns were:

- Concern about their ability to keep their company in compliance;
- Concern about their ability to successfully implement proactive environmental programs; and
- Complaints about insufficient resources, regulatory overload, a lack of corporate awareness at all organizational levels, and a high perceived lack of management support or interest in proactive environmental initiatives.

In many organizations, the management of environmental matters is uneven. The focus is disproportionally placed on compliance and remedial measures at the expense of planning, pollution prevention, and waste minimization. Where there is a greater level of control, the integration is not complete. One fundamental element of an EMS is top management commitment. A second is an integration of environmental issues at every stage of the business process. The principle is simple: Get the right people involved and raise the appropriate questions. Consider the following two case studies.

Case Study No. 1: Chemical Plant Operations Working with Government to Draft Regulations to Fit Community Needs

The company has 10 sites under remediation, with three closed facilities being regarded as significant sites. Cleanup efforts at the three significant sites will continue throughout the next 20 years. The rest of the sites will be remediated to nonresidential levels.

Within the corporate structure, the remediation department of the environmental unit is responsible for the cleanup of the facilities. Risks are assessed to determine appropriate cleanup levels and they are applied to an expected nonresidential end use. End uses are projected, but not subject to any sort of marketing inquiry.

Remediated properties are inventoried and disposed of by the corporate real estate department. This process nominally commences as the site is nearing remediation, but begins only in earnest after the site work has been completed.

To date, the company has not been able to transfer a single property. The effort to establish useful brownfield uses for three properties has failed, in spite of a significant corporate level commitment.

This case study addresses an "end-of-pipe" problem, one that is presented in cases in which plants are decommissioned. Corporate environmental departments and engineers saw the problem as one that was to be engineered, assessing a level of risk and designing a remediation plan that was appropriate to the end use. This was a failure of the planning process.

The governing U.S. environmental laws affecting both the remediation and the resulting transaction were created and implemented from 1973 to 1989. When these laws and regulations were crafted:

- Government never foresaw the transfer of contaminated properties as an option;
- Banks and insurance companies never anticipated providing financial security to contaminated property; and
- Industry never contemplated buying contaminated property.

The case study corporation's efforts to date have failed for three reasons. First, the infrastructure and administrative processes that would be necessary to accomplish the mission have not yet been created. EPA, at the federal level, is working on a series of pilot administrative programs, but has no favored option to date. There are several state pilots, but these are inconclusive. Banks and insurance institutions are years behind the agency's efforts and there is little work under way to develop the appropriate vehicle. Industry can handle the liability issues that would be associated with the transfer of properties, but this tends to be an ad hoc, case-by-case approach dealt with by legal departments.

Second, within the corporation, the decision to commence the initiative was not inclusive. Several key departments and personnel were left out of the decision process. Because the planners saw the problems as being, first, one of engineering, and then of a real estate transfer, the legal department was consulted only for real estate and liability advice. The corporate acquisitions and insurance departments, both staffed by personnel who would have raised other questions, were not in the loop. This was a systems or management-of-change failure.

Third, there was a quality control failure. Some project transfers failed because the buyer lacked sufficient information about the site. The level of risk assessment that was required for the selection of a remedy was far less than that which was required to satisfy the information needs of a buyer or a financial entity. This failure point, experienced by the real estate department, was never carried back to the remediation group and the pattern of information gaps continued.

ISO 14000 envisions a fully integrated management and process decision loop, with performance indicators and quality checks, many of which were not evident by this process.

Case Study No. 2: Chemical Plant Operations Integrating Business Systems to Reduce Losses to Workers

A chemical plant, a manufacturer of adhesives and coating compounds, operates seven plants in the United States. In 1989, workforce injuries accounted for 2,700 lost work days. The company had an aggressive environmental, safety, and health program, but it had failed to reduce the number of worker injuries. Direct salaries and worker benefits paid were in excess of $1.08 million. Medical and compensatory payments would exceed $2.40 million.

Direct loss dollars for worker injuries accounted for $3.48 million. In the United States, a company will spend, on average, $7 for every $1 in direct loss payments for worker retraining, replacement staff, administration, and lost productivity. This left a significant projected bottom-line impact.

The first level of analysis in any systems approach is a review of the business procedures and consideration at the company. How do the pieces fit together? We can begin by asking such questions as:

- Where do you start within the organization?
- What really needs to be done?
- How are you managing the scope of the effort?
- Who is responsible for profit within the organization?
- What are the costs of a product?

In this instance, top management reached the conclusion that while plant operations were held responsible for cost, profit, and loss, reward systems—paid out in terms of bonuses and raises—were computed on the older formula of "material + labor + overhead = costs." Overhead was defined to include administrative costs, fixed assets, and incidental operating expenses at the plant, but failed to capture direct losses that were attributable to worker injuries. Direct costs associated with worker injuries were charged off against corporate books, rather than the plant operations.

Top management altered the performance award schedule for plant managers and other senior plant level personnel. Bonuses would be paid out only if there were both a profit **and** no lost-time injuries for the labor force. A profitable bottom line, with losses to the workforce, was simply not acceptable under the new structure. The direct and indirect costs of worker injuries were charged back to the divisions.

The core existing environmental, health, and safety programs remained the same. There was a greater emphasis placed on the programs, along with heightened training efforts. Audit and performance goals were, as before, left to the discretion of the responsible line management. Some new programs were added as needs were identified, and efforts were made to reduce hazards and to engineer for solutions. The sole significant change in this instance, however, was top management commitment to the program.

In 1994, this company sustained three lost work days from injuries. The next phase of the company's program was to consolidate environmental and safety and health operations. In the United States, worker safety issues are regulated by the Occupational Safety and Health Administration (OSHA) under the Occupational Safety and Health Act. OSHA has been concerned with a variety of worker safety issues, including those dealing with chemical and process hazards, but its jurisdiction ends at the plant boundaries. OSHA programs involve training, recordkeeping and reporting requirements, audit protocols, and process safety.

The Environmental Protection Agency (EPA) regulates the treatment, storage, and disposal of hazardous waste. EPA regulations also govern active waste streams, involving plant emissions and wastewater discharges. Worker safety and emergency planning regulations evolved that were specific to the chemicals and hazards associated with the controlled compounds, but developed at a slower pace than those promulgated by OSHA. There are extensive recordkeeping and reporting requirements.

The Department of Transportation (DOT) regulates the transportation of chemicals and hazardous waste. It, too, developed regulations involving worker safety, reporting and recordkeeping, and spill control.

OSHA tended to develop its process-oriented safety regulations first. For industry, the natural corporate interface was the human resources manager or risk manager. Over time, OSHA compliance was vested in these departments. EPA's initial regulations involved permitting and releases, and eventually the siting and management of hazardous waste treatment and disposal facilities. These were recognized as process or operational issues. At this level, the EPA interface was a plant manager or plant operations supervisor.

With the onset of the Comprehensive Environmental Response, Compensation, and Liability Act (CERCLA) in 1980, a law governing closed—and often abandoned—facilities, industry faced significant liability for closed and inactive sites. The EPA interface for these facilities tended to be senior management or the legal department on a financial basis, and plant-level personnel on an operational basis.

DOT regulations were accepted and recognized as a transportation issue and rested with terminal operations.

Upon review, OSHA, EPA, and DOT regulate the same areas. Each provided a regulatory framework, with training, recordkeeping, and reporting requirements. Each governed aspects of process safety, emergency planning, and spill control. Because industry established its own response mechanisms on a piecemeal basis (largely in response to separate agency directives), most U.S. industries have three to four individuals dealing with the same or similar hazards and materials at each plant or facility. Our case study company's current management plan is to reduce the administration cost of a successful and improving environmental, health, and safety program by consolidating information databases and operational responsibilities.

The belief is that this leaves less room for oversight and it will almost certainly result in operational efficiencies. Our case study client will manage the hazard, task, or result, rather than the agency. There will be one training program that is fully responsive to all of the governing regulations, rather than nine programs responsive to the directives of three agencies and the state government. New regulatory directives issuing from an agency, regardless of the agency, will be measured against the existing programs. In most instances, the company expects to be required to make few or no changes.

ISO is also a management system that strikes to form, not simply culture. Integrated management has two meanings, integrating environmental decisions with all other business. The second order of management would be modifying the structures of business. This requires a reshaping of the U.S. business and governmental systems.

Business Considerations and Transaction Costs

The environmental statutes and regulations of the United States impose a high cost on business. There are fundamentally two types of costs: substantive costs, which relate to an act of compliance or site cleanup, and transaction costs. Some environmental statutes create a liability. Under these statutes, the substantive costs may take the form of investigation expenses, remediation costs, fines, and penalties.

The cost of doing business with the government represents a transaction cost. Congress and the several states have, in effect, created a parallel, and sometimes overlapping, scheme of environmental regulations. The authority to promulgate, regulate, and enforce environmental laws has been widely dispersed among EPA, state and local authorities, and various other federal agencies. A single "event," whether it is a site cleanup or an accidental release, may force a company to deal with as many as three or four agencies.

Transaction costs are the hidden costs associated with environmental laws in the United States. There is an interlocking web of procedures and rules for any given site, chemical, or waste release. The approval of a federal agency does not necessarily guarantee the blessing of a parallel state agency with jurisdiction over the site. The reverse also holds true, because a state agency can not speak for the federal office. A company's administrative mistakes can be costly. A single compliance or regulatory oversight may delay a plant project for years or result in the imposition of severe fines. Under these circumstances, a company's understanding of the requirements and procedures of the environmental laws becomes an essential part of the business planning in the United States.

Generally, a company's structure allows it to operate within a given regulatory and business environment. If it does not, it simply does not survive. Environmental liability is, in part, a function of how a company reacts to the environmental laws. In the United States, there is a highly regulated and "punitive" enforcement system that taxes the resources of business. In this climate, the expectation is that business will concentrate on reporting and regulatory issues, rather than on prevention and safety. Environmental departments, to the extent that they exist, would be consumed by the sheer task of keeping up to date with regulations. Remediation, waste minimization, and loss prevention would be, under these circumstances, back-burner issues for many companies. In short, we might find that the diverse federal and state scheme of environmental regulation is taxing the resources of many of the companies that do business in the United States.

Corporations often find themselves unprepared to meet the challenges presented by changing technologies or markets. Granted, they may have effective administrative procedures and systems for present business concerns, but these systems often lack the flexibility to handle new regulatory initiatives.

ISO 14000's concept of an EMS may fairly be regarded as fundamental change in business and management principles. Top management commitment to the environment, a systemic integration of environmental issues into the decision-making process of an organization, and the reengineering of governmental and business systems, taken together, may be the force that drives the next generation of economic powers. Government and industry, working together, can implement a change that drives down the cost of doing business *and* improves the quality of life. The mission will be to build it better, faster, cheaper, and cleaner.

There are two possible futures. If no single industry/nation partnership emerges, ISO 14000 may still be a force. The changes will come about gradually, perhaps as a result of piecemeal application of the principles of EMS, but it will nevertheless occur. The early signs are that the concept will take hold. If however, industry/national pairings do emerge, the change is likely to be dramatic.

Early Leaders

Early indications are that the Asian and Scandinavian economies will latch onto and adopt ISO 14000. Their motivations and starting points may be different, but the process is under way.

Asia is the likeliest candidate. According to the 1993 World Bank study, titled the *East Asian Miracle,* eight Asian economies supplied 9 percent of the exported goods 30 years ago. Today, that figure exceeds 21 percent. Japan, Hong Kong, Singapore, and Taiwan are powerful economic forces. South Korea, Malaysia, Thailand, and Indonesia are rising economic powers. These countries focus on the international economy, manage long-term issues, and focus on creating a favorable economic climate. They see not adopting ISO 14000 as a trade threat, a potential barrier. They will move quickly to certify to ISO 14001, rather than risk a disruption of their industries and economics. Understanding the culture of ISO 14000 and its benefits should soon follow.

Create a favorable environment, and domestic economics will flourish. Eliminate redundancies in business structures and government administration, and direct transactional costs that are tied to the management of the environment will drop. Plan for the environmental consequence up front, anticipate the issue on resulting harm, and the bottom-line impact will dissipate. In the United States, the electronics and semiconductor industry has, directly or indirectly through higher insurance premiums, spent hundreds of millions of dollars on sites with TCE and TCA groundwater contamination. If even a fraction of that expense is avoided on the next environmental problem, the industry will be stronger and better suited to manage its growth.

Build it better, faster, cheaper, and cleaner, and whoever builds it first may win.

Stephen A. Watson, III, Esq. is director of regulatory services for Foster Wheeler Environmental Corporation. Mr. Watson has strategic and operational responsibility for Governmental Affairs and Regulatory Services. He is his company's principal corporate spokesperson before governmental bodies and industry associations. Mr. Watson manages the Regulatory Services Division, a unit that provides environmental consulting services to a wide range of domestic and international clients. Mr. Watson is a delegate and U.S. technical expert to the U.S. Technical Advisory Group (TAG) to ISO TC207, participating on SubTag 4, Environmental Performance Evaluation.

12

Preparing for ISO 14000

Thomas P. Ambrose

The U.S. Environmental Protection Agency has expressed a keen interest in environmental management system (EMS) standards for use in its cooperative programs. The agency has played an active role in drafting ISO 14001 and NSF 110, and is now sponsoring demonstration projects to evaluate how implementation of an EMS can improve a company's environmental management and compliance performance. The two EMS standards are being used as benchmarks in these demonstrations.

With the adoption of the British and U.S. standards and the introduction of ISO 14001 in 1996, companies need to identify what opportunities exist to merge environmental and quality systems for a total quality environmental management (TQEM) approach.

Corporate environmental, health, and safety (EH&S) performance is increasingly becoming a critical business issue. Four important challenges are driving this change:

1. The expansion in number and complexity of EH&S regulations affecting industry, together with more sophisticated government programs that increase enforcement pressure;
2. Global competitiveness to reduce waste, use raw materials more efficiently, and lower costs through sustainable manufacturing and pollution prevention technologies;
3. Voluntary industry initiatives in response to growing community concerns and stakeholder interest in corporate environmental performance; and
4. Growing demand for products that reduce environmental burdens through their use and disposal.

Worldwide public expectation for organizations to disclose the facts behind the claims of environmental performance is increasingly coupled with the growing recognition that "environmental improvement is good business." Published EMS standards and ISO 14001 provide organizations of all types with the template for developing or improving sound environmental practices to meet these critical business challenges.

EMS and Quality—Sharing a Common Basis

NSF 110, BS 7750, and the ISO 14001 EMS standards differ in some areas and in specific important requirements, but they share the core elements of environmental management that are also common to quality management clauses in the ISO 9000 series standards.

Environment and quality management systems have a number of similar approaches for establishing and documenting formal procedures to demonstrate that the system is working and conforming to internal standards and established policy. The NSF International correspondence between NSF 110 and ISO 9001 indicates these similarities (Table 12.1). However, the management mind-sets in establishing implementation processes differ in the following very important respects:

- *Quality* is a contract between a supplier and customer (e.g., "producer" and "buyer"), which places the ultimate focus on increased buyer satisfaction. The goal is to connect everyone's daily effort in the producer's organization with understanding what the buyer wants and delivering a product or service that consistently meets or exceeds those expectations. The quality process integrates fundamental management techniques in an organized, disciplined system focusing on the continuous improvement cycle.
- *Environment* has stakeholders beyond the producer-buyer relationship who have legitimate interest in the process and influence over the outcome. In addition to meeting buyer expectations, the focus of the producer is to comply with government requirements, minimize environmental impacts, and address community concerns in order to continue its "license to operate." New regulation, heightened buyer awareness, and society's acceptance of the producer's operations and products are the additional forces that drive EMS continuous improvement.

Moving Ahead—Creating an Effective TQEM System

Environmental management systems and programs should be designed for flexibility to meet the needs of the organization's individual operating units, while providing a sharp focus on continuous improvement and meeting strategic goals for the total organization. An effective system should be built around nine key management process areas, to ensure:

Table 12.1 Correspondence between NSF 110 and ISO 9001

Note: A checked cell indicates that the relevant elements of the two standards share similar requirements.

Elements of ISO 9001	Elements of NSF 110								
	3.1	3.2	3.3	3.4	3.5	3.6	3.7	3.8	3.9
	Policy	Organization and personnel	Objectives and targets	Program implementation	Control procedures	Emergency preparedness	Verification and review	Documentation	Communications
4.1 Management responsibility	✓	✓					✓		
4.2 Quality system				✓				✓	
4.3 Contract review									
4.4 Design control									
4.5 Document and data control								✓	
4.6 Purchasing									
4.7 Control of customer-supplied product									
4.8 Product identification and traceability									
4.9 Process control					✓				
4.10 Inspection and testing									
4.11 Control of inspection, measuring, and test equipment									
4.12 Inspection and test status									
4.13 Control of nonconforming product									
4.14 Corrective and preventive action							✓		
4.15 Handling, storage, packaging, preservation, and delivery									
4.16 Control of quality records								✓	
4.17 Internal quality audits							✓		
4.18 Training		✓							
4.19 Servicing									
4.20 Statistical techniques									

1. Compliance with government laws, regulations, and standards;
2. Conformance to company policy and externally subscribed standards;
3. Management responsibility and accountability;
4. Objectives and targets that minimize significant environmental impacts;
5. Periodic assessment of potential major risk;
6. Emergency planning and response;
7. Adequate training and awareness programs;

8. Appropriate communication channels and information management systems; and
9. Performance evaluation and audits that measure progressive improvement.

The effectiveness of these activities should be measured routinely against internal and external expectations to ensure that policy goals remain valid. Additional EMS performance metrics should cover the underlying management system, including the company's supplier-to-customer chain.

Environmental Management System Baseline Assessment

Within the above core framework, the following crucial components of the management system should be critically accessed initially and on a defined cycle:

- *Policy*—Has a formal policy statement been issued by senior management and endorsed by the governing board? Is it relevant in scope to the organization's activities?
- *Organization*—Is an integrated structure in place in which accountability and responsibility are defined, understood, and carried out?
- *Continuous Improvement*—Are clear, specific, challenging goals and objectives set and aligned with defined, measurable annual targets? Is a tangible commitment to meeting set goals and resolving problems visible?
- *Implementation*—Does the environmental planning process include all levels of management and result in programs and procedures to implement corporate policy?
- *Legal Compliance*—Does each operating unit clearly understand relevant environmental laws, regulations, and permit conditions and have implementation procedures? Is an audit program in place with sufficient content and cycle frequency to evaluate issues and their degree of complexity? Is a process present to respond to legitimate employee complaints?
- *Risk Management*—Have known environmental risks associated with the company's operations, products, and services been identified? Does risk assessment exist to address reasonable sudden events or long-term situations? Are identified significant risks being managed appropriately to minimize the potential for major liability?
- *Emergency Planning*—Is a process in place for responding to unexpected events? Do emergency response plans exist that define appropriate actions required to address potential incidents?

- *Quality Assurance*—Are progress and performance regularly measured against the policy to verify that objectives and targets are being met? Are identified problems corrected in a timely manner and preventive measures installed? How does the organization's governing board know that the EMS is working?

An organization operates in a dynamic atmosphere. An effective EMS strives to integrate environmental considerations into other routine business management processes and everyday decision making. Teamwork, starting with a firm top-management commitment and forging support from those that will implement the EMS, is the underlying formula for an effective TQEM system.

Getting Started

The TQEM system should be designed with environmental performance as an integral component of the company's business success plan. To begin effective integration into business planning, the following are some critical action steps that utilize the organization's cross-functional expertise to implement sound technical programs and solutions:

- Conduct quick surveys and hold short "brainstorming" sessions with individuals dealing with the company's main functions and issues.
- Form a multidisciplinary team made up of experts who have decision-making capability for all the organization's key activities. Ask questions that challenge the core assumptions of the assembled team on the quality of the organization's environmental performance.
- Using the team's input, establish specific performance criteria for your program and conduct a self-assessment against the core elements in the EMS standards to rank and evaluate any identified "major gaps."
- Hold working sessions attended by EH&S staff and business and operations managers who will be charged with taking improvement action. Decide what to do, who will do it, and by when. Build a mechanism into your program to track progress on the "to do's" in order to evaluate how and when to adjust course as conditions unfold.
- Summarize the results for all participants, allowing comparisons against the standards and internal criteria to be used as part of the ongoing process to set priorities.
- Once the system has been designed and implemented, commission third-party audits periodically to obtain an independent, objective evaluation of how well the system is working and areas that need improvement. Implementation is not an end, but one crucial step in the continuous improvement cycle.

Creating Ownership

Like quality, environmental management that goes beyond meeting basic needs depends on bringing all employees into the decision process to share a common proactive goal. The key to an effective TQEM effort is designing a system that makes sense to all the people being asked to implement it.

Managers should educate senior management on "why" and "what's in it for us" in order to obtain their visible support and commitment that environmental improvement is a core value for business success at all levels of the organization. The next step is to communicate an approach that works best in the corporate culture to obtain a consensus on moving ahead with the new initiative with internal stakeholders such as R&D, accounting, marketing, general managers, and facility management.

To further ownership, hold "shirt sleeves" sessions with all employees to discuss the new policies and solicit suggestions for improvements in their work areas of responsibility; involve business unit and facility management in the setting of stretch objectives and targets that provide implementation flexibility in line with the environmental impacts and competitive market forces associated with their operations; and finally, develop feedback loops and information tracking systems to identify continuous improvement opportunities and methods to communicate steady progress toward reaching the goals to both internal and external interested parties.

Conclusion

It is fundamental to an effective TQEM effort to identify, access, and prioritize significant environmental effects that relate to an organization's operations, products, and services. Conducting an environmental effect analysis is the most important feature that differentiates the ISO 14001 environmental

Involve nonenvironmental people in the process and to validate judgments. Consider normal and abnormal conditions.

Systematic procedure:

1. Assemble a cross-functional team that knows the organization's activities and issues.
2. Devise a structured process to identify environmental aspects of operations, products and services (e.g., flow charting, checklists).
3. Establish boundary conditions on *what you will manage.*
4. Set criteria in line with the scale, severity, and duration of each aspect.
5. Develop a first-cut list of obvious and nonsignificant aspects (ask questions that challenge core assumptions of the team).
6. Refine the list—Seek out individuals throughout the organization with multidiscipline expertise (e.g., R&D, marketing, production, law) to obtain input and feedback.
7. Rank aspects that can have a significant impact to set initial priorities.
8. Develop objectives and targets and metrics to measure progress to reduce impacts.
9. Hold quarterly team updates—annual senior management strategic review.

Figure 12.1   Suggested Process for ISO 14001 Aspects/Impacts Analysis

standard from ISO 9000. The commitment to reduce environmental impact is at the heart of the ISO 14001 environmental management system and a systematic aspects and impacts planning step (see Figure 12.1) is the key to the underlying continual improvement idea of the EMS standard.

Once the organization's significant environmental impacts have been identified, measurable objectives need to be set and action plans developed that minimize real or potential impacts. The goal is to work toward a consistent level of environmental performance across the organization. Further progressive improvement will also come from incorporating pollution prevention into day-to-day operations and designing environmental considerations into products and services.

Sustainable, proactive total quality environmental management happens when the freedom is present to choose "what works best in our culture" and when each individual's TQEM effort is linked with achieving the organization's strategic business goals.

Thomas P. Ambrose is a health, safety, and environmental (HSE) management advisor providing audit/assessment services to a variety of organizations. He is a past president of the Environmental Auditing Roundtable and is a Qualified Environmental Professional (QEP).

13

Implementing ISO 14000: Overcoming Barriers to Registration

Rodger A. Jump

An initiative within an enterprise begins with an idea originating from one person. That initiative gains its impetus because the originator of the idea assumes the role of the proponent. The proponent needs to sell the idea to others within the enterprise if it is to win support and succeed in having the idea become an initiative. How are the proponents of ISO 14000 to win support for their position that registration under ISO 14000 is good for their enterprise?

Current literature on ISO 9000 and ISO 14000 already offers numerous articles about what the chief executive officer or president of a firm must do to implement registration under the standards. This we can refer to as the top-down approach. However, not all CEOs or presidents of companies are first in their company to see the need for registration under an ISO standard. This article addresses the bottom-up approach, in which lower-level staff can take actions to overcome barriers and move their firm toward registration.

The barriers to ISO 14000 registration that this article will address are:

- Lack of hard data to demonstrate cost-effectiveness of registration
- Agency costs arising from opposing and unsupporting parties
- Assertion of barriers to trade
- the assertion that ISO registration is not in synch with "reengineering the corporation"

Fortunately, there are definite actions that the lower-level staff can take to deal with all these barriers.

Cost-Effectiveness

A crucial step is to justify implementation of ISO 14000 to the decision makers who have the authority to allocate resources. The proponents must put themselves in the shoes of the CEO of a firm, who must justify the expense of ISO 14000 registration to shareholders, or the CFO, who must justify the expense to superiors. And, in the case of privately held small businesses, the proponents must answer the question, "Will the expense of registration create an intangible asset that will generate an increase in net income greater than the cost of registration?" There are always proposed activities in a firm that compete for funds and the proponents of ISO 14000 registration need to furnish decision makers with the ammunition to justify the expense of going forward with the registration process. It is not unusual to find cases cited in the literature where firms have saved significant amounts of money carrying out environmental initiatives. The skeptic will ask, however, "At what cost were these benefits gained?" This question must be addressed before the decision maker will be persuaded to support registration.

The proponents of ISO 14000 registration must provide information based on disciplined budgeting and tracking of environmental quality costs so that the decision makers can defend their decision to support registration. Russell, Skalak, and Miller, in *Environmental Cost Accounting: The Bottom Line for Environmental Quality Management,*[1] make an excellent case for estimating and tracking environmental quality costs, along with the use of such data for investment analysis and capital budgeting. In addition, the question of registration under ISO 14000 should be subject to both a life-cycle and cost/benefit analysis based on documented assumptions. The life-cycle analyses should present best, nominal, and worst-case scenarios and provide a system for tracking costs and benefits and periodic evaluation.

Identifying contracts won, increases in gross revenues, the value of good will generated, and so forth as a result of implementing ISO 14000 will, of course, often be a matter of opinion and debate. However, tools for making such forecasts are a matter of routine in most enterprises. In cases where the item to be forecast may be a little "fuzzy," using the Delphi method of evaluation may offer a way to develop a consensus. (The Delphi method is a strategy for arriving at a consensus by polling a group of experts who respond without consulting one another. The responses are averaged to arrive at a nominal result.)

Proponents of ISO 14000 registration often turn to outside consulting firms to gather information to support their case for registration. Therefore, firms that are in the business of "selling" the implementation of ISO 14000 should be prepared to offer prospective clients the information needed to justify registration to their decision makers. Where might vendors get such information? An initial strategy would be to demonstrate the cost-effectiveness of registration under ISO 9000 and draw as many parallels as possible with ISO 14000. Then, as registrations under ISO 14000 accumulate, it would be wise for firms who sell services for preparation for ISO 14000 registration to collect cost-benefit data throughout the process. Some of the information collected may be hard cost data but, as mentioned above, much of it may be anecdotal or "fuzzy" data. However, large amounts of fuzzy data will show trends and is better than no feedback at all on costs and benefits. Once entered into a well-designed relational database, this information will be a valuable marketing tool for the vendor.

This data collection would not be an appropriate function for the auditors. So, it behooves the audit preparation vendors to follow up after registration to collect information on customer satisfaction and for feedback for improving their services.

Agency Costs

An essential part of management's decision to go forward with registration under ISO 14000 must address the threat of agency costs. It is a characteristic of human behavior that members within an organization do not invest their best efforts in an activity unless that effort is consistent with maximizing their own welfare (self-interest). This situation gives rise to what are referred to in the field of economics as agency costs: costs that arise due to parties within an organization not "pulling in line" with the most cost-effective vector of the organization. Suppose that the most cost-effective solution for a dispute between a company and its vendor is to mediate a compromise. However, suppose the head of the legal department wants the prestige of a publicized court case, even though that action will distract management for a year from responding effectively to an attack on the company's market niche by a competitor. The difference in cost of litigation over mediation is termed agency costs—costs arising due to an agent within the firm electing an alternative other than the most cost-effective one for the firm.

How are agency costs relevant to ISO 14000? Suppose the proponents of ISO 14000 registration within a firm win the support of the decision maker and are given the go-ahead for implementation. It is essential to identify those parties or agents (people and organizations) within the firm who will either actively resist the effort or will not support it. Once these parties have been identified, management must devise a strategy to align their interests with those of the firm to facilitate the registration under ISO 14000. To bypass this step is to invite failure of the registration process or to suffer unnecessarily high costs of implementation.

Therefore, *identification of passive and resisting parties* and *alignment of interests* are two activities that should appear on a flowchart and be tracked just as any other vital activity or milestone. These activities should not be overlooked or given short shrift because people whose interests are not aligned with the effort can impair and increase the cost of success.

Barriers to Trade

Another argument against registration under environmental standards that proponents will need to overcome is that such standards act as barriers to trade.

Most people familiar with ISO 9000 and the Eco-labeling and Audit Scheme are acquainted with the assertion that standards such as these are a luxury afforded only by developed economies and act as barriers to trade with emerging economies. This argument is based on the tacit assumption that environmental quality, embodied in registration under standards such as ISO 14000, yields a negative net present value as an investment, or, at best, a noncompetitive return compared to alternative investments. The approaches presented here for winning the support of decision makers within a company should aid decision makers in emerging market enterprises to see that it is possible to support ISO 14000 registration and still be competitive. In fact, ISO 14000 registration may place the registered firm at a competitive advantage with prospective clients who use environmental criteria as a discriminator in vendor selection.

The suspicion that these standards pose barriers to trade may be unfounded. There is evidence that ISO 9000 registration is taking hold in emerging economies, as demonstrated by ASCERT International having certified more than 100 ISO 9000 auditors in Mexico in May 1995.

Reengineering the Corporation and ISO 14000

Registration under ISO 14000 must be in harmony with the reengineering process because so many companies are using reengineering principles to cut any activities deemed nonessential to the fundamental processes of the firm. Implementation of ISO 14000 will be stillborn if it is perceived to be merely the latest pet project of the quality assurance staff. Registration under ISO 14000 must be shown to be a vital part of the fundamental function of the company's business process and provide more benefits than costs.

There is an element of convergence between reengineering and ISO standards: It should be easier to implement ISO 9000 and ISO 14000 in firms that have been reengineered because there will be fewer fragmented divisions within the company and, therefore, fewer opportunities for "hand-off" errors.

Reengineering consists of

- Clearly and concisely stating the customers' wants and needs;
- Identifying outputs that will meet customers' wants and needs;
- Structuring the value-added processes essential to generating the identified outputs; and
- Planning for the inputs required for generating the outputs.

Looking at these four activities, where does ISO 14000 registration fit in? More fundamentally, does it even fit in? The answer depends, in part, on who the customer is. For example, if the customer is an enterprise that is soliciting proposals from candidate vendors, the customer may require that the vendor be registered under ISO 14000. If the customer is a retail end user, the customer may not even know what ISO 14000 is and, therefore, ISO 14000 is not a discriminator in the decision to purchase. However, it may still be cost-effective, in this case, to produce goods or deliver services in accordance with ISO 14000 if two conditions are met: The quality of the goods or services is pleasing to the customer and the value added to the goods either costs no more or appears worth the price increment over the competition.

As Hammer and Champy noted in *Reengineering the Corporation,* "Quality programs and reengineering share a number of common themes. . . . However, the two programs differ fundamentally."[2] So, it is incumbent on the proponents of ISO 14000 registration to make it harmonize with reengineering, even to the point of making the ISO 14000 process systemic to the reengineered processes of the firm rather than having ISO 14000 as an appurtenance.

Conclusion

What can proponents of ISO 14000 registration do to address the decision makers' skeptical questions, "Why should I support ISO 14000 registration? What's in it for me?" The in-house proponents must:

- Present their case for registration in terms of cost-benefit to the decision maker. They must enable the decision maker to defend the decision to register under ISO 14000.
- Commit to a businesslike implementation by agreeing to track costs and benefits and to assess and report them on a regular basis.
- Gain the support of top management for the identification of passive and resisting parties and alignment of interests in order to improve the probability of success.
- Understand the reengineering process and be prepared to implement ISO 14000 registration in harmony, if not systemically, with reengineering.

What can the vendors of services for the preparation of the audit for ISO 14000 do to support the prospective client?

- Collect data on cost-benefit of registration under ISO 14000 as experience accumulates and build databases even if much of the information is anecdotal.
- Offer cost-benefit data and/or anecdotal evidence supporting the cost-effectiveness of registration under ISO 14000. In the near term, this information may be related to ISO 9000 registration with parallels drawn to ISO 14000.

- Look for cost-benefit data on ISO 14000 registration in the emerging economies to address the assertion that such standards pose barriers to trade and, it is hoped, increase registration in those nations by citing successful experiences.

Notes

1. W.G. Russell, S.L. Skalak, and G. Miller, "Environmental Cost Accounting: The Bottom Line for Environmental Quality Management," in J.T. Willig, ed., *Auditing for Environmental Quality Leadership* (New York: John Wiley & Sons, Inc., 1995), pp. 109–119.

2. M. Hammer and J. Champy, *Reengineering the Corporation* (New York: Harper Collins, Inc., 1993), p. 49.

Rodger A. Jump, P.E., is a business mergers and acquisitions consultant with Proforma West, LLC in Denver, Colorado. He was formerly president of International Business Consultants (IBC) in Rockville, Maryland, and was program manager on the startup of the Environmental Restoration Program for the U.S. Department of Energy at Oak Ridge, Tennessee, and at DOE headquarters in Washington, DC.

14

Registrars, Accreditation, and ISO 14001

Scott Foster

The International Organization for Standardization (ISO) has published the first international environmental management system standard: ISO 14001. While the ultimate impact of this standard is subject to heated debate throughout the industrial and environmental communities, this chapter will focus on one aspect of the standard: the process of certification/registration.

ISO 14001 is a voluntary initiative; companies will need to decide for themselves whether or not to pursue certification. As indicated in Section 1: Scope of ISO 14001,

> This International Standard is applicable to any organization that wishes to
>
> a) implement, maintain and improve an environmental management system;
>
> b) assure itself of its conformance with its stated environmental policy;
>
> c) demonstrate such conformance to others;
>
> d) *seek certification / registration of its environmental management system by an external organization;*
>
> e) *make a self determination and declaration of conformance with the standard.* (Emphasis added.)[1]

As the introduction to ISO 14001 makes clear, "The specification contains only those requirements that may be objectively audited for certification/registration and/or self-declaration purposes." Any additional "guidance . . . will be contained in other international standards."[2] To avoid confusion, these other international standards tend to be called guidelines.

Of particular interest to those associated with the certification and registration of systems to ISO 14001 are the three guidelines for environmental auditing. Officially these are referred to as:

- ISO 14010: Guidelines for Environmental Auditing—General Principles;
- ISO 14011: Guidelines for Environmental Auditing—Audit Procedures—Auditing of Environmental Management Systems; and
- ISO 14012: Guidelines for Environmental Auditing—Qualification Criteria for Environmental Auditors.

There are essentially four levels of parties involved in the registration of a company to ISO 14001 (Figure 14.1). At the top of the registration pyramid is the company that is claiming to have an EMS that can be certified to the ISO 14001 standard. The next level is the registrar, which has three distinct elements: (1) the registration body, which is a supervising company such as Underwriter's Laboratories or Lloyd's; (2) the audit team, which is employed by the registration body and composed of auditors and technical experts; and (3) the approved training programs that each auditor must complete prior to being able to perform an audit in the field. Each of these three elements—the registration body, the auditors, and requisite training courses—is accredited by the national accreditation program (NAP) that most countries will establish to regulate these parties.[3] In turn, the NAP will reflect the input of a variety of stakeholders, including industry, government, public interest groups, consultants, and registrars. The broader the interests represented, the more credibility the national program will have, both within the country and internationally.

ISO Involvement with Registrations

It is important to note that ISO has no official involvement with any of these levels. Its official participation ends with the publication of the standard, and will be felt only in the continuing revisions of the standard. Due to the structure of ISO technical committees, however, national members of ISO (such as ANSI) and individuals associated with the development of ISO 14001 as an

Figure 14.1   Parties Involved in ISO 14001 Registration

ISO standard will be involved at every level of the pyramid. To fully understand how this is possible, and the potential issues involved, the methodology of the development of an ISO standard, as well as the structure of the personnel involved, must be better understood.

While ISO does have some permanent staff, they are not generally involved with the development of the different standards. This role is left to experts within the respective fields. These experts are organized into technical committees (TCs), which decide if a standard is needed and then draft the standard following ISO procedures. Each technical committee is organized around a particular topic and has a secretariat and chairman responsible for oversight of the TC and for convening meetings. According to the chairman of TC 67, Cyril Arney of Marathon Oil, the role has little additional authority beyond upholding the ISO constitution with respect to TC procedures.[4] Within each TC, there are numerous subcommittees (SCs) and/or working groups (WGs) that are organized to address a particular facet of the TC's subject area. Within TC 207, for example, there are 6 subcommittees and one working group, with each subcommittee having from two to five working groups subordinate to it. Each subcommittee has a separate secretariat, while each working group has a convenor and sometimes a secretariat. Generally, the secretariat positions are designated to a country or the respective standards organization of the country that is the actual member of ISO.[5] Commonly, the structure of the ISO TC is mimicked by a similar structure within each nation, including the subcommittees and working groups, in a technical advisory group (TAG). This is certainly the case with respect to the U.S. and Canadian representation in TC 207. By organizing the national effort in a similar pattern, the process of selecting national representatives to attend the international meetings (where space is limited) can be made more efficient. Additionally, representatives will have a better understanding of the perspective that its TAG wishes to present on a given issue that may only be discussed in one particular subcommittee.

All persons involved with the subcommittees or working groups, both at the national and international levels, normally has full-time employment with a private or public sector employer. Thus, even though they participate in the ISO/TC/TAG process, this participation is normally secondary to their other employment. However, there is a flip side to this scenario. Since there are only a limited number of individuals involved in the process, these individuals have effectively cornered the market of expertise with the standard, and will be using this position to influence the future of registrations within the United States. Thus, while ISO does not have any official influence over the registration process, the individuals that make up the ISO process will have an influence.

These individuals and organizations are already leveraging their experience with the standard and its development and their professional contacts to gain an influence over others in the registration process. For example, ANSI is leveraging the fact that it is the "organization which serves as the ISO Member Body"[6] to become the recognized national accreditation body. NSF International recently announced its intention to become a registrar and a consultant on the ISO 14000 series, which is convenient since Gordon Bellen of NSF International was the head of the U.S. delegation to the TC 207/SC 3 meeting in Oslo, Norway. Additionally, Andrea Jensen of NSF was a U.S. expert to TC207/SC4.

Numerous Fortune 500 companies, such as AlliedSignal, Merck, IBM, Georgia-Pacific, Champion International, Exxon, International Paper, Motorola, Procter & Gamble, ALCOA, and 3M have sponsored their employees' involvement with the process at the international level. Countless others have sponsored employees at the national level. In addition, different branches of the government, including EPA and the U.S. Army, are involved, as are numerous nonprofit groups (Environmental Defense Fund) (EDF) and Environmental Law Institute (ELI), consultants (Roy F. Weston, ERM, Coopers & Lybrand), industry groups (CMA and the American Forest and Paper Association) and law firms of various sizes.[7] Each of these organizations sees a strategic advantage to participation in the process.[8]

To Register or Not to Register?

Returning to the registration pyramid, there are myriad issues within each level of the pyramid. For the company, there is the initial decision whether or not to implement an ISO 14001-compatible EMS, followed by the decision to register the system through an official registrar. For each company, this will be a individualized decision based on the perceived benefits and costs associated with registration.

For the most part, having an environmental management system of some nature is customary for most multinational corporations. The percentages drop if smaller and medium-sized companies are taken into account.[9] Generally, it is also undisputed that EMSs have a positive impact on the bottom line. Statistical data supporting this contention is sparse; however, a pilot program in Mexico monitoring the implementation of ISO 14001-like EMS guidelines documented an 80 percent increase in profit margins.[10] Thus, the initial decision on whether to pursue an ISO 14001 equivalent system is typically not a hotly debated issue for most larger companies. Registration and certification are another matter.

Under ISO 14001, a company may decide to register to 14001 using a third-party registrar, or could decide to self-declare. Self-declaration is just that: The company's management presents a press release indicating that the company has complied with the tenets of ISO 14001. While it is obvious that this will have less credibility when compared to claims that are verified by a third-party registrar, there are some advantages to this method. Primarily, the costs are greatly reduced (the actual costs of registering will be discussed later). However, very few companies are actually planning to self-declare. A recent survey conducted by Arthur D. Little (ADL) of 260 U.S. and Canadian companies with senior EH&S managers (there were 115 respondents, most with more than $1 billion in annual sales) reported that 68 percent of respondents said that third-party certification was potentially important or very important to their companies' future business success.[11] As motivators for certification, 70 percent indicated that certification would be important to demonstrate EH&S due diligence to regulators, while 61 percent noted the potential competitive advantage in acquiring customers.

The statements coming from EH&S officials within U.S. Fortune 500 companies have indicated that most companies will pursue an official certification at a few sites, and will then decide if it is cost-effective to pursue this on a companywide basis. Most of these companies simultaneously indicate that they already have an EMS that meets most of ISO 14001's requirements; however, they stop short of self-declaration. The ADL survey indicated that 87 percent of respondents felt that even if certification was not pursued, it was important or very important that their EMS was equivalent or at least consistent with ISO 14001.

Given this current trend toward achieving actual registration, the next question is which registrar to use. This is a very complicated question. At the moment, there are no registrars available for ISO 14001; however, the ISO 9000 registration process is similar enough to use anecdotal evidence to provide a perspective on the probable relationships to be developed between registrars, NAPs and companies. The most important decision is whether to use an accredited registrar or one that has not be accredited. The fact that unaccredited registrars exist may come as a shock to some, but even in the realm of law schools, there are a few that are unaccredited yet still prepare graduates. However, the degrees are not comparable in terms of marketability. Generally this is the same case with registrars, though there may be reasons for pursuing a nonaccredited registrar particular to one company. As Jill Quist, vice president of Lloyds Register Quality Assurance, explains, "It's the difference of having an Ivy League degree and a degree from a community college."[12] For the most part, companies that pursue certification will choose a registrar that is accredited. However, being accredited is not the end of the inquiry. Depending on where the company will do business, it may need to choose a registrar that has been accredited by a particular NAP. For example, with respect to ISO 9000, companies doing business with the Canadian government must be registered by a registrar that has been accredited by the Standard Council of Canada (mutual recognition of

NAPs will be discussed later).[13] The scope of the accreditation, or the areas of expertise that the registrar demonstrated sufficient knowledge, is also an important issue.

Accredited Registrars

An accredited registrar is made up of three distinct elements: the registrar itself, the audit team (with a lead auditor), and technical experts. The later two are described in ISO 14010, Section 3: Definitions:

3.5   Audit Team: Group of auditors, or a single auditor, designated to perform a given audit; the audit team may also include technical experts and auditors-in-training.

3.7   Auditor (environmental): Person qualified to perform environmental audits.

3.10   Lead auditor (environmental): Person qualified to manage and perform environmental audits.

3.13   Technical Expert: Person who provides specific knowledge or expertise to the audit team, but who does not participate as an auditor.

There are other guidance documents relating specifically to "Certification/Registration Bodies" prepared by the Committee on Conformity Assessment (CASCO). CASCO was established to periodically develop international guides to facilitate assessment procedures for conforming to the requirements of ISO standards, and is composed of delegates from ISO-member bodies.[14] ISO/IEC Guide 61 refers to the general requirements for these registration bodies, while Guide 62 refers to quality systems registrars.[15] It is still unclear when revised documents for environmental management systems registrars will be available. ISO/IEC Guide 2 provides terms and definitions "concerning standardization and related activities." According to this guidance document (as cited by ANSI), a "registration body" (or registrar) is a "third party which assesses and registers the environmental management system of an organization with respect to the ISO 14001 environmental systems specification standard." In order to become an accredited registrar, each registration body must gain "accreditation" from an "accreditation body" (NAP).

While the trend to have industry-specific registrars is recent with respect to ISO 9000, ISO 14001 registrars are expected to be accredited only in certain areas, based on their level of technical expertise. If the registration follows the pattern established by BS 7750 and EMAS, the registrar will advertise its scope. Some examples found in a recent edition of *IESU* include:

"Scope: Bodyshops for passenger cars and small vans and building in sun-roofs."

"Scope: Extraction of crude white marble."

"Scope: Development, production, and supply of luminaries and optices for indoor lighting in standard, as well as project, versions."

The benefits of having a registrar familiar with a particular industry arose over time with respect to ISO 9000 certifications, as companies found it easier to communicate with a registrar that understood the basics of an industry. The reasons for requiring a scope of accreditation for ISO 14000 registrars has less to do with communication and more to do with the complexity of environmental issues. Technical experts may be used to fulfill or expand the scope that a registrar is certified to cover.

In addition to requirements that the registrar must meet to become accredited, members of the audit team must also be accredited by the NAP. ISO 14012 provides "guidance on qualification criteria for environmental auditors and lead auditors."[16] The guidelines were designed to apply both to external third-party auditors (such as those employed by a registrar) and internal auditors that a company uses on a more regular basis. The primary qualifications that ISO 14012 requires are education and work experience. All auditors should have completed at least secondary education, defined as the stage of education "completed immediately prior to entrance to a university or similar establishment." If an auditor has completed only secondary school, then he or she is expected to have at least five years of work experience "which contributes to the development of skills and understanding in some or all of the following:

a) environmental science and technology;
b) technical and environmental aspects of facility operations;
c) relevant requirements of environmental laws, regulations, and related documents;
d) environmental management systems and standards;
e) audit procedures, processes and techniques."

If an auditor has completed some post-secondary education relating to any of the above mentioned topics, up to one year may be reduced from the five-year requirement. If an auditor has a "recognised national or international degree . . . through a minimum of three years formal" study, then, typically, a minimum of four years' work experience is required, unless the degree focuses on one of the above-mentioned topic areas, which may entitle the auditor to a reduction of the work experience requirement to two years. Additionally, an auditor must complete an approved training program on environmental auditing, and have at least 20 work days of on-the-job environmental auditing training. Section 7 of ISO 14012 lists six "personal attributes and skills" considered necessary for the job. Among these are the ability to clearly express concepts and ideas, both orally and in writing; interpersonal skills; the ability to make sound objective judgments, combined with the ability to maintain objectivity in auditing situations; demonstrated sensitivity "to the conventions and culture of the country or region"; and organization skills.[17] Auditors must also know the language in use at the site, or obtain communication support, and must subscribe to a code of professional ethics.

Despite the relatively high bar established for entry-level auditors, becoming a lead auditor is very easy. If an auditor has completed three full environmental audits for a total of 15 working days, and was acting as a lead auditor under the guidance of another lead auditor for at least one of these audits, he or she is considered to be qualified according to Section 8 of ISO 14012. If this is not possible, then an auditor can demonstrate readiness to be promoted to lead auditor simply by means of interviews, observation, references, and/or assessments of auditing performance made under quality assurance programs. Thus, an auditor could be advanced based, in large part, on reviews of his or her performance not from an educational or experience-based perspective, but from a quality perspective. The difference in skill and education level between an auditor and a lead auditor is not proportional to the increased responsibilities of a lead auditor.

ISO 14011 provides a detailed description of the audit process, including specific responsibilities of the audit team, the auditors, and the lead auditor. The auditor's responsibilities are little more than following the directives of the lead auditor in collecting, analyzing, and documenting audit evidence and preparing audit findings. The lead auditor is the crucial link between the audit team and the auditee, and sometimes to the client, which may or may not be the auditee. This situation may arise with respect to larger companies where the corporate office is the client that commissions the audit, while the site or facility is the auditee. The lead auditor must be in communication with the site prior to the audit, to ensure that there is enough documentation and evidence to substantiate an audit, and to prepare a qualified team with skills and knowledge relevant to the facility or site. Part of this initial communication includes a review of the auditee's documentation, including the environmental policy statement, programs, records, and manuals. A detailed audit plan must be prepared and agreed to by the client and auditee before the team arrives. During the audit, the lead auditor needs to be able to resolve conflicts, and to recognize when audit objectives are unattainable for a variety of reasons. The lead auditor is responsible for all communications with the client and auditee, and must inform them of any "critical nonconformities." The lead auditor also has the final word on determining the significance and description of audit findings, although disagreements with the client and/or auditee should be resolved, if possible, at the closing meeting.

An important theme that runs through ISO 14011 is the avoidance of a conflict of interest between any of the parties. This is mentioned no fewer than four times in the guideline; however, this is typically addressed more severely by the accreditation process. For the most part, a registrar is not allowed to offer consulting services on ISO 14001. Some firms have circumvented this requirement with regard to ISO 9000 by establishing separately managed groups under the same corporate umbrella.

Another theme that is conspicuously underplayed in the guideline is the confidentiality of the audit. ISO 14011 stops short of recommending that the audit, its findings, or any "critical nonconformities" are to be held confidential, in part out of recognition that this is an international standard, and different nations have different perspectives on this issue. Even in the United States, different states have decidedly different opinions on the matter. While ISO 14011 does not specifically require the lead auditor to discuss and determine the level of confidentiality that will be maintained with respect to the audit, confidentiality is one of several items that should be discussed. For example, confidentiality requirements should be included in the audit plan, along with such basic information as the date and time of the audit, and the intended scope and objectives. Any working documents involving confidential or proprietary information should be suitably safeguarded by members of the audit team. Finally, a statement of the confidential nature of the contents of the final report may be included in the report, which is considered to be the sole property of the client, whose "confidentiality should be respected and appropriately safeguarded by the auditors."[18] Despite all of these recommendations, no mention is made of whether an auditor is required to disclose a critical nonconformity of a criminal or environmentally catastrophic nature to relevant authorities. This issue, which is of particular importance to U.S. clients, is typically addressed by the NAP when it establishes its accreditation program.

The National Accreditation Program

The third level of the registration pyramid is perhaps the most essential, important, and influential piece of the process. The NAP balances the concerns of the stakeholders in determining what criteria should be established, consistent with ISO 14010-14012, for registrars, auditors, and approved training programs. The nuances of the NAP are best illuminated by exploring actual examples of NAPs, which are discussed below.

Stakeholders

The inclusion of stakeholders at the foundation of the registration pyramid is appropriate, given their number and the ultimate credibility that they offer to the entire process. A stakeholder is a term used to mean any group that has an interest, or stake, in a company's actions—not merely owners (who are often called shareholders). The term arose in the 1700s in the frontier, where individuals that agreed to work the land were given a "grub-stake" and were referred to as stakeholders. Stakeholders in the registration process include environmentalists, companies, registrars, consumers, and, potentially, the government (this list is by no means complete, and will adjust depending on the country). If a broad enough cross section of the stakeholders believes in the credibility of a certain NAP, then it will have the support necessary to operate effectively as an accreditation body. If a NAP does not have enough support, its accreditations may be considered worthless, and, as a result, registrars that are accredited by that NAP may have difficulties in having their registrations or certifications taken seriously. In the final analysis, the entire process turns on whether enough stakeholders believe in the process. However, as seen by the dotted lines in Figure 14.2, the stakeholders are the consumers of the process at different levels. The only party that is not considered a stakeholder is the NAP, which, at least in the case of the United States, may be composed of stakeholders. Somehow, by weaving a gossamer web of faith on top of another gossamer web, a substantial and reliable system emerges.

National Examples

The United States

Within the United States, most registrations of ISO 9000 registrars, auditors, and training courses are overseen by joint venture of ANSI and the Regis-

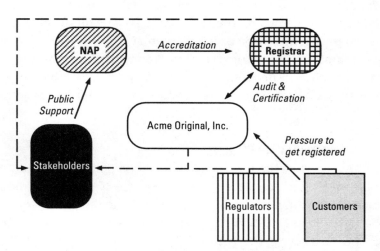

Figure 14.2 Stakeholders in an Organization

trar Accreditation Board (RAB). There are a few exceptions. For example, the Independent Association of Accredited Registrars (a trade group representing ISO 9000 registrars in North America) claims to accredit some auditors and training courses, although few seem to subscribe to this accreditor. It is also possible for a U.S. registrar to seek accreditation from another NAP, such as the highly esteemed Dutch body, Raad voor Certificate (RvC).

ANSI is a private nonprofit organization that coordinates the U.S. voluntary standards system, bringing together interests from the public and private sectors. ANSI is the official U.S. member body to ISO and IEC. ANSI's membership includes about 1,300 national and international companies, 35 government agencies, 20 institutions, and 260 professional, technical, trade, labor, and consumer organizations. RAB was founded in late 1989 as a separately incorporated affiliate of the American Society for Quality Control (ASQC). It is a not-for-profit corporation that derives its income from accreditation and certification operations.[19]

The ANSI-RAB arrangement was the product of intense negotiations and agreements. Many expected these two groups to reunite forces to accredit ISO 14001 registrars, auditors, and training courses; early in the process, however, it became clear that not only were there more parties coming to the table, but ANSI and RAB would also be acting as competitors and not teammates.

The U.S. TAG tried to kick-start the process of identifying an accreditation body for ISO 14000 by turning to a newly formed group of stakeholders called the Standards Conformance and Registration Group (SCRAG). SCRAG prepared a list of criteria for an organization to meet in order to demonstrate that it has the resources and credibility to be the nation's central accreditation body. The criteria were simple and direct. The organization should:

1. Be in place when ISO 14001 becomes an official standard;
2. Already have national recognition and credibility (for potential U.S. governmental endorsement);
3. Be able to establish international recognition and credibility (to promote universal acceptance of ISO 14000 and universal acceptance of the accreditation);
4. Have sufficient human and financial resources; and
5. Demonstrate objectivity and independence.[20]

At that time, no single organization seemed to fit all of these criteria.

Negotiations between ANSI and RAB began soon thereafter, and continued for several months until October 1995. Apparently, as negotiations continued, RAB sought a more predominant role in the accreditation than ANSI was willing to concede. It is important to remember that ANSI is the member body to

ISO, and is able to leverage this position. On October 11, ANSI officially withdrew from the negotiations, throwing the entire U.S. accreditation scheme into question, not only for ISO 14001, but for ISO 9000 as well. Fortunately, RAB president George Lofgren was quick to emphasize that RAB would not drop its ISO 9000 relationship with ANSI.

RAB

Shortly after the end of negotiations, RAB and ANSI began jockeying for recognition as the organization that best met SCRAG's criteria. Even before the official announcement, both were thought to be exploring other options. The rumors were so strong that in July 1995, the trade newsletter *Quality Systems Update* (a sister publication of *IESU*) performed and published a survey of ISO 9000 registrars. The survey showed that more than one-half of the group supported RAB as the sole accreditor, while only 30 percent supported a team of RAB and ANSI.[21] None supported ANSI operating solo. With this level of support from one critical stakeholder group, RAB aggressively pursued (and is continuing to pursue) plans to be involved with the accreditation process.

While the registrar community supported RAB, few others shared this group's fervor. In fact, RAB was "criticized for its insular way of conducting business and [for] its lack of environmental management credibility."[22] While RAB claimed that it would address this issue, it suffers from a cart-horse problem. In March 1996, RAB presented its draft of criteria for accreditation of registrars for EMS for public comment. This draft was prepared by "a small number of RAB officials" with 'indirect' contributions from stakeholder groups." At that time, RAB had not yet established an EMS policy committee, but was planning to do so. One RAB official summarized the approach to the entire process as focused on the customer, the registrar. In a move to consolidate support, RAB announced in December 1995 that it would pursue only an accreditation system for registrars, leaving training course accreditation and auditor certification to others. RAB has, for the large part, cornered the market of support from the *existing* registrars, but it has failed to recognize the broad-based support necessary to substantiate an EMS accreditation system.

ANSI

ANSI officials were much more methodical in their approach to preparing draft criteria, and have thus gained greater and broader support from stakeholders in the process. Starting in October 1995, ANSI announced its intention to establish an EMS accreditation program, and established a task group on EMS accreditation chaired by Gerald H. Ritterbusch.[23] This was already a significant departure from RAB's actions. For one, ANSI established the task group not to develop EMS accreditation criteria, but to assess whether ANSI was the right organization to accomplish this effort. Secondly, ANSI appointed a seasoned environmental manager familiar with voluntary standards and audit procedures to serve as the chair of this group: Mr. Ritterbusch is the manager of product safety and environmental control for Caterpillar, Inc.

As soon as ANSI announced its intention to develop an accreditation program, it received votes of confidence from two key players in the U.S. TAG. Mary McKiel, who is the director of the Standards Network at EPA, the vice chair of the U.S. TAG, and (conveniently) an ANSI board member, stated that "EPA recognizes and supports ANSI's role as the sole U.S. representative to the ISO community . . . [and] . . . looks forward to continuing its work with ANSI, the U.S. TAG, and others to ensure that the ANSI-run accreditation system is credible to U.S. stakeholders and is internationally accepted."[24] Joe Cascio noted that "ANSI is uniquely poised to be" "the one organization that speaks for the U.S."[25] A few months later, Cascio reiterated his comment, but went on to note that the U.S. TAG would likely not take a position as to which organization should oversee U.S. accreditation.

ANSI also addressed a key concern of the quality registrar community by noting that "registrars already accredited to the ANSI-RAB ISO 9000 program will only be required to demonstrate compliance with any additional requirements that apply specifically to EMS activities."[26] Previously, this was one of RAB's major points as to why it would be the better choice. Most observers assumed that many quality registrars would also begin to offer EMS registration, and would want "one-stop" shopping for accreditation. Many feared that if this were not arranged, U.S. registrars would abandon both the RAB-ANSI ISO 9000 accreditation program and ANSI's ISO 14000 accreditation program, and would turn to European or Canadian accreditation bodies. ANSI's statement, while not offering the maximum comfort, made it clear that turning to foreign competitors would be considered unacceptable.

ANSI's next major step was to hire John Donaldson as vice president in charge of all conformity assessment issues. Mr. Donaldson was previously employed by the National Institute of Standards and Technology (NIST) as the chief of applications and services. Donaldson was also the U.S. representative on CASCO. In this position, he would oversee any EMS accreditation program that developed. ANSI's hiring of Donaldson was seen as a serious indication of its commitment to developing a solid accreditation program. Joe Cascio captured the importance of the move when he noted that "Donaldson is probable the best known and biggest name on conformity issues in this country."[27]

ANSI's concerted effort to include a broad spectrum of stakeholders in the 18-member EMS Council was apparent from the initial appointment of the chair and vice chairs. In addition to Rittenbusch as chair and McKiel as a vice chair, Erik Myers, general counsel for the not-for-profit Environmental Law Institute, was named the second vice chair. Other members include:

Brian Unter Director, Corporate External Standards, Hewlett-Packard

John Master Consultant, Chemical Manufacturers Association, and Chairman of U.S. TAG SC4

Joel Charm Director, Health Safety and Environmental Sciences, Allied Signal, Inc, and Chairman of the U.S. TAG SC1

Mary Saunders Assistant to the Director, National Institute of Standards Technology

Larry Stirling Environmental Protection Specialist, Office of Environmental and Assistance, U.S. Department of Energy

LeRoy C. Paddock Assistant Attorney General, Minnesota EPA

Dr. Robert Stephens Chief, Hazardous Materials Lab, California EPA[28]

Barbara Haas Director, Corporate Conservation Council, National Wildlife Foundation

Molly Kingston International Program Trade and Policy Analyst, Environmental Defense Fund

Jean McCreary President, Environmental Auditing Roundtable

Richard McLaughlin Representative, Institute for Internal Auditors

James Highland Management Systems Analysis, Inc. (representing auditor training providers)

Marshall Courtois President, Independent Association of Accredited Registrars

George Krafcisin President, Kemper Registrar Services, Inc. (representing registrars)

Joseph Cascio Chair of the U.S. Technical Advisory Group (TAG) to ISO/TC 207 on environmental management (the *official* liaison member with the U.S. TAG)

The EMS Council has published two draft policies for public comment: One covers the self-imposed requirements for the ANSI-run NAP (EMS 1) and the other contains "General Requirements for Bodies Operating Registration of Environmental Management Systems (EMS 3)." These standards were developed in conformance with ISO/IEC guides, ISO 14001, ISO 14010, ISO 14011, ISO 14012, and ISO 10011-1:1990 (Guidelines for Auditing Quality Systems—Part 1: Auditing).

There are a few important clarifications and additions to the requirements not found in ISO documents. To preserve integrity, Section 6 of EMS 1 requires that any member of the EMS Council involved in an accreditation audit of a registrar cannot take part in the actual decision on accreditation. These individuals will obviously be able to present their findings and make recommendations, but will not be allowed to vote, and will probably be excused from any serious debate. Section 4.2 (o) of EMS 3 discusses measures to ensure an impartial registrar:

> [The registration body shall] ensure that activities of related bodies and subcontractors do not affect the confidentiality, objectivity, or impartiality of its registrations and shall not offer or provide:
>   i.   the services that it registers others to perform;
>   ii. consulting services to the organization being registered to obtain or maintain registration;
>   iii. services to design, implement or maintain environmental management systems to the organization being registered.
>
> Note—Other products, processes or services may be offered, directly or indirectly, provided they do not compromise confidentiality, or the objectivity or impartiality of its registration process and decisions.

It is yet unclear exactly what this section means; however, it appears likely that any organization that does not keep any consulting operations quite distant from any registration services will risk losing its accreditation. While this section seems to be addressing overly compensating registrars, Section 9.4 makes an allowance for an audit team member who may have a grudge against a company by requiring the registrar to inform the company of the names of the audit team members and preserving the company's right to appeal the appointment of certain personnel.

Confidentiality

The confidentiality of the audit is covered in Sections 4.9.1 and 4.9.2. Essentially, the registrar must have adequate arrangements to safeguard confidentiality of any information obtained during the audit, Additionally, if any information must be legally disclosed to a third party, then the registrar must inform the organization of what information was provided, and to whom. The most volatile confidentiality issues arise in regard to auditing compliance with Section 4.2.2 of ISO 14001, which concerns legal and other requirements.

The current draft of EMS 3 does not specifically address what level of detailed evidence a registrar must review to assure that the EMS is in compliance with the provisions of ISO 14001. The CASCO has prepared language concerning this issue that a registrar "shall always require that a site complies with . . . legislation related to environmental protection." Joe Cascio has proposed that the EMS Council adopt this language modifying one word: changing *complies* to *conforms*. In an issue paper attached to the EMS 3 draft, the EMS Council has solicited views as to the following:

- What would be the appropriate EMS audit topics regarding compliance with legal requirements?
- Should noncompliance with legal requirements disqualify an organization from registration?
- Would an explicit commitment toward compliance and a procedure to be in compliance with legal requirements be sufficient for registration, assuming that the EMS auditor is capable of determining that the process is working?

Clearly the answers to these questions are the tip of the iceberg. The EMS Council realizes that the future acceptance of ISO 14001 will, in large part, turn on what interpretation it chooses. If the standard is interpreted as too lax, then its credibility with environmental watchdog groups and regulators will be substantially weakened. However, if a company will need to demonstrate to the auditor continuous compliance with all legal requirements to achieve certification, then few companies will want to take that risk. If the standard is rigidly interpreted, and there is no audit privilege protection offered by state legislation, then a company could conceivably have a top-notch EMS, and have a stellar compliance record, but have one drum of waste mislabeled (a minor violation of the legal requirements) on the day of the ISO 14001 audit. As a result of this one mislabeled drum (or another minor infraction), the company might not only fail to achieve certification, but might also have the registrar inform the authorities (as required by law) and be subject to a hefty fine. For the moment, this issue remains unsettled. The ANSI EMS Council is, however, adding to its credibility by addressing this difficult issue head-on.

Mutual Recognition

One remaining important issue for the ANSI EMS Council to confront is mutual recognition of its registrars in other nations. The council has taken certain steps to help guarantee recognition—in particular, assembling a diverse, talented, and recognized team, and in following the CASCO and ISO guidance documents religiously. Bilateral arrangements may be worked out in the near future, but these would be limited to the groups party to the arrangement. Either type of recognition would increase the value of an ANSI accreditation, since a U.S. registrar would not need to be accredited by another group to perform registrations in other parts of the world for the same multinational corporation.

Canada

The Canadians' methodology for developing accreditation bodies is slightly different from the Americans. For one, it involves a more official and higher level government involvement. There are also a few more parties in the process.

The Standards Council of Canada (SCC) is the secretariat for the entire TC 207 and shares these duties with Canadian Standards Association (CSA). Their relationship seems to be similar to that of ASTM and ANSI. In December 1995, SCC announced that is had begun developing its accreditation program, presumably for all Canadian registrars. However, a year earlier, the Canadian Institute of Chartered Accountants (CICA) operating with assistance of the federal Environmental Department, began developing a larger framework document that recognizes SCC's role but goes further in identifying other parties in the process. CICA organized an impressive array of stakeholders, including CSA, the Canadian Manufacturers Association, the Canadian Chemical Producers Associations; the Air & Waste Management Association; Noranda; the Canadian Environmental Industry Association; Environment Canada; the Canadian Bar Association; the Canadian Bankers Association; the Institute of Certified Management Consultants of Canada; the Society of Management Accountants of Canada; and the Canadian Council of Professional Engineers.

By amassing such broad support early in the process, CICA was practically able to dictate the policy to SCC. Specific terms of the arrangements include SCC agreeing to led other groups assess and accredit registrars and course suppliers, while another group will certify individual auditors. Fortunately, CICA was not trying to put SCC out of the picture, but was trying to clarify the picture for future systems. The framework that is established will be able to encompass certifying Phase I and Phase II site assessment practitioners, as well as other environmental auditing personnel for other programs.

Other Countries

Information about the relationships and negotiations leading up to an established systems is more difficult to locate on other countries, especially European groups. This is, in part, due to the fact that they have had a system in place longer, both for ISO 9000 and the two European-based environmental standards, BS 7750 and EMAS. However, the number of parties and the plethora of acronyms seems to continue to be status quo in all nations.

Notes

1. ISO/DIS 14001, p. 6. Hereinafter 14001.
2. 14001, p. 4.
3. While it is possible for one country to have more than one national accreditation body, it is unlikely, for a number of political and logistical reasons that will be discussed later.
4. Phone conversation with Cyril Arney, March 15, 1996. Hereinafter Arney 1996.
5. This is a subtle, yet important point. While there are more than 100 nation-members of ISO, generally only the standards organizations within these nations are members of ISO, rather than the governments themselves. I have not been able to find out exactly why this is the case, although too much governmental involvement would probably defeat the original mission of

ISO, which is to facilitate the exchange of goods and services and foster mutual cooperation. (From the CSA flier entitled "The International Organization for Standardization".) An American National Standards Institute (ANSI) pamphlet states that "[e]ach country is represented in ISO by an organization which serves as the ISO Member body. In the United States this body is" ANSI. (From the pamphlet entitled "Environmental Management Standards: Background, Benefits & Impact," undated, hereinafter ANSI EMS Doc1.)

6. ANSI EMS Doc 1.

7. From a memo dated June 16, 1995, that lists the approved U.S. delegates to the Oslo meeting.

8. From personal experience, the time and money involved in attending one TAG meeting resulted in consulting contracts that paid the investment back more than five times in less than one year.

9. Sixty-four percent of respondents to a survey of the 1,000 largest companies in Canada, along with 400 smaller firms, and 187 hospitals, universities, or municipalities, reported having an effective environmental management system, according to KPMG consultants. Within manufacturing firms, 85 percent indicated having an EMS, along with 95 percent of the natural resource/energy companies and 85 percent of service sector firms. See "Quality of Canadian EMS has Risen," *Eco-Log Week,* April 26, 1996. Hereinafter *Eco-Log Week.* For a copy of the survey, contact Daren Frizzell via fax at (416) 777-3077.

10. BNA International Environmental Daily, Feb. 1, 1996.

11. This survey was reported in a variety of magazines and journals. One of the most thorough articles was located in *International Environmental Systems Update (IESU),* August 1995, pp. 11–12.

12. "Choosing the Right Registrar to Audit your ISO 9000 Quality System Standard," *Facilities Design & Management,* Vol. 14, No. 7, July 1995, p. 37.

13. "How to Choose an ISO 9000 Registrar," *Appliance,* Vol. 52, No. 3, March 1995, p. BG11.

14. *IESU,* Vol. 3, No. 3, March 1996, p. 15.

15. ISO/IEC refers to documents that are authored by ISO and its sister organization, the International Electrotechnical Commission, which is responsible for drafting standards that relate to electrical and electronic engineering. From the CSA flier entitled "The International Organization for Standardization."

16. DIS/ISO 14012, 1995 draft, p. 1. Hereinafter ISO 14012.

17. ISO 14012, Sec. 7, pp. 3–4. These requirements could eliminate many in the legal field from becoming auditors.

18. ISO 14011, Sec. 5.4.3, p. 8.

19. PR Newswire, "American National Standards Institute, Registrar Accreditation Board Not to Pursue Joint ISO 14000 Accreditation Program," October 13, 1995.

20. *IESU,* Vol. 2, No. 3, March 1995, pp. 6–7.

21. *Quality Systems Update,* Special Report, July 1995, p. SR-7.

22. "Who Will Accredit ISO 14000 Registrars? No Easy Answer," *Chemical Week,* Vol. 157. No. 16, November 8, 1995.

23. PR Newswire, "American Standards Institute (ANSI) to Establish EMS Accreditation program," October 31, 1995.

24. *Id.*

25. *Id.*

26. *Id.*

27. *IESU,* Vol. 2, No. 12, December 1995, p. 5.

28. Paddock and Stephens will share one position.

Scott Foster is a third-year law student at the University of Connecticut, where he is a Managing Editor of the *Connecticut Law Review*. He is also a member of US TAG and the ISO 14000 Legal Issues Forum. Prior to law school, he worked as an environmental consultant focusing on environmental metrics, ISO 14001, information systems, pollution prevention, and environmental management. Following graduation, he will be an associate with Wiggin & Dona in New Haven, CT.

Implementation and Integration Issues, Impacts, and Tools

Chapters in this section by Lawrence Cahill and Dawne Schomer, and Jim Dray, and Cynthia Unger, give managers key information on how various groups and operations will be affected by the new efforts and how they can leverage their current resources to optimize the ISO investment. Companies searching for solutions will be encouraged by the advice of these leading authorities. The theme of integration is continued by Judith Cichowicz for companies that have embarked on an ISO 9000 program. Alerting and linking efforts with critical partners in the organization, such as the information systems group, will be necessary to make ISO 14000 successful. These chapters will show you what needs to be done to make it happen.

15

Should ISO 14000 Be Linked with ISO 9000?

Judith A. Cichowicz

ISO 9000 is a series of international standards that address the structure of quality management systems. The quality management system objective is to provide the purchaser of a product or service with confidence as to a specified level of quality performance by the product or service provider. Its focus is systems that enable you to verify consistency of quality processes.

Its requirements cover an array of functions, from purchasing, to process control, to training. Verification of conformance to these requirements can be achieved through

- Self certification;
- Customer certification; or
- Third-party certification by a registrar.

Should ISO 14000 be linked with ISO 9000? The short answer is yes, but how did we reach that conclusion? In this chapter, we discuss this issue and

1. Analyze the cost factors that affect a decision to implement management systems;
2. Define the clear linkages between the two standards; and
3. Describe some "real life" examples of how these linkages are being successfully achieved.

Why is there never time to do it right, but always time to do it over? Whether speaking about quality management systems such as ISO 9000 or environmental management, that question underlies the inability of organizations to successfully implement programs and projects.

In quality management, the ISO 9000 standards strive to assure consistency of products and services delivered through implementation of a structured and systematic approach to their production. When similar management principles are applied to environmental issues, improvements occur that reduce both actual and perceived environmental and regulatory liabilities. But only if you want to do it right, not if you have to do it over.

With increasing competition for limited financial and human resources, organizations that link ISO 9000 and ISO 14000 have the opportunity to develop a consistent management system that is cost-effective and represents a higher chance of complete implementation success.

What are the consequences of doing it over? And can they provide the economic incentive for doing it right by optimizing integration of quality and environmental management systems?

Quality management research estimates that the costs of rework, lost orders, and customer aggravation comprise about 25 percent of expenses in manufacturing and an astounding 40 percent in services.

While the development of sophisticated accounting for measuring environmental costs lags, we know certain facts that point to spending extra money. These are:

- Environmental liability insurance, if available, is expensive;
- Regulatory fines for noncompliance are not cheap;
- The indirect costs to managers of "working with the lawyers" to respond to or reduce a fine can be excessive, grueling, and personally painful; and
- Environmental cleanup or remediation, in response to "past practices," drains today's capital resources.

Publicly held companies further weaken their capital positions by a requirement to report on environmental liabilities in their 10-Ks.

If these are the costs of not doing it right, the argument for preventive action, either in matters of quality or the environment, is made. The management challenge then becomes one of controlling the preventive costs associated with operating quality and environmental management systems. This is useful to keep in mind because early figures indicate that the direct costs of achieving ISO 14000 registration will be about 30 percent higher than those for ISO 9000.

One solution to controlling preventive costs requires "planting internal egos by the door" and integrating management systems used to achieve ISO 9000 and/or ISO 14000.

The areas most adaptable to this type of integration include:

- Document and data control;
- Process control;
- Training; and
- Internal auditing.

Using those factors, let's consider how links are forged. In order to make the examples more meaningful, let us assume that we are a specialty chemical manufacturing company that:

- Sells throughout Europe;
- Uses and produces chemicals subject to SARA Tier 2, Chemical Inventory Reporting requirements; and
- Is subject to the OSHA Process Safety Standard because at least one of its raw materials, chlorine, is a highly hazardous chemical.

If the devil is in the details, then integration of document and data control can make you or break you. Consider that although the actual documents and data used for quality and environmental management may be different, the processes for achieving document and data control can and should be systematized.

If your organization has a formal record retention process, then integration can be a simple matter of applying that process to environmental recordkeeping.

Let's relate this to the environmental issue of SARA Tier 2, Chemical Inventory Reporting. ISO 9000 requires that storage areas be designated to prevent damage or deterioration of the product. SARA Tier 2 reporting requires that storage locations be reported to regulatory authorities to assist in emergency response planning.

When a storage area is defined and assigned to a product, this information becomes data. These data are records that can be used to verify that things are stored where they should be so they don't deteriorate and require emergency response. But if the quality manager and the environmental manager refuse to build this link, the company has at least two separate systems for collecting and retrieving these data. These are not redundant systems; they become competitive systems. And what they are competing for are your limited managerial resources.

Mismanagement in document control can easily cost you money. Think personal computers; think Beauty and the Beast. The beauty of personal computers is that they open new doors for communication. They speed up the process and remove some of the horribly tedious things we had to do in the past to analyze and communicate.

The beast of personal computers is that they are personal. And we Americans cherish our freedoms. So when someone creates a document describing how a SARA Tier 2 report is prepared, it gets some unintelligible name, is probably not backed up anywhere, and is eventually lost in disk land.

Successful companies set up a structure not only for formatting documents, but also for naming them on disks so they can eventually be retrieved or otherwise become a document within the document control process.

This is not "rocket scientist" stuff. But without it, whether you are a quality manager or environmental manager, you are out of control. I would wager that most managers can think of at least one horror story in which someone left an organization, and it took a great deal of effort to make sense of the computer disks left behind.

The point is, don't fight this systematization, but embrace it for the tool that it is. You don't have to redesign the wheel. Once this concept is accepted, the issue becomes retrofitting and/or reworking your current procedures and data retention into the new document/data control process.

Process Control

Next, let's discuss just one feature of "process control." ISO 9000 states that a controlled condition includes: "Suitable maintenance of equipment to ensure continuing process capability." ISO 14000, through operational control, has companies planning for activities including maintenance. Additionally, the OSHA Process Safety Standard requires a documented system for "mechanical integrity" associated with our hypothetical company's handling of chlorine. That sounds like maintenance to me.

Our model company uses specifics of that OSHA regulatory requirement to address implementation of both ISO 9000 process control and ISO 14000 operational control. Additionally, this preventive maintenance results in an elimination of releases or spills of chlorine, thus reducing costs associated with worker injuries, emergency response, and insurance premiums.

Training

The training link between quality and environmental management once again returns to the administrative procedures. These include:

- Assigning training requirements to employees; and
- Tracking implementation of those requirements.

Again, it does not make any difference what the actual training requirements are or whether they are used to support ISO 9000, ISO 14000, or both. The idea is to use a systematic approach for documenting the requirements and tracking their implementation.

Internal Auditing

This leads us to internal auditing. Both ISO 9000 and ISO 14000 require some internal audit system. Irrespective of who conducts those audits within an organization, having common administrative systems for data collection, retention, document control, and the like facilitates this process and helps you and your organization identify errors or exceptions to your processes. From there you can make decisions about improving your systems for accomplishing your quality and/or environmental objectives. From an environmental standpoint, it is nicer to find your mistakes before a regulator or activist group does.

Conclusion

Despite these linkages, there is a notable philosophical difference between quality management systems and environmental management systems. Specifically, ISO 9000 insists on consistency in performance, while environmental management standards, such as ISO 14000, focus on implementing systems that lead to improvement in environmental performance. It requires the identification of measurable performance goals or metrics to verify improvement.

This discussion has considered:

1. Cost factors that affect a decision to implement management systems;
2. Linkages between ISO 9000 and ISO 14000;
3. "Real life" examples of how these linkages are being successfully achieved.

The objective in implementing any type of standard is exactly that: achieve standardization. By linking together compatible elements of different standards through common administrative and/or regulatory response systems, you achieve your objective in the least costly manner.

Judith A. Cichowicz is general manager for Compliance Systems Inc., a Seattle-based consulting firm focusing on design and implementation of management systems for companies with environmental exposures. She is a RAB Certified Provisional Auditor for ISO 9000 and an Environmental Management Systems Auditor. In these capacities, she serves as an authorized representative for NSF International (Ann Arbor, MI); and an ISO 9000 and EMS registrar.

16

The Potential Effect of ISO 14000 on Environmental Audits

Lawrence B. Cahill and Dawne P. Schomer

Environmental audit training in the United States has become something of an industry in and of itself. Videotapes, books, and articles abound. There has been a proliferation of training courses and seminars as well. However, there is often uncertainty over whether an individual course teaches environmental auditing or property transfer environmental liability assessments. This is an important distinction and, therefore, "let the buyer beware." The ISO 14012 environmental auditor qualification guidelines[1] expect that environmental auditing will be the subject of the training.

The courses come in a variety of forms:

- *University certificate programs.* Several universities provide certificate programs in environmental auditing. For example, the University of California at Irvine's Extension Program offers an extensive certificate program in environmental auditing. The certificate is awarded to those who complete at least 180 course hours with a grade of "C" or better in each course. On the other hand, the University of Texas offers a one-time, two-day seminar in environmental auditing. This seminar is not part of a larger program, and no formal certification is offered.
- *Professional organizations' certificate programs (with examinations).* Several professional organizations offer two- to three-day certificate programs that typically include examinations. Programs are offered by the National Association of Safety and Health Professionals, the National Registry of Environmental Professionals, and the Environmental Assessment Association, among others.
- *Commercial, open programs.* Organizations such as Government Institutes, Federal Publications, and Executive Enterprises have offered environmental audit courses for more than 10 years. There are now some relatively new entrants in this business, such as the Environmental and Occupational Health Sciences Institute. These programs range from

two to three days and are held in hotels. Instructors are likely to be from consulting firms, law firms, and/or industry. There are no prerequisites and typically no examinations. Continuing education units (CEUs) and certificates of completion are awarded to participants.

- *In-house, internal, and third-party programs.* Some of the best training programs are in-house programs developed by large companies. These programs last from three to five days and, most importantly, usually involve a "mock audit" as part of the curriculum. This mock audit allows the participants to apply the techniques they have been taught in the classroom. Hence, these programs are often held at or near a plant site. Instructors are likely to be experienced, in-house auditors and/or consultants.

- *Consulting firms.* Many consulting firms teach environmental auditing skills and techniques. These programs are mostly taught at a client's site. In some cases, the training takes place at the offices of the consultant. Certificates are often awarded for completion, but generally their distribution is not dependent on the results of a rigorous examination.

One of the most important things to remember about the current status of auditor certification in the United States is that there is no single, generally accepted "certification" or "registration" program for environmental auditors. That is, there is nothing comparable to the PE, CSP, or CIH; at least, not yet.

Thus, one must be very careful in evaluating an individual training program and one must review the true meaning of any certification. The ISO 14012 guidelines currently set the requirements for environmental management system (EMS) auditing. In the future, training organizations may want to certify auditors that meet these EMS auditing guidelines, as well as other types of audits (e.g., compliance audits) that the guidelines currently do not address.

An important development that might affect training organizations in the United States is the recent initiative of the Environmental Auditors Registration Association (EARA), a United Kingdom-based "independent, non-profit making organization representing the interests of both the providers and recipients of services relating to environmental auditing and environmental management systems."[2] The EARA has both an auditor certification and a training course accreditation program, under which it is now licensing groups in other countries to conduct auditor certifications and training program accreditations using the EARA model. The first licensee is the Asian Pacific Institute for Environmental Assessment. Its members include Singapore, Malaysia, the Philippines, and Borneo. The EARA has had minimal impact in the United States, although the EARA has registered environmental auditors who are based in the United

States. EARA's impact could expand if the United States does not develop some form of national response to the ISO 14000 guidelines.

The ISO 14012 Guidelines

The ISO 14012 guidelines provide guidance on qualification criteria for environmental auditors and lead environmental auditors. These include education, experience, and training criteria. Among the criteria, the guidelines require that "auditors should have completed both formal training and on-the-job training, to develop competence in carrying out environmental audits."

The ISO 14012 guidelines state that the formal training should address:

- Environmental science and technology
- Technical and environmental aspects of facility operations
- Relevant requirements of environmental laws, regulations, and related documents
- Environmental management systems and standards against which audits may be performed
- Audit procedures, processes, and techniques.

In addition, the current draft of the guidelines calls for "on-the-job training including 20 equivalent work-days of auditing, and for a minimum of four audits, occurring within a period of not more than three consecutive years. This should include involvement in the entire audit process under the supervision and guidance of the lead auditor."

Like most ISO 14000 standards, there has been an attempt in ISO 14012 to achieve harmonization with the in-place ISO 9000 standards. Some of the consequences of this philosophy are discussed below.

U.S. Implementation of the ISO 9000 Standards: A Standing Precedent

The ISO 9000 registration process has been in effect for some time now in the United States. Since many of ISO 14000's standards are being modeled after the ISO 9000 quality standards, it would be helpful to understand how that process works in this country. As shown in Figure 16.1, the Registrar Accreditation Board (RAB), under the direction of the American National Standards Institute (ANSI), has taken the leadership position in the U.S. ISO 9000 registration, accreditation, and certification process. The RAB, a nonprofit organization, is an affiliate of the American Society of Quality Control (ASQC), which formed the RAB in 1989 as a separate, self-supporting organization.

The RAB performs several functions.

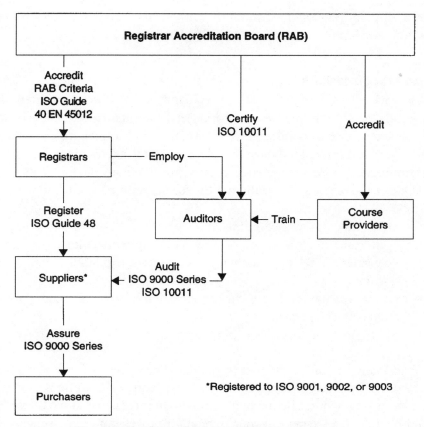

Figure 16.1   Accreditation and Registration Process

RAB accredits third-party organizations, known as registrars, using criteria based on internationally recognized standards and guides. Registrars, in turn, audit and register suppliers also using international standards and guides. The ultimate intent of RAB's accreditation process is to assure purchasers that their suppliers have implemented proper quality systems as defined by the ISO 9000 standards. To support the registrar accreditation program, RAB operates the U.S. program for quality systems auditor certification and an accreditation program for auditor training courses.[3]

Many of the terms used in the ISO 9000 process discussed above are quite similar and easily confused. The highlights are as follows:

- The RAB accredits registrars;
- Registrars register companies (i.e., suppliers) to ISO 9000;
- The RAB accredits training programs;

- Accredited training program providers train auditors; and
- The RAB certifies auditors.

A similar, but probably not identical, approach for registration, accreditation, and certification will be developed under the ISO 14000 standards. The RAB and ANSI are developing independent ISO 14000 registration/certification programs. It is possible that these programs will eventually be joined. With respect to the impact on environmental audit training programs in particular, note that, under ISO 9000, trainers do not certify auditors; the RAB does. In part, this is because the qualification criteria include an evaluation against education, experience, training, and personal attributes and skills, not simply a person's ability to successfully complete a training program.

Potential Effects

In this dynamic setting, there likely will be some significant effects on the current environmental audit training business in the United States. It is difficult to anticipate all of the consequences of ISO 14012, but, upon reflection, some are apparent. These are discussed below.

Accreditation, Oversight, and Certification: The Lack of Autonomy

Under ISO 14000, it is likely that there will be one organization in the United States that will accredit environmental auditor training organizations. This hypothesis, consistent with ISO 9000, will have various consequences on the training business. First, in order to accredit trainers, these oversight organizations will have to review the structure of the programs and audit one or more seminars. This is an outside control that many of the organizations have not had to face historically. Also, the costs associated with these activities will be borne by the trainers. If nothing else, this will raise the price of the training seminars. And, finally, certifications currently provided by the training organizations may not have significant impact on the profession if, like ISO 9000, auditor certifications are made by the accrediting organization.

Length and Type of Courses: A Variety of Demands

Most U.S. environmental auditor training organizations make no distinction among the various levels of experience that trainees may have. However, under ISO 9000, there are different training requirements for associate auditors, auditors, and lead auditors. For example, the RAB grants accreditation for two types of courses. A 36-hour course meets the requirements for its auditor certification program, and a 16-hour course, along with an ASQC certified quality auditor (CQA) certificate, meets the identical requirements for the RAB's auditor certification program.

Similarly, the ISO 14012 guidelines classify individuals as auditors or lead auditors, depending on education, experience, and training. Thus, it is likely that environmental auditor trainers will have to acknowledge the varying degrees of experience and qualifications of their customers and will have to design programs accordingly, especially in the first few years of ISO 14000 implementation, when many individuals will wish to be "grandfathered" with minimal training.

Also, ISO 9000 and ISO 14000 both call for refresher training in order to assure that auditors maintain their skills and currency with evolving audit methodology improvements. This will mean that training-program providers should provide refresher training programs. EARA recommends that this training address the following:

- Ensuring that auditors' knowledge of environmental management systems standards and requirements is current;
- Ensuring that auditors' knowledge of environmental laws and regulations, auditing processes, procedures, and techniques are current; and
- Ensuring that auditors' experience in the execution of audits is current.[4]

Meeting these requirements can also be accomplished through on-the-job training, but assurances to the marketplace will be less clear under that scenario.

Class Size: Too Small to Be Economical?

Under ISO 9000, the RAB has issued a guidance document entitled "Requirements for Accreditation of an Auditor Training Course (Rev. 1-930421)." These requirements apply to ISO 9000 training providers in the United States. RAB requires that the number of students not exceed 20 and that there be at least two instructors for each course. There is a possibility that there will be equivalent requirements under ISO 14000, regardless of who accredits trainers. This class-size constraint will affect the economics of many current programs, which have no limitations on class size and, in fact, achieve acceptable profitability *only* when class sizes are *above* 20.

One should also note that, at the same time course sizes may be limited, course costs will be increasing due to accreditation fees. For example, U.S. ISO 9000 course providers wanting to receive accreditation from the RAB are expected to pay between $10,000 and $15,000 in one-time application fees and up-front program audits and evaluations, and between $4,000 and $6,000 in annual fees. Similarly, EARA, under ISO 14000, requires an application fee of about $1,500 and annual fees of about $15 per student taught, or $300 for each 20-person program.

Course Content: The Shift to Management Systems

In the past few years, most audit programs in major companies have changed their focus toward evaluating management systems and from more conventional, detailed compliance reviews. In practice, however, this reemphasis has been difficult to achieve fully. The reasons are varied. First, evaluating management systems requires a "paradigm shift" that many auditors have found difficult to achieve (Figure 16.2). It implies that the auditor looks at issues almost at right angles from what he or she is used to in conducting compliance audits. Second, many auditors are scientists and engineers, and they find it difficult to conduct an evaluation that they feel is more in line with what an MBA might do in an organization study. And, third, conducting management systems audits means that one is attempting to identify root causes—asking the "whys," not just the "whats." This takes substantially more time and typically is not as "clean" as a compliance audit.

ISO 14012 does, in fact, require training programs to formally address management systems audits. Thus, audit training programs in the future will have to emphasize the techniques used in management systems evaluations. This may be as difficult for the instructors as it is for the students.

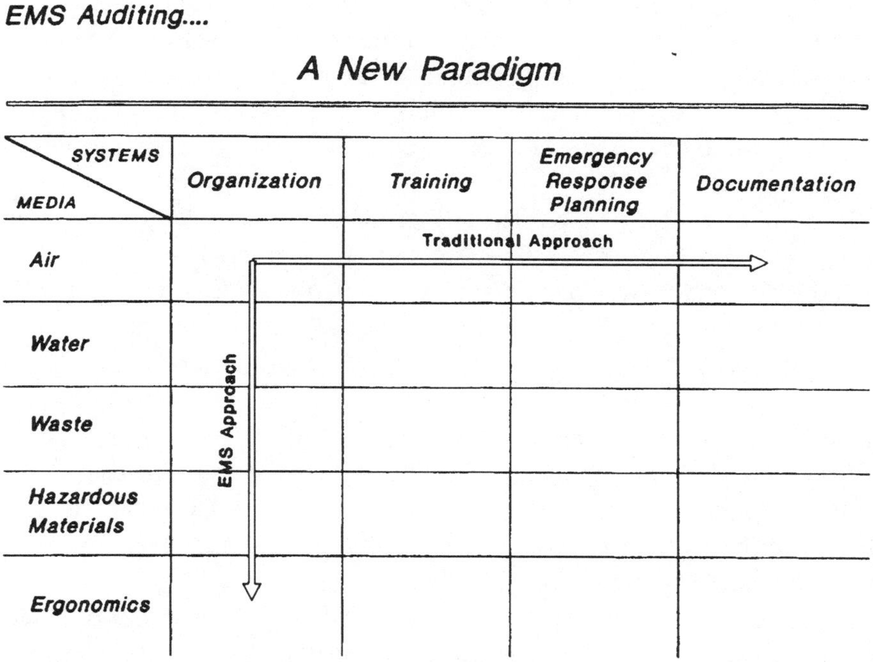

EMS Auditing....

A New Paradigm

SYSTEMS / MEDIA	Organization	Training	Emergency Response Planning	Documentation
Air		Traditional Approach		
Water				
Waste				
Hazardous Materials				
Ergonomics				

Figure 16.2   Evaluating Management Shifts

Course Content: Teaching Relevant Regulatory Requirements

As stated above, ISO 14012 requires that a training program address "relevant requirements of environmental laws, regulations and related documents." Most current environmental audit training programs address regulatory requirements in some fashion. In the United States, this can be an overwhelming challenge. For example, does this regulatory review mean that the trainer needs to discuss all federal environmental laws and regulations? This would be a daunting task, since there are now more than 12,000 pages in Title 40 of the U.S. Code of Federal Regulations. How should state regulations be covered—none, a sampling, or all 50 states? And, if the auditors are likely to conduct international audits, how are regulations in other countries to be covered? All of these issues will need to be resolved by the accrediting organization.

Course Content: Field Exercises

One of the most effective auditor training techniques is to conduct a "mock audit" as part of a program. This, of course, requires that the class be able to visit a location that might have a regulated unit (e.g., hazardous waste accumulation point) and audit that unit. Typically, the site will set up some situations of noncompliance or breakdowns of management systems. The class would review (altered) records, interview (actor) operators, and observe the (altered) unit.

The ISO 14012 guidelines are silent on the use of this technique. However, EARA-accredited courses "must include at least one practical exercise/site visit. . . . [The presumption is that] the training organization running the courses will be able to provide or secure, with the cooperation of a local company, a site visit."[5]

Responding to this requirement or suggestion will be easier for some training organizations than others. The commercial programs held in hotels will find it difficult to do anything but conduct simulations of the mock audit using slide photographs. On the other hand, industrial on-site programs typically incorporate this technique already.

Course Examinations: Evaluating Personal Attributes

Under ISO 14000, examinations will be expected at the conclusion of the training courses. If expectations are comparable to those of ISO 9000, the exams will last two hours. This provision is not found now in many auditor training courses, but could be incorporated easily.

However, the ISO 14012 guidelines expect auditors to meet not only technical qualification criteria, but also "interpersonal attribute" criteria. Namely, the ISO 14012 guidelines suggest that auditors possess attributes and skills that include, but are not limited to:

- Competence in clearly and fluently expressing concepts and ideas, orally and in writing;
- Interpersonal skills conducive to the effective and efficient performance of the audit, such as diplomacy, tact, and the ability to listen;
- Ability to maintain independence and objectivity sufficient to permit the accomplishment of auditor responsibilities;
- Skills of personal organization necessary to the effective and efficient performance of the audit; and
- Ability to reach sound judgments based on objective evidence.

It may be that the trainer will not be expected to provide this "softer" evaluation. Under ISO 9000, it is done by the auditor accreditation organization, the RAB. If course providers are expected to evaluate participants against these criteria, however, the situation could become problematic. Many of the criteria are quite subjective, and written exams are not a good measure of an individual's capabilities.

As a consequence, trainers will likely be expected to place participants in role playing situations and evaluate their interpersonal skills—a difficult task for both trainer and participant. And, what if the trainer finds the participant wanting and no certification of successful course completion is awarded? Will there be an appeals process? There is one under ISO 9000.

Additionally, some auditors with less than perfect personal attributes (e.g., they are dogged in their verification efforts but not very personable in how they go about it) can be valued team members on certain types of audits when coupled with the right partner (e.g., "good cop, bad cop"). These individuals may unnecessarily get the "heave-ho" in a training course.

Documentation: New Expectations

In the future, training organizations will have to be considerably more rigorous about maintaining records. The course syllabus, course manuals, results of examinations, and the like will have to be available to auditors from the accrediting organization. Yes, auditor trainers will be audited; this will be quite a turn of events.

Conclusion

It is likely that environmental auditor training in the United States will change considerably over the next few years due to the finalization of the ISO 14012 guidelines. Programs will need to meet conformance criteria to be recognized as accredited trainers under ISO. The current version of ISO 14012 addresses only certification and accreditation for conducting and training for environmental management systems audits.

In the future, there may be additional requirements set for other types of audits as well. For example, the door remains open for the development of requirements for compliance audits. Training providers should watch the evolving developments closely. There should be excellent opportunities under a national environmental auditor training accreditation program.

Notes

1. Draft International Standard ISO/CD 14012: "Guidelines for Environmental Auditing—Qualification Criteria for Environmental Auditors," August 10, 1995. The ISO 14012 guidelines are part of the larger ISO 14000 environmental management standard-setting scheme, under which guidelines will also be developed for environmental management systems, environmental performance, life-cycle analysis, and the like. These standards are "close cousins" of the ISO 9000 quality standards, which have been widely adopted by industry worldwide.

2. Environmental Auditors Registration Association brochure, undated.

3. The source for both the text and the Figure 16.1 is an undated document titled "Registrar Accreditation Board (RAB) Overview," provided by the RAB.

4. Bacon, Ruth A., "The Environmental Auditors Registration Association (EARA) Scheme," prepared for the ISO SCRAG meeting on September 27, 1994, Baltimore, MD.

5. Environmental Auditors Registration Association brochure, undated.

Lawrence B. Cahill is a senior program director with Environmental Resources Management, Inc. **Dawne P. Schomer** is the corporate ESH audit program manager with Texas Instruments. Both participate actively in the U.S. involvement in the developing ISO 14000 environmental auditing standards, including holding leadership positions on the Standards Conformance and Registration Advisory Group (SCRAG) to the U.S./ISO/TC207. They are the current co-chairs (with Doug Matkins of Clorox) of the Environmental Auditing Roundtable's Auditor Training and Qualifications Work Group.

17

ISO 14000 and Information Systems: Where's the Link?

Jim Dray and Scott Foster

The first of the ISO 14000 family of standards, ISO 14001, will be published as an international standard defining a company's environmental management system (Figure 17.1). Like ISO 9000 before it, conformance to ISO 14001 may become necessary for industries whose primary customers demand it.

Many larger companies are announcing their intention to conform to the standard's requirements, although most have deferred a decision about whether to seek certification. Among other things, each company will develop a policy statement, identify where its operations, services, or products affect the environment, establish specific objectives and targets for environmental performance, measure progress toward these targets, and ensure that all employees receive proper environmental training to comply with the standard. In addition, there are requirements for monitoring regulation, controlling documents, designating responsibilities and specifying operating procedures. Figure 17.1 outlines the five sections of the environmental management system standard ISO 14001.

As the ISO 9000 standards became a requisite to doing business in the international manufacturing market, and lately in the U.S. market, many software developers focused on providing easy, off-the-shelf software solutions to companies of all sizes. ISO 9000 was well suited for this type of solution, given the emphasis on documentation. Many of these same software developers are seizing on ISO 14001 with the same fervor and the same approach. It remains to be seen whether certification to ISO 14001 can be standardized across companies in a way that would allow an off-the-shelf ISO 14001 software package to be genuinely useful.

Environmental Management Information System (EMIS)

Largely independent of ISO 14000, most companies are working feverishly to reduce overhead, reengineer, and simplify their environmental functions. Often, this involves systems that help handle the information required for environmen-

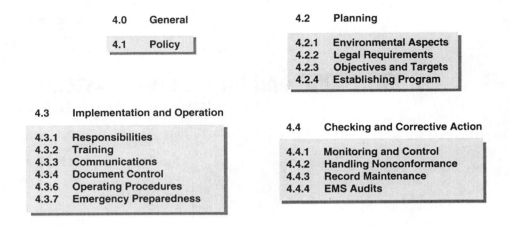

Figure 17.1   The Five Sections of ISO 14001

tal management. Many companies that have tried to tackle EMIS in one giant custom project have been frustrated with the results and the cost; others that have tried to select only off-the-shelf software have found that they have a proliferation of "point solutions" with no coherent way to harvest the synergy. Most companies are now looking for a middle ground, a semi-custom EMIS that can be implemented fairly quickly at moderate cost and can be scaled up as appropriate.

At first glance, there is an apparent contradiction between ISO 14001, which requires documentation and systematization of practices, and the drive to reduce environmental overhead. Often, in fact, there is a short-term increase in effort required in order to harvest the benefits of systems later. Without appropriate planning, both ISO 14001 and EMIS can consume large quantities of management attention without much payback.

Figure 17.2 illustrates a process that can help ensure that companies get payback from their efforts for both ISO 14001 conformity and for information systems. The process is based on some of the accumulated wisdom of environmental information systems development, as well as the quality management systems in use by many companies, and is seasoned by the experience of companies that are currently preparing ISO 14001-compatible approaches.

Step 1: Identify Stakeholders and Their Concerns

There are many stakeholders for an EMIS, some of whom are illustrated in Figure 17.3. It is critical to understand the perspective of all stakeholders and to give them an opportunity for input as the plan evolves. Failure to do so can

	ISO 14001 Link	Information System Link
Step 1: Identify stakeholders and their concerns.	14001 mandates that key players, internal and external, be recognized.	Without understanding stakeholders and including them, they will not use the system.
Step 2: Assess the current state, including constraints and resources.	14001 plan must be realistic for company to minimize overhead and maximize acceptance. 14001 plan must be appropriate to the nature, scale, and impact of a company.	A successful system must build on available data, technology, and culture.
Step 3: Agree on the desired future and priorities.	14001 allows wide variance in environmental objectives, as long as they are documented.	Consensus on aspirations and priorities is the single most important criterion for successful systems development.
Step 4: Develop an implementation plan to get to the desired future.	Develop a phased plan for meeting 14001 that puts early payoffs and simplification up front.	Determine what makes sense to computerize at each stage and what does not.
Step 5: Implement, monitor, and revise the plan as necessary.	Monitoring is required by 14001 and will ensure continued relevance and payback.	Technology, user, and regulatory shifts require ongoing course correction.

Figure 17.2   Steps toward an EMIS that Reinforces ISO 14000 Payback

result in systems that are not used. Each stakeholder will also have "land mines," some more predictable than others, that must be avoided in the development process. It is much easier to include stakeholders in the design up front, than it is to design a system and then convince stakeholders to use it.

Step 2: Assess the Current State

Most Fortune 500 companies have elements of an environmental management system already in place. Unless there are major technical barriers, consider developing a cost-effective solution that incorporates systems that already exist. At a minimum, a new EMIS that replaces an antiquated system should strive to appear familiar to the user.

Figure 17.4 shows some of the key questions that must be addressed during an analysis of the current state. In this analysis, it is important to be realistic about the company's culture. An EMIS that encourages communications across levels will not fit with a very centralized and structured company. Alternatively,

Typical Stakeholder	Concerns	Keys for Success
Project sponsor (senior management who approves budgets and priorities)	Cost justification, fit with environmental strategy.	Designing for early wins, getting consensus on priorities, and sticking to plan.
End users (environmental and other operating personnel who will be day-to-day users of the system)	Is this a "program du jour"? How can I find time to invest in order to save me time later? Will I be able to figure out how to use this?	Providing opportunity for input on what would make their jobs easier, maximizing ease of use and support options.
Developers (internal or external staff who will design and support the system)	Predictability of scope, unrealistic expectations of users, shifting technology, need to understand both I.S. and environmental jargon.	Agreeing on a specification that everyone understands, providing opportunity for input along the way without pulling up the roots; rapid prototyping using a platform that can adapt in the future.
Other company management (line managers, CEO, other function managers)	Demonstrate payback; avoid reinventing the wheel.	Understand how environmental data are mapped to other business processes.
External groups (regulators, environmental groups, industry associations)	Credibility of data, access to data in usable formats.	Plan for flexibility and security in how information can be reported.

Figure 17.3   Typical Stakeholders and Their Concerns

an EMIS that relies on strict lines of authority and centralized decision making will not succeed in a decentralized company that empowers business- and site-level employees. Note that ISO 14001 requires a clear chain of authority "in order to facilitate effective environmental management." (See Section 4.3.1, Structure and Responsibility.)

Step 3: Agree on a Desired Future and Priorities

This is a crucial, and often neglected, aspect of the planning process for both ISO 14001 and EMIS. The most successful systems begin with a planning effort that brings together representatives of all the stakeholders identified in Step 1. They work through a disciplined process that includes reviewing the results of steps 1 and 2, and they address the following key questions as a group:

- Where does the company want to be in environmental management in five years?
- What are the major differences between that vision and the current state?
- Of those differences, which have priority in terms of impact and need?

Topic	ISO 14001 Link	Information Systems Link
Understanding of environmental impacts and issues	What are key "environmental aspects?"	What current business processes are related to the environment?
Readiness of systems	What documentation is available on training, performance, and standards?	What information systems are now in use, and what are their strengths and weaknesses?
Availability of data	What data really exist and how credible are they?	In what form are the data stored, and who has access?
Linkage to business plan and strategy	To what degree are environmental concerns integrated with corporate business strategy?	What data and processes are shared between environmental and other areas? What are the information systems' plans for the company?

Figure 17.4   Typical Questions about the Current State

Many managers resist having an inclusive planning process because it appears to jeopardize their control over the effort or can lengthen the development time if the process gets out of hand. We have found that the bulk of this planning process can usually be accomplished in an intensive two-day meeting. It requires very careful planning and preparation, including development of appropriate formats for brainstorming, facilitator guidelines, and appropriate technologies for showing the group the results of their brainstorming as the meeting is in progress. For example, we have used a software tool, In Control™, to show the participants on a live basis the results of their prioritization of action items.

Step 4: Develop an Implementation Plan

An implementation plan must take the results of the planning process and factor in the following considerations:

1. Availability of budget and staff resources;
2. Appropriate phasing of action items into understandable chunks, usually six months to one year each; and
3. Balancing of high-impact items with "quick wins" in each phase in order to build momentum. For example, areas related to ISO 14001 in which an EMIS can have a quick impact on business productivity are
   • Automating quantitative metrics collection and display;
   • Tracking environmental training (Section 4.3.2);

- Tracking compliance efforts and upcoming regulations (Section 4.2.2);
- Facilitating documentation requirements of Section 4.3.4; and
- Addressing external stakeholders' concerns through discussion databases and on-line information (Section 4.3.3).

Step 5: Implement and Monitor

Finally, any project of this magnitude requires ongoing monitoring and a mechanism for course corrections to ensure that the company is getting the payback that it intended. Figure 17.5 shows some of the key criteria that companies may choose to monitor.

Conclusion

Using the five-step process that we have outlined for designing and implementing an environmental management information system can increase the

Criteria	ISO 14001 Link	Information Systems Link
Budget and Deadlines	Missing targets may be a valuable signal that there is more complexity involved in implementation than initially realized.	Watch for early warning that scope is ballooning out of control.
System Usage	Evaluating business processes to determine whether ISO 14001 systems are being complied with.	Frequency of use, timeliness of key data can suggest whether real value is being obtained.
Stakeholder Satisfaction	If the system is not meeting documentation needs or measurement needs, this needs to be assessed immediately.	Formal and informal user feedback is critical to maintaining momentum, correcting problems early.
Financial Payback	Marketing value (e.g., ability to market ISO 14001 conformity) is often hard to measure, but worth the effort A 14001 EMS may also positively affect quality and productivity.	Time saved often can be measured on a before/after basis. Linkage to existing financial systems can document resource and other savings.
Strategic Value	Is the company achieving its strategic environmental goals? Is environmental activity being appropriately integrated into business functions?	Is the information system allowing environmental professionals to add more value? Are other users being incorporated?

Figure 17.5   Sample Monitoring Criteria during Implementation

likelihood of success in ISO 14001 compliance and can increase the chances for generating ongoing value. Clearly, the steps and questions outlined here are only a beginning, and companies will bring their own subtleties to the process. Nevertheless, the process does not have to be a daunting one. Planning is the key. A concrete plan with phased action steps, time lines, and responsibilities will allow all parties to concentrate on the common goal. As Yogi Berra said, "If you don't know where you are going, you are likely to end up somewhere else."

Jim Dray, vice president of RPM Systems, New Haven, Connecticut, is a specialist in business management and development, and in creating change with information systems. He has consulted many Fortune 500 companies on designing environmental strategies, environmental management information systems, and environmental performance measurement systems. **Scott Foster** is a third-year law student at the University of Connecticut, where he is a Managing Editor of the *Connecticut Law Review.* He is also a member of US TAG and the ISO 14000 Legal Issues Forum. Prior to law school, he worked as an environmental consultant focusing on environmental metrics, ISO 14001, information systems, pollution prevention, and environmental management. Following graduation, he will be an associate with Wiggin & Dona in New Haven, CT.

18

ISO 14000 and Environmental Performance Evaluation

Howard N. Apsan

Renowned baseball manager Casey Stengel, "The Ol' Perfessor," was fond of taunting his occasionally incredulous audience with the challenge, "You can look it up!" He used it masterfully as an argument closer; but alas, in many cases, you really could not look it up because it either was not documented or, in rare situations, it never actually occurred. While Casey may have been able to get away with some rather liberal interpretations of fact, we in the environmental arena are seldom afforded the same luxury.

Environmental Performance Evaluation in the ISO 14000 Scheme

One of the essentials of total quality management is having a "scorecard." It ensures the ability to measure progress—to enable any interested party to "look up" the level of improvement at any stage of an operation. In the environmental arena, the effort to establish uniform standards for environmental performance (EP) has been evolving for years. Many of these standards, in the United States and elsewhere, are established by statute and regulation. Others are established by the limitations of technology. Still others are developed by individual organizations, or by umbrella associations, to set minimum standards for environmental behavior on a corporate or industrywide basis.

The evolving ISO 14000 program would provide an integrative, worldwide standardization scheme for environmental management. Most environmental professionals welcome the promise of standardization under ISO 14000, particularly its potential to bring more consistency and stability to some of the non-quantitative and unregulated aspects of the environmental field.

The six key components of ISO 14000 are:

- Environmental Management Systems
- Environmental Auditing
- Environmental Performance Evaluation

- Life-Cycle Assessments
- Environmental Labeling
- Environmental Aspects in Product Standards

Of these six, three are geared toward organizational evaluation and three are geared toward product evaluation. The relationship of these three components is interactive (Figure 18.1).[1]

To illustrate this relationship, the EPE process is dependent on a number of key issues that must be established or evaluated through the broader-based environmental management system.[2] These include: integration of interested party analysis, determination of organizational targets and objectives, establishment of widely agreed-upon priorities and needs, and organizational boundaries or jurisdictional limitations of EPE. Naturally, these issues depend on effective communications, both within the organization itself and from the interested outside community.

EPE as a TQM Tool

EPE provides an effective TQM tool by establishing both a road map for continuous improvement and a model for understanding the varying analytical perspectives, or evaluation areas. It is broadly defined as follows:

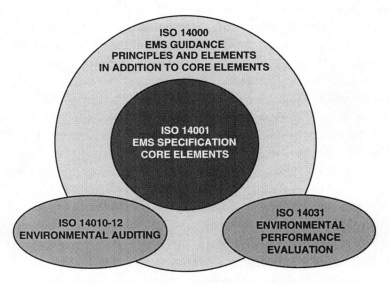

Figure 18.1   Relation of Various ISO 14000 Documents

EPE is an internal process and tool which can provide management with reliable, objective, and verifiable information usually linked to the achievement of an organization's environmental objectives and targets. EPE assists management to focus on trends in environmental performance, changes in performance, and the reasons for them.[3]

The description concludes in a TQM vein by highlighting that "EPE is an integral part of the process of continual improvement of environmental management."[4] For its continuous improvement focus, EPE addresses five areas (Figure 18.2):[5]

- *Commitment to EPE.* This includes not only a philosophical commitment to EPE, but also a set of formal EPE policies designed to establish EPE as a core component of organizational activities.
- *Planning for EPE.* This component should include reviewing environmental aspects, determining the scope of the EPE process, establishing the sources and extent of necessary management information, determining the scope of participation, setting objectives and targets, and selecting and validating environmental performance indicators.

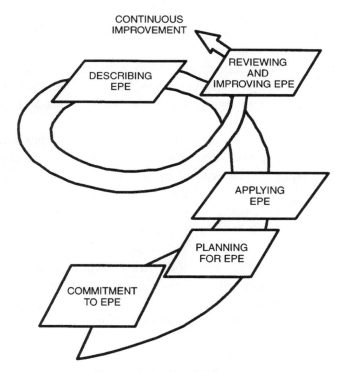

Figure 18.2   The EPE Process

- *Applying EPE.* This is the implementation stage. It includes collecting and analyzing data and aggregating and assessing information.
- *Describing EPE.* This is the communications aspect. It includes ensuring effective communication within the organization and providing open lines for external communication.
- *Reviewing and improving EPE.* This is the crux of the continuous improvement process. It is designed to focus on improving the EPE process itself, using EPE to improve the overall EMS process, and ultimately improving the organization's environmental performance.

To understand the different levels of analysis, or evaluation areas, EPE attempts to integrate the management system and operational system perspectives.

> The management system includes people at all levels of the organization, as well as all of the procedures and activities related to the organization including planning resource allocation, control of operational processes, feedback and verification of performance information and results. The basic input to a management system is information concerning legal requirements, issues from interested parties, the operational system, and the state of the environment; the outputs are decisions and information. . . . The operational system includes the design and operation of the physical plants, equipment, and the mass and energy flows required for the generation of product and services. EPE of an operational system should take into account linkages among activities, plants, and sites.[6]

The EPE process looks very carefully at the relationship between these two systems; at how they interact with the environment, in terms of the use of resources, the production process, and the generation and handling of wastes; and at how they interface with the surrounding community from a local, regional, and global perspective (Figure 18.3).[7] It also tries to give us a better understanding of who the interested parties may be, both inside and outside the organization.

The combination of these two models for EPE allows this segment of ISO 14000 to take a hard look at empirical, relevant data, and ground a philosophical enterprise in the essential quantitative language of business. From a TQM standpoint, it also provides the essential measurements for continuous improvement.

The Inside Pitch

Most environmental managers have countless competing demands pressuring them every day. If they are not already beginning to get up to speed on

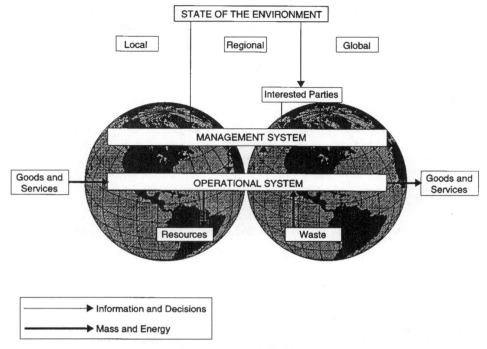

Figure 18.3   Evaluation for EPE

ISO 14000 issues, they have at least an evolving sense of its imminence. Nevertheless, if it is not something that has to be addressed today, most of us will tend to put the issue on the back burner. In the case of EPE, that may be a costly mistake.

The current state of the EPE process includes recommendations for establishing an EPE system and evaluating EP indicators. It provides these recommendations within the framework discussed above. Naturally, any effective performance evaluation system will do the trick, and the number of variations available is virtually infinite. However, at some point, when ISO 14000 begins to establish a baseline for overall environmental management, it may be advantageous to have an EPE system that is consistent with the ISO scheme.

Conclusion

When Casey Stengel assumed the helm of the newborn New York Mets in 1962, his first draft pick for the expansion club was Hobie Landrith, a veteran catcher. When questioned about the sagacity of this selection, Casey responded that without a catcher, there will be no one to stop all the pitched balls from rolling to the backstop. The logic was unassailable—at least to Casey.

For environmental managers preparing to venture out into the untested waters of ISO 14000, EPE is our veteran catcher. Where the environmental management and environmental auditing components of ISO 14000 are invaluable players, EPE will likely become the anchor of the ISO 14000 team. Without establishing the ground rules for measuring environmental performance, you might as well let all the pitches roll to the backstop.

Notes

1. The EPE figures and text quoted in this article are drawn from the May 10, 1995, draft of ISO/TC 207/SC 4, "Environmental Management—Environmental Performance Evaluation," p. 1. Revisions to this draft have been under consideration.

2. *Id.* at 4.

3. *Id.* at 1.

4. *Id.*

5. *Id.* at 2, with variations on pp. 5, 8, 12, 14, and 16. An outline of this summary is found on p. 5.

6. *Id.* at 6, 7.

7. *Id.* at 6.

Howard N. Apsan, Ph.D., is regional director of environmental management services for Clayton Environmental Consultants, Inc., in Edison, New Jersey, and also serves on the faculty at Columbia University. He advises clients on environmental management and compliance issues.

19

Environmental Corporate Reporting: Do We Really Need a New Standard?

Cynthia A. Unger

More and more companies are concluding that issuing an environmental progress report to the public makes good environmental and business sense. Some companies publish environmental progress reports annually (e.g., Monsanto Company, Sun Company); other companies report less frequently, every two or three years (e.g., Bristol-Myers Squibb Company, Chevron Corporation). Although the number of companies issuing environmental progress reports is relatively small (approximately one-third of the Fortune 250 industrial corporations), the number has been increasing yearly, as pressures mount from stakeholder groups seeking more information about companies' environmental records. These groups (or audiences) include employees, shareholders, communities, government agencies, the media, and the general public.

During the past several years, corporate environmental progress reports have become more ambitious, have presented more candid assessments of progress made, and have better balanced the needs of different stakeholder groups. Companies reporting periodically are improving their reports with each edition, while first-time report issuers are making sophisticated efforts to advance the state of the art. Companies with several years of reporting experience are beginning to share their knowledge with others. Several industry initiatives have developed guidelines for voluntary environmental reporting. In addition, several environmental management system principles and standards (e.g., ISO 14000, EMAS) to which companies may subscribe call for public communication/reporting of environmental information; however, few provide much in the way of substantive environmental reporting guidelines.

Unlike annual financial statements prepared by public companies, no generally accepted standard format exists for companies to voluntarily report environmental information to the public. As a result, stakeholders are unable to compare one company's environmental progress against another or, for that matter, compare one company's environmental performance against itself from year to year.

Although corporate environmental reporting has advanced out of infancy, it has not yet reached the level of full maturity. Companies are still seeking help and guidance in preparing and/or updating their environmental progress reports. Three organizations recommend specific guidelines for reporting environmental information:

- The Coalition for Environmentally Responsible Economies
- The Public Environmental Reporting Initiative
- The United Nations Environmental Programme

The specificity and detail provided for in these organizations' guidelines make them noteworthy. However, companies in the process of preparing an environmental progress report would be well advised to review other reporting guides as well (e.g., European Chemical Industry Council: *CEFIC Guidelines on Environmental Reporting for the European Chemical Industry,* Global Environmental Management Initiative's (GEMI) Primer: *Environmental Reporting in a Total Quality Management Framework,* and World Industry Council for the Environment: *Environmental Reporting—A Manager's Guide*).

The Coalition for Environmentally Responsible Economies (CERES)

CERES, recognized for its issuance of 10 principles originally known as the "Valdez Principles," requires signatory companies to submit detailed information concerning how well they are complying with the mandate of the principles. The 10 principles pertain exclusively to corporate environmental accountability. Company information is detailed each year in a publicly available report, which may or may not follow a specific format developed by CERES. The CERES format includes 12 reporting sections:

1. Company Profile
2. Environmental Policies, Organization and Management
3. Materials Policy
4. Releases to the Environment
5. Workplace Hazards
6. Emergency Response and Public Disclosure
7. Hazardous Waste Management
8. Use of Energy
9. Product Stewardship
10. Supplier Relationships
11. Audits
12. Compliance

Although most CERES signatories choose to use the CERES report format, all signatory companies are committed to completing and making public the information required by CERES, perhaps the most thorough and comprehensive of the existing environmental reporting requirements.

In order to give some perspective to the CERES report requirements, some background about CERES is necessary. CERES is a nonprofit organization consisting of diverse stakeholders: investment and research professionals, environmental groups, churches, labor unions, and public and private entities entrusted with investment duties. According to CERES, these groups represent more than 10 million people and $150 billion in invested assets. CERES developed the principles in response to national outrage over the grounding of the Exxon Valdez oil tanker in Alaska's Prince William Sound.

G.J. Carpency wrote that the principles are intended to accomplish two objectives.[1] First, CERES expects that signatories to the principles will commit to a corporate governance ideal that promotes implementation of responsible environmental practices. Second, CERES believes the principles will "help investors make informed decisions around environmental issues." Carpency stated that the principles operate on two levels. One level is symbolic: Signatories demonstrate commitment to environmental protection. The other level is pragmatic: Signatories must submit to CERES an annual report regarding their environmental status.

The CERES report, which requires standard, specific information from each signatory, provides corporations with one form of voluntary environmental reporting guidance and provides investors with information to make informed investment decisions. The CERES report represents an effort to establish uniform and easily understood standards for corporate environmental performance.

The Public Environmental Reporting Initiative (PERI)

In 1992, a group of 10 companies (Amoco, BP America, Dow Chemical, DuPont, IBM, Northern Telecom, Phillips Petroleum, Polaroid, Rockwell International, and United Technologies), known as the Public Environmental Reporting Initiative (PERI), convened to develop a specific framework for corporate environmental reporting. In so doing, PERI was responding to growing demands from investors, consumers, environmental groups, and others for more detailed information on corporations' environmental performances and programs. PERI's initial guidelines (issued in 1993) placed a major emphasis on environmental disclosure; a second iteration of the guidelines, published in June 1994, incorporated reporting issues applicable to multinational companies and nonindustrial companies, such as banks and other service organizations.

The PERI guidelines provide 10 core components for comprehensive reporting on environmental performance that can be added to, or built on, as an organization achieves its goals or as reporting situations change. The core reporting components include:

1. Organizational Profile
2. Environmental Policy
3. Environmental Management
4. Environmental Releases
5. Resource Conservation
6. Environmental Risk Management
7. Environmental Compliance
8. Product Stewardship
9. Employee Recognition
10. Stakeholder Involvement

According to PERI, the intent of the guidelines is to help companies anticipate and influence demand by stakeholders for environmental information, to develop more credible and comprehensive reports, and to respond to requests for information. Company reports prepared in accordance with the guidelines will provide the public with a mechanism to weigh a company's environmental progress and to create an open dialogue. The guidelines do not dictate a required format or style of document, but, rather, they leave these decisions to the discretion of the company. Companies that subscribe to the PERI guidelines generally state in their environmental reports that the report is prepared in accordance with the PERI guidelines, providing their audiences with a certain level of assurance regarding the content of the report.

The United Nations Environmental Programme (UNEP)

The UNEP Industry and Environment Office, together with SustainAbility Limited, a European environmental communications and consulting company based in London, published an environmental reporting framework in 1994. The framework identifies 50 "reporting ingredients" grouped into five broad topics:

1. *Management Policies and Systems:* This topic includes 13 reporting ingredients meant to set the tone and strategic direction of the report.
2. *An Input/Output Inventory of Environmental Impacts of Production, Processes, and Products:* This topic includes 17 reporting ingredients that provide data on all key inputs, process management approaches, and outputs. For example, information regarding mass balances, energy

efficiency, water supply and quality issues, accidents and emergency response, Superfund cleanup and remediation projects, process emissions (e.g., TRI), and other types of information are included in this topic.

3. *The Financial Implications of Environmental Actions:* This topic includes six reporting ingredients that seek to integrate environmental factors into economic decision making. For example, this topic includes company data on environmental spending, environmental liabilities, discussion regarding environmental cost accounting systems, charitable contributions, and more.

4. *Relationships with Environmental Stakeholders:* This topic includes 10 reporting ingredients that emphasize sound, two-way stakeholder communication as a result of an effective environmental management system. This topic may include information regarding employees (e.g., numbers of employees trained, internal award schemes, results of employee surveys), legislators and regulators (e.g., discussion of government relations), local communities (e.g., community liaison activities), investors, suppliers, customers and consumers, industry associations, environmental groups, science and education programs, and media (e.g., proportion of "good" versus "bad" articles or programs).

5. *Sustainable Development Agenda:* This topic includes four reporting ingredients that demonstrate "how a company is helping to meet the present generation's needs for goods and services, while minimizing environmental impacts and resource use so that future generations can meet their own needs." This topic embraces all of the ingredients of the previous four topics but goes further to address social and economic issues.

The 50 reporting ingredients were identified based on a combination of various reporting frameworks (i.e., CEFIC, CERES, GEMI, PERI, and WICE) and through an analysis of what companies are currently reporting and what they may need to report to meet emerging stakeholder expectations. The UNEP emphasizes that the 50 reporting ingredients should be viewed not as a reporting standard, but rather as a set of building blocks companies can use to construct their reports according to their own priorities.

Conclusion

The reporting guidelines discussed in this chapter provide diverse perspectives and varying levels of specificity, which offer companies guidance in preparing corporate environmental progress reports. The CERES report is probably the most prescriptive and specific guideline, requiring signatories to submit information on approximately 99 data points. The PERI guidelines are less rigorous in that they provide a framework for reporting based on a company's perception of its stakeholders, as well as its company culture, management system, industry, and scope of business activities. In a similar way, the UNEP's 50 "reporting ingredients" provide a framework; however, the framework is aimed toward sustainable development reporting. Each of these organizations has provided valuable insight into the emerging field of environmental progress reporting.

Different approaches to environmental reporting should be encouraged; the lack of a generally accepted standard format for environmental reporting stimulates innovation. The various audiences for a report should direct the content of a report, not a specific reporting guideline. How can one approach to environmental reporting fit all? Before preparing an environmental progress report, a thorough analysis of the company's audiences, coupled with an analysis of the various elements, components, and "reporting ingredients" mentioned in the CERES, PERI, and UNEP guidelines, should be undertaken. Following these analyses, company management should "pick and choose" those elements, components, and reporting ingredients that are most appropriate to its audiences' concerns, as well as those that reflect the company's culture and values. This "cafeteria approach" to environmental reporting may be an effective alternative to the constraints imposed by a particular guideline in conveying your company's message to its stakeholders.

Note

1. G.J. Carpency, "The Valdez Principles: A Corporate Counselor's Perspective," *Wake Forest Law Review*, 1991, pp. 11–37.

Cynthia A. Unger is a senior associate in the Environmental Management Consulting Services Practice of Coopers & Lybrand. She has more than 15 years' experience as an environmental consultant and has extensive experience in conducting environmental management system reviews; preparing environmental reports, policies, and plans; and conducting research and analysis for environmental due diligence.

SECTION FIVE

Advancing Sustainable Development and Creating Competitive Advantage

As we approach the new millennium, the global goal of sustainability will increasingly become a major consideration for companies. In this section, many timely chapters from industry experts, such as Paul Bailey, Peter Soyka, and Michael Lenox and John Ehrenfeld, show how managers need to rethink their accounting and manufacturing practices to continue making environmental and economic progress. New frameworks for incorporating these changes are highlighted in case studies of AT&T and Chrysler. In order to continue their ISO 14000 momentum, life-cycle assessments and labeling issues and practices will need to be addressed. Chapters by Stan Rhodes, Linda Brown, and Ellen Huang and David Hunkeler provide the vital information needed to make these informed decisions.

20

Leading the Competition to a Greener Environment through Sustainable Development

Lynn Johannson

The competitive challenge for business is to achieve sustainable development—environmentally sustainable economic growth. The global marketplace has embraced the concept already (Figure 20.1). The irony of the situation is that while governments have guaranteed sustainability and businesses have promised it, few are ready to deliver better environmental performance. Under reengineering, some managers feel they are losing ground on the accomplishments made to date based on short-term thinking. One company that has acknowledged the depth and breadth of the challenge is Dow Chemical. Under the environmental leadership of David Buzzeli (vice president, International EHS), Dow has created a strategic vision to allow it to produce sustainably developed product by the year 2020 (Figure 20.2).

However, in a conversation with the vice president of a major institution in Canada, the vice president commented that while the institution had an environmental policy that stated support for sustainable development and had signed the UNEP's charter for sustainable development, no one in the organization could define or defend it.

Nonetheless, all four key stakeholders of the global marketplace outlined in Figure 20.1 have signed on to the concept of sustainable development. This forms the focal point for a global growth vision (Figure 20.3). With this buy-in comes a timeline that varies slightly, centering around the close of this century and the start of the third millennium. It requires the concerted effort of all stakeholders, not just one or two.

What Does This Buy-in Mean?

Competing for the future is competition for opportunity share, rather than market share. It will require cooperative alliances along the supply chain, which is really an interconnected service chain that starts with the customer and comes back around to the customer.

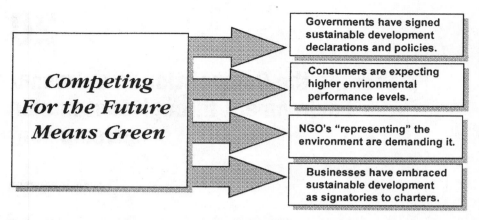

Governments have signed sustainable development declarations and policies.

Competing For the Future Means Green

Consumers are expecting higher environmental performance levels.

NGO's "representing" the environment are demanding it.

Businesses have embraced sustainable development as signatories to charters.

Figure 20.1   The Buy-In for the Concept of Competing Green Has Already Been Accepted

What Does This Mean for Competing in the Emerging Global Marketplace?

Competition requires a redefinition of strategy. With this comes a redefinition of top management's role in creating strategy. Rather than transforming the organization belatedly in a crisis atmosphere, in which resources have already been wasted, top managers will forge their organizations' futures with foresight. The goal is a transformation that is evolutionary in execution, and revolutionary in result.

There is a strategy crisis today. Why? Many strategic plans have "died on the vine"; hence, strategic planning has fallen out of vogue. Why? For the most part, these strategies were not visionary in nature; they were justifications for action plans already in play.

Strategy is a process. It enables you to understand and shape competitive "forces" and fosters discovery and purposeful improvement. These forces of

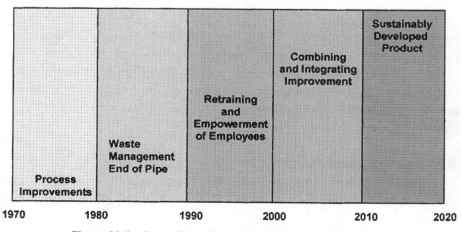

Process Improvements

Waste Management End of Pipe

Retraining and Empowerment of Employees

Combining and Integrating Improvement

Sustainably Developed Product

1970   1980   1990   2000   2010   2020

Figure 20.2   Dow's Time Chart for Sustainable Development

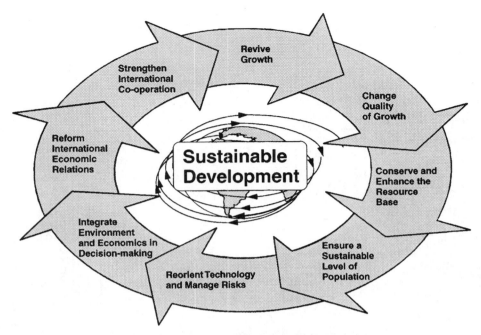

Figure 20.3   The Key Elements in Sustainable Development

change, highlighted in Figure 20.4, will be a melange of self-initiated actions and activities brought forward by customers in competitive organizations.

Strategy is a synthesis of the following underlying elements:

- Relationships (interlinking players along the service chain, requiring partnerships)
- A collective structure (the accumulation of individual entities)
- Directed employees (knowledgeable workers who can incrementally save resources)
- Commitment by internal activists (a team of people with an intense desire to improve and add value to the service offered)
- Benefits-led (internally *and* externally defined customer needs and desires)
- Core competence (the connective threads that hold together seemingly diverse portfolios)

Can you ignore sustainable development in your core business strategy? No. A successful strategy starts with envisioning the future. Leaders will be the first to incorporate sustainable development for competitive advantage. If your organization does not have the commitment to be a leader, are you tracking the trends pushing and pulling sustainable development? Is your plan to catch the

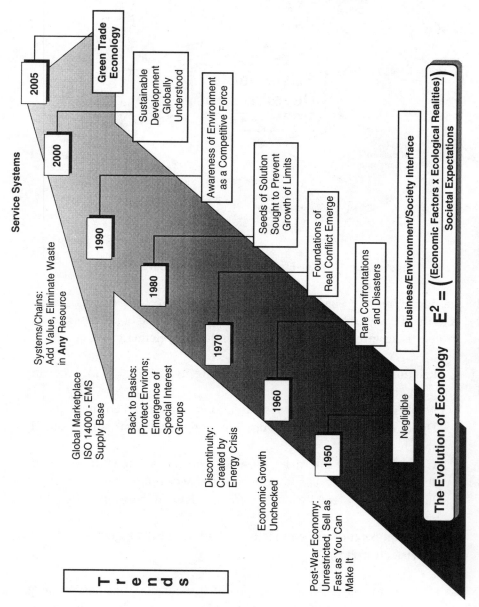

Figure 20.4 The Forces of Change

wave as it explodes through the S-curve of innovation? Or are you devoting your energies to preserving the past?

What Action Should You Be Taking?

While a competitive strategy is about creating the future, competing today means competing *within* the current marketplace. If you have not already started, you need to establish an environmental management system. There are a number of self-assessment tools to help you, including:

- Canadian Standards Association's (CSA's) Z750-94, A Voluntary Environmental Management System (CSA)
- *Competing Leaner, Keener and Greener,* CSA's EMS workbook for small and medium-sized enterprises
- CGLI's TQEM Primer and Self-Assessment Matrix (based on Baldrige criteria)
- GEMI's Environmental Self-Assessment Program (based on the ICC Charter for Sustainable Development)

Competing today requires your organization to operate as a lean, keen, and green service system.

Are You Convinced That Sustainable Development Is Crucial to Your Future?

No? Add to the discussion the acknowledgment of 34 nations at the Summit of the Americas held in Miami in December 1994 that "sound environmental management is an essential element of sustainable development." The declaration signed by these countries *guarantees* sustainable development. Action plans include sustainable development as part of the free trade negotiations to be completed by 2005.

While some may excuse this activity as political posturing, it is not isolated, nor has the process for dialogue slowed. The Hemispheric Trade and Commerce Forum held in Denver, Colorado, in July 1995 followed on the groundwork laid in Miami. Regional partnerships have been formed with "the goal of ensuring that economic integration of the region occurs in an environmentally sustainable manner."

Is This a Consumer Preference?

Some perceive that consumer interest in environmental issues has waned because the environment is not in the press every day with the same voracity as it was in the period from 1988 to 1991. Think again.

A consumer boycott forced Royal Dutch/Shell, an oil producer, to drop plans to dump an off-shore storage buoy called Brent Spar. The company had intended to send Brent Spar to the bottom of the ocean. Boycotters refused to buy the company's gas. Not only were the consumers' wishes a contributing factor to forcing the company to bring Brent Spar ashore for disposal, their efforts were supplemented by Greenpeace, whose activists landed on the buoy by helicopter to prevent it from being sunk.

Over the last 25 years, environmental issues have shifted from being concerns of vocal minorities to a background expectation of the silent majority. Polls in many countries indicate that the consumer will become more demanding. As public participation in decision making in corporate and government policy increases through the information superhighway, no public or private organization can dismiss customer-driven environmental concerns.

Why Is There Such Emphasis on Compliance in the U.S. Market?

As long as corporate priority focuses on the bottom line without adding value to the community in which it operates, the public good will be enforced through these expensive measures. The costs associated with compliance are estimated as high as 5 percent to 8 percent of revenue.

Preservation is a restrictive growth path. Hanging onto outmoded management practices by trying to prevent the forces of change is not productive. Just as you cannot freeze-dry and containerize the environment, you cannot stop market fluctuations and cycles. This is contrary to the key elements of sustainable development. A fear-driven response is not sustainable. The future lies in improving productivity, in new technology that maximizes the throughput per unit of resource expended, and in retraining the workforce to understand the power of each action taken to achieve these goals.

What Impact Will ISO 14000 Have on Spurring on the Greening of Competition?

Plenty. The development of an international standard was requested by participants of the United Nations Conference on the Environment and Development, held in Rio de Janeiro in June 1992. Its goal was to minimize the non-tariff trade barriers that were emerging as countries strove to meet society's growing expectations of technological advancements, jobs, and a clean and healthy environment. The International Standards Organization (which includes 74 countries) overwhelmingly agreed to forward the committee drafts of the ISO 14000 standards on environmental management systems and environmental auditing to draft international standards status at the Oslo meeting in June 1995. This four-year effort is a relatively quick turnaround for an international standard.

Is There Opportunity? Are There Benefits?

In addition to broader trade issues, ISO 14000 standards may be used in regulatory reform measures now under discussion. The presence of an ISO 14000-aligned environmental management system may replace the command-and-control approach to environmental protection. This would afford organizations more flexibility and autonomy in deciding how to meet regulated requirements. Those with ISO 14000 standards in place within their organization may be privileged with expedited treatment with regard to permits. This may help to reduce the cost of compliance. Preferential supply status could be another benefit.

However, the possibility exists that ISO 14001 (the specification standard against which an organization can be audited) will be used by countries as a trade barrier and by companies as a means of streamlining their supply bases.

What Is the Bottom Line?

Business and governments have offered sustainable development as a selling feature for growth in a global marketplace. Customers in all sectors have placed their orders for sustainable development. If your organization is truly committed to meeting and exceeding customers' expectations and becoming the preferred supplier, you must be prepared to distribute by "tomorrow." As part of the settlement for services, environmental management is a requirement for the return of benefit to the service provider. Leaders in competing "green" will not only listen to their customers, but also will support the customers' own discovery of what sustainability means. In most organizations, regardless of size or sector, this requires a fresh start. Overnight success in green ventures can take five years. The clock is ticking. Will you be ready?

Lynn Johannson is president of E2 Management Corporation, an environmental management consulting firm in Georgetown, Ontario, Canada. E2M specializes in assisting clients to integrate environmental issues into the organization's business using quality management systems and alignment to the ISO 14000 series.

21

Making Environmental Accounting Work for Your Company

Paul E. Bailey and Peter A. Soyka

Environmental accounting comprises a set of tools that serve the management of an organization. Its function is to provide useful information to support plans and decisions, without regard to the interests or opinions of external parties (e.g., environmental or accounting regulatory bodies). Accordingly, two points should be kept in mind when developing an environmental accounting initiative. The first is that any program that you create should serve your needs as you see them, rather than what others outside the organization might believe are higher priorities or better methods. The second is that the primary reason that companies should practice environmental accounting is to make better plans and decisions.

Where you start will depend on where you, as an agent of change, are in your organization, your scope of authority, "fellow travelers" who share your interest in environmental accounting, the nature of any senior management mandate for action, and, of course, the environmental aspects (type and magnitude) of your organization. We recommend starting out modestly. There are several dimensions for applying environmental accounting, each of which reflects a continuum that ranges from the most attainable to the most ambitious. The key dimensions include the following:

- *Scale:* It is easier to apply environmental accounting to discrete processes and systems than to products and product lines. As you go up the scale from process to department to facility to division to business unit to the entire corporation, the number of key stakeholders and cross-cutting issues will rise.
- *Scope:* It is easier to address conventional, and even "hidden," environmental costs than it is to incorporate future costs, contingent costs, image and relationship costs, upstream and downstream life-cycle costs, and social costs (externalities) into environmental accounting. As desired, environmental accounting can get "fuller" over time by

expanding the scope of costs considered. Some firms (e.g., nuclear power generators) should address these more difficult issues, while others need not. Some organizations have deliberately chosen to focus on external costs or upstream and/or downstream life-cycle costs as a matter of corporate philosophy.

- *Sensitivity:* It is easier to begin with applications that are farthest removed from (i.e., ancillary to) core products and how they are produced. Such ancillary activities include:
  - Waste management and recycling (as opposed to waste minimization or source reduction)
  - Maintenance of nonproduction equipment and structures (e.g., painting external transformers)
  - Utilities (e.g., heating, lighting, air conditioning)
  - Cleaning materials
  - Plating, coating, and painting to the extent not integral to the product
  - Storage and distribution systems

The literature is replete with examples of successful interventions in such ancillary areas that have resulted in "win-win" situations, while examples of the application of environmental accounting to product and process design are fewer, though still substantial, in number. Change that might affect the functionality and perceived quality of the product is very threatening and is not likely to be a propitious starting point for applying environmental accounting.

Given some of the important practical limitations to implementing environmental accounting, a good operating practice is to start small; that is, don't overreach. It is more prudent to achieve initial successes and build on them than it is to attempt immediately to create and implement a broad restructuring of important business management functions.

Interestingly, even leading firms are at the early stages of implementing environmental accounting. A discussion on "Green Accounting" at the March 1996 Global Environmental Management Initiative (GEMI) conference illustrates the different starting points recommended by three major companies: Amoco recommended focusing on wastes as a large area of cost; DuPont countered that waste disposal costs were only a small part of its environmental costs, adding that lost ingredients were more important; and Dow agreed that while attention initially focuses on waste management, pollution prevention often is found to be more important. As organizations work their way through the relatively uncharted terrain of incorporating environmental accounting into their planning, operations, and decisions, some common patterns are starting to emerge. Companies experience success with applications that are tangible and easily understood; it is a plus if such applications also are important from the standpoint of improving the bottom line (e.g., if expenditures on waste management can be turned into revenues from waste recycling).

In this chapter, these starting points are described as locations on two complementary "maps" reflecting broad-scale paradigms for applying environmental accounting to strategic and operational issues, respectively. The paradigms place these starting points in a larger context and thereby identify further directions for progress. Following discussion of these paradigms we present an overarching approach, applicable to both paradigms, that describes critical activities needed to embed environmental accounting principles into an organization so that they continue to influence behavior over time and help companies successfully confront the many environmental issues that arise in a dynamic society and marketplace.

Strategic Decisions and Environmental Accounting

Figure 21.1 illustrates a hierarchy of "big decisions" that can benefit from consideration of environmental issues. The types of "big decisions" considered are of significant strategic import, are difficult and costly to reverse, and individually involve relatively sizable commitments of funds. As shown in Figure 21.1, strategic decisions can become increasingly more difficult, entail greater business risk, and involve more senior levels of decision makers. These different actors and decision makers may not appreciate fully the environmental aspects of their decisions, and, therefore, environmental professionals will need to do two things to be effective in describing strategic plans and decisions: (1) express

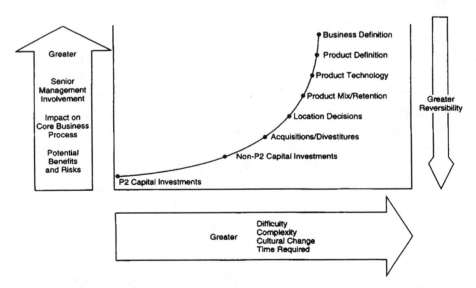

Figure 21.1   Strategic Decisions Influenced by Environmental Accounting

environmental aspects in financial terms, and (2) tailor the level of detail to the audience to avoid eye-glazing discussions of the nuances of environmental management. Fortunately, doing the former may help in accomplishing the latter; the latter, on the other hand, is no substitute for the former.

Although strategic decisions are detailed in Figure 21.1, we do not mean to imply that there is a necessary sequence for applying environmental accounting to strategic decisions, nor that all of these decisions are equally relevant to every company. An organization's competitive situation and corporate culture will strongly affect the priorities it gives to various strategic topics. The relevance of environmental aspects to each topic also will vary. On the other hand, as a company applies environmental accounting to more strategic issues, it makes further progress in integrating environmental considerations into business planning, decisions, and operations, which we believe is important for business success. During a December 1995 meeting hosted by ICF Kaiser on the topic of methods of and barriers to implementing pollution prevention (P2), representatives from organizations such as Dow Chemical, Kennecott Utah Copper, and the NASA Kennedy Space Flight Center agreed that extending and mainstreaming environmental accounting is a high priority.

Capital budgeting decisions are strategic because they can affect the future competitiveness and productivity of organizations in significant and relatively long-lasting ways. Increasingly, the environmental dimension of such decisions has important implications for both the expected return on the investment (as indicated by standard measures such as net present value (NPV) and payback period) and its business risk. Environmental accounting can contribute in direct and fundamental ways to improving the accuracy of predictions related to both of these capital investment analysis aspects. Analytical tools (written guidance, workbooks, and software) for evaluating prospective pollution prevention capital investments are widely available and can be applied more extensively, with or without modification, to capital projects having no direct, visible environmental implications. This means of "harvesting low-hanging fruit" has been successfully used by a number of major corporations and could be applied by organizations of virtually any type or size.

The application of environmental accounting techniques to capital budgeting requests for P2 projects is a logical starting point for several reasons. First, tools are readily available that are extensions of conventional capital budgeting methods that have been taught for years to business managers. Second, this application rarely involves changes to management systems; rather, it brings P2 projects into existing decision-making processes. Third, necessary cross-functional coordination may be the most manageable, primarily involving conversations with accounting staff and production people to develop cost inputs. As noted in the *Pollution Prevention Benefits Manual*, some P2 projects may be justified based on a few numbers that are relatively easy to acquire (e.g., materials costs, waste disposal cost, utilities), whereas, for others, a more complete assessment of costs and benefits will be needed.[1] Fourth, this area can be a training ground for corporate environmental, health, and safety (EH&S) personnel to learn to speak the language of business, which is necessary for them to have meaningful input to a wider range of strategic corporate plans and decisions.

Incorporating environmental aspects into capital spending decisions that do not originate in the environmental department is more challenging. Absence of awareness or sensitivity to the environmental aspects of such decisions, coupled with a lack of easy access to information expressing environmental aspects in terms of dollars and cents, can lead to decisions with substantial hidden environmental costs. If decision processes and tools for evaluating capital investments have been properly designed, the dollar values of environmental aspects will be required inputs. For example, some companies are updating their capital investment decision processes to de-emphasize environmental compliance-oriented qualitative checkoff lists (e.g., Does the proposed project create compliance problems? Will permits be required?) and, instead, seek more meaningful and monetized input. Ontario Hydro, for example, has added a "sustainable development" screen to its review of all major capital projects, applying full cost accounting principles to get at environmental impacts and costs that were previously not a critical part of the review process.

If decision aids and processes were to provide opportunities for input from a company's environmental managers, would most EH&S people be able to put the environmental consequences of prospective operations and investment decisions in terms of dollars and cents? Or do EH&S staff need professional training to learn how to fashion effective inputs? Discussions with EH&S managers confirm that existing staff capabilities often will need to be enhanced to provide the input needed for new management processes to successfully reflect the environmental aspects of business decisions.

As shown in Figure 21.1, other big decisions that could be better informed by environmental accounting include the following:

- Acquisitions and divestitures (where the current focus is largely on environmental liabilities associated with property transfer);
- Location decisions (both macro—state x versus state y—and micro—where to locate structures and facilities on a given plot of land);
- Product mix and retention (proper environmental accounting may allow managers to better distinguish the real winners and losers);
- Product design (e.g., "green" cars, computers, and buildings); and, ultimately,
- The definition of the business itself.

The key business definition issues that are being driven by environmental considerations include: (1) Are you selling (or buying) a product or its function? (2) Are you selling (or buying) a product or leasing it (i.e., returning the product for the seller to take back after use)? General Motors, for instance, is putting in place chemicals management contracts based on its suppliers' providing a chemical service to GM facilities rather than selling chemicals on a per-gallon basis. More than half of GM's North American plants already have such contracts in place, resulting in a reported average reduction of 30 percent in chemical usage and up to $750,000 savings per year.[2] The Safety-Kleen Corporation similarly has successfully developed its primary line of business by defining it as the sale of services (recycling used automotive and industrial fluids), not chemicals. In response to an apparent trend, the potential costs of product take-back are being reviewed by a variety of North American assemblers and manufacturers that are monitoring take-back programs initiated in Europe. When such programs are in effect, efficient handling of returned products for recycling can confer a competitive edge.

Management of Operating Costs

Another major opportunity for applying environmental accounting is in the area of purchases of goods and services and performance of operations that involve smaller individual commitments, are relatively reversible, and for which there may be many substitutes or alternatives. This area, which includes logistics management, involves a different set of managers than those who typically deal with more strategic issues. Notwithstanding the smaller scale of individual operating expenditures, they are substantial in most companies when considered as a category. In the aggregate, organizations spend only half as much annually on capital investments for pollution abatement and control as they spend on operating expenses for pollution control. Similarly, nonenvironmental operating expenses tend to far exceed nonenvironmental capital spending in most companies. Thus, the potential payoff from applying environmental accounting to operational decisions is great.

As shown by Figure 21.2, there are a variety of normal, everyday activities whose performance can be improved and/or costs reduced through use of environmental accounting as a decision support tool. We distinguish between ancillary activities that do not directly affect product production from activities that have a more direct impact on products. Applying environmental accounting to the former will require less cross-functional coordination and will be easier to implement than addressing the latter.

The curve in Figure 21.2 does not mean that there is a sequence that companies must follow in implementing environmental accounting, but experience reveals a path of least resistance that revolves around relatively noncore activities.

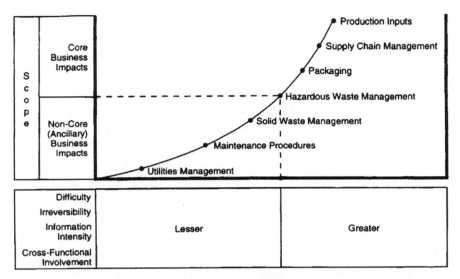

Figure 21.2 Operating Decisions Influenced by Environmental Accounting

The dividing line is, of course, a simplification. For example, packaging can be considered more or less important to the image and sales of a product; thus, its position on the curve might vary for different companies. There are two reasons why hazardous waste management is on the cusp between core and noncore activities. First, for some businesses, generating hazardous waste is a necessary by-product of core processing or formulating activities. Second, for virtually all businesses that generate them, hazardous wastes pose significant management costs and contingent liabilities that can affect the firm's financial viability.

Aspects of manufacturing operations and logistics that are less intimately tied to product production have proven to be successful starting points for environmental accounting. Energy, environmental, and financial savings from "greener" approaches to illumination of work and office space and other energy-saving techniques have produced eye-popping returns. Similarly, through recycling, reuse, and source reduction, the daily costs and environmental impacts of solid waste management can be drastically reduced. Firms have applied environmental accounting to water use practices; cleaning, repair, and maintenance procedures; and even packaging and distribution. For many firms, inventory wastage is a much bigger issue than waste disposal costs. To address this, as one example, the U.S. Navy has successfully implemented a "pharmacy" concept for hazardous materials that has resulted in substantial net cost savings. Nonetheless, environmental accounting has only just begun to be applied to many operating activities.

Companies are starting to pay more attention to the environmental costs that accompany purchases. For example, firms employing classic life-cycle assessment techniques and "root cause" thinking have found, in a number of cases, that the environmental cost burden of a product is heavily influenced by the processes used by manufacturers further up the supply chain. To address these concerns, the Chrysler Corporation, for example, requires its tooling and equipment and production part suppliers to certify as to material contents of detail components and substances of concern. Until recently, EH&S expenditures were one of the largest non-measured cost areas, and Chrysler has initiated a program to better tie such costs to purchased products.[3] Any organization can apply environmental accounting to root out the hidden environmental costs of goods and services purchased, and thereby make smarter buying decisions.

For instance, several electric utilities have started to use lifecycle accounting principles in a variety of applications, with significant savings in operational costs. Niagara Mohawk, for example, expects to save more than $30,000 per year from recycling wood pallets formerly disposed of as waste (a large percentage of the company's purchases are shipped on pallets, which alone comprise 15 percent of its trash by volume). Duke Power determined that switching to a new type of sealed lead-acid battery to provide emergency power at substations and generating facilities would save the company $600,000 per year. Other utilities have used environmental accounting to evaluate alternative painting activities. These applications are all ancillary to the core business of generating and distributing electrical power. In fact, one utility estimated that 75 percent of all direct costs at its generating facilities arise from general maintenance, compared to 15 percent from waste treatment, 8 percent from fuel oil combustion, and 3 percent from power sources. Bearing in mind that the majority of operating costs incurred by manufacturers are "overhead" (i.e., indirect) costs, the potential for cost savings and improved environmental performance (e.g., reduced resource consumption and waste) is staggering. There seems to be no dearth of low-hanging fruit, once an organization starts looking for it. Companies can go further and initiate "buy green" programs, using environmental accounting to assess how much extra, if any, they spend on "greener" goods and services (e.g., recyclable equipment, supplies and equipment with recycled content).

Critical Activities

Any successful environmental accounting initiative will include one or more of the following key activities, although, depending on the situation, some of them may receive greater or lesser emphasis:

- Define desired behaviors.
- Perform a diagnostic/assess capabilities.
- Enhance capabilities.

- Identify and quantify environmental costs.
- Allocate (reallocate) costs.
- Examine and realign incentives.

While recognizing the considerable variability that exists across organizations with respect to objectives, capabilities, resources, and priorities, some of these activities should precede others. One logical sequence begins with an analysis of how the objectives of the initiative translate into desired behaviors, then proceeds into an assessment of existing organizational and individual practices and capabilities to carry out these behaviors. Depending on how actual practices and capabilities compare to desired behaviors, corrective measures, such as providing training, tools, and information, may be necessary. Other important activities involve the "nuts and bolts" of both identifying and quantifying key environmental costs to make them more visible and the process of (re)allocating environmental costs and benefits to those responsible for them. We also recommend that organizations critically evaluate and, as necessary, realign existing incentive structures to promote the behaviors required to attain the desired objectives. We describe each one of these activities of our model environmental accounting process in turn.

In general, we recommend that a clear focus of any environmental accounting initiative be on identifying decision and action points that have environmental drivers, influences, and/or consequences (aspects) and resulting costs or benefits, as well as on the data, especially financial information, that are directly tied to these decision points. This approach shifts the emphasis from identifying, quantifying, and allocating costs (the traditional emphasis of managerial accounting efforts) to a process of improving organizational effectiveness. It is neither necessary nor desirable to count, measure, or estimate the cost or value of everything. Indeed, such an exercise would almost certainly be difficult, time-consuming, and expensive, and yet might not yield an outcome that would be of lasting benefit (through lower costs or increased revenues) to the firm. Instead, a more practical approach is to address only those costs that matter to the decision makers who can benefit from environmental accounting information, and that are directly tied to the objectives of the environmental accounting initiative.

Define Desired Behaviors

A critical first step in making environmental accounting an operational reality in any organization is to define the linkages between the objectives of the initiative and the specific behaviors that will be needed to accomplish them. As we have discussed elsewhere,[4] because environmental accounting can be used to address a number of different issues (e.g., capital budgeting, purchasing) and can vary with respect to scope, scale, and sensitivity in various applications, it is very important to be clear about what one hopes to get from environmental accounting, and to ensure that multiple objectives, if they exist, are assigned priorities and are not in conflict with one another.

Likewise, for any given objective, there is a corresponding set of desired behaviors on the part of various individuals whose decisions and activities influence the occurrence, timing, and magnitude of costs incurred and revenues generated by the firm. If an environmental accounting initiative is to succeed, people (and, often, many people) will need to change the ways in which they make decisions and do things. Bringing this about should not be left to chance, "common sense," or wishful thinking, but must be planned and worked toward through the careful establishment of appropriate incentives. As a necessary step toward developing any needed incentives, one must first define how the organization wants groups and individuals to perform their respective duties and to interact with one another. For example, if the objective is to ensure that environmental accounting is used to make better capital investment decisions, the desired behaviors might include forming multidisciplinary teams to evaluate investment options, using formal decision-making processes that explicitly consider indirect and contingent environmental costs (e.g., using the *Pollution Prevention Benefits Manual*), and applying these and other appropriate techniques to both environmental and nonenvironmental investments.

Perform a Diagnostic/Assess Capabilities

Some leading companies have initiated environmental accounting activities using a diagnostic as an initial step. This can be a useful starting point when there is no consensus on what desired behaviors should be. Or, performing a diagnostic can follow agreement on objectives and desired behaviors. For example, because DuPont wanted to optimize decisions about the $600 million-plus it spends annually on environmental operating costs, it established an objective of developing a best practice on environmental cost accounting. To achieve its objective, DuPont decided to inventory its current practices in order to define what needed to be done to improve. Not surprisingly, surveys revealed that most DuPont sites did not have a process to collect and report environmental costs and did not identify an "owner" of environmental costs. While only a few sites split out the environmental portion of nonenvironmental cost items, most sites reported including environmental costs, if significant, in capital budgeting analysis.

DuPont also sought to profile who receives reports of environmental costs, how the reports are generated, whether reporting has influenced decisions, and how costs are charged to products. Every site representative responding to the survey wanted to see the overall results of DuPont's initiative. Because most large businesses operate in a fairly decentralized way, a diagnostic survey may be the only way to develop a sufficiently complete understanding of environmental management and costing practices across the organization.

Another prominent company, AT&T, developed a "status survey" as a self-assessment tool.[5] Its Green Accounting Team designed the survey instrument to draw attention to how decisions are made and what information is used or needed, but unavailable; how costs are classified in accounting systems; and whether environmental aspects are reflected in product and process costing. A major focus of the survey was whether decisions about product design features, production and handling processes, sourcing and make-versus-buy choices, capital investments, or facility investments or divestment consider environmental impacts and cost tradeoffs and, if so, which costs are considered and how they are handled. The questions addressed frequently overlooked costs such as future costs, potential liabilities or contingent costs, and so-called intangible costs (and benefits), such as brand image and customer relations costs. The survey also posed questions about the *process* used to evaluate cost tradeoffs for environmental impacts, including *when* environmental managers are consulted on decisions about equipment and facility acquisitions.

These types of "diagnostic reviews" serve multiple purposes, including raising awareness of the potential importance of environmental aspects of business decisions. They also can help in developing focused interventions to improve performance. In the near term, both raising awareness and focusing efforts will likely be priorities for environmental accounting.

Enhance Capabilities

Another critical activity for success in transforming behavior is to provide the training and tools needed to enhance capabilities. Information alone may not be sufficient to effect organizational change; even with appropriate incentives in place, there likely will be a need for training and tools.

Training is important because environmental accounting is inherently cross-functional. An organization must supply both the information and the concepts that people require for successful communication and coordination. Just as EH&S professionals need to learn to speak the language of business, accounting professionals need to understand how environmental issues affect the costs of doing business. In a recent series of full cost accounting workshops presented by one of the authors, the financial and accounting personnel were particularly interested in learning how facility and process life cycles and environmental requirements affect expenditures and financial needs over time. Conversely, the environmental professionals in attendance were challenged to view environmental expenditures as costs they can control rather than as fixed budgets to spend. Companies implementing unfamiliar or state-of-the-art approaches to environmental accounting also have used training seminars. For example, Ontario Hydro has conducted training sessions for its senior managers, line managers, and key support staff to explain its approach to full cost accounting, and it has tailored presentations to specific business unit needs for line managers and working level staff.[6]

Tools are likewise critical to make the potential complexity of environmental accounting manageable. For example, a tool can allow a company to monetize (i.e., quantify in dollar terms) the potential liabilities of off-site waste disposal to facilitate more informed decisions about waste management practices. In one specific application, the U.S. Air Force developed a life-cycle cost accounting tool to help in selecting among different materials used in aircraft maintenance. Product designers are testing a variety of tools to make manageable choices among product and process design features that have environmental aspects. To be most helpful, tools should be user-friendly, transparent, and flexible.

Identify and Quantify Environmental Costs

Once it is clear what environmental accounting is to help accomplish, and how and by whom, the process of collecting relevant information (e.g., on environmental costs and benefits) should begin. Sometimes, however, organizations dive into this activity without well-defined objectives, apart from learning about the magnitude and nature of environmental costs. Performing this activity, even in isolation, may help companies to better articulate desired behaviors or to simply draw management attention to the importance of environmental costs. In most cases, this process will require involvement of internal staff having diverse responsibilities, from purchasing to EH&S management to financial/management accounting to maintenance. Identifying and tracking down environmental cost data can itself yield some eye-opening findings and catalyze new thinking, but the key role played by this step is to provide the information needed to evaluate, and perhaps redeploy, the use of the firm's assets (i.e., make better investment decisions). One of the extensions of this exercise is often a reexamination of the value added by each of the activities imposing environmental costs, that is, whether that activity is necessary and if so, whether it could be replaced by a less costly alternative.

The types of costs (hidden or otherwise) that are attributed to environmental management activities fall into four distinct categories, as originally described in the *Pollution Prevention Benefits Manual* published by the U.S. Environmental Protection Agency (EPA) in 1989 and in a number of subsequent publications, most recently EPA's *An Introduction to Environmental Accounting as a Business Management Tool: Key Concepts and Terms* (1995). Using this framework, environmental costs are considered either conventional, potentially hidden, contingent, or image and relationship costs.

- *Conventional costs* cover the items that receive the most attention in traditional managerial accounting systems, such as capital equipment, raw materials, labor, utilities, and supplies, and, in this context, include the costs associated with the tangible environmental aspects of these entities and activities.
- *Potentially hidden costs* are the costs of up-front, operational, and back-end activities required to comply with environmental laws and any additional corporate environmental policies, commitments, or initiatives. Examples (just a few of many) include monitoring, recordkeeping and reporting, emergency preparedness, and training.
- *Contingent costs* include the expenses that may (or may not) be incurred due to future regulatory costs, remediation activities, fines and penalties, compensation claims, legal expenses, and natural resource damages, among others.
- *Image and relationship costs* involve the perceptions of and relationships with the stakeholders of the firm, as well as other external parties (e.g., local communities, regulatory agencies). Although difficult to quantify, environmental performance can improve or damage the firm's relationships with these parties, and these impacts may have cost and/or revenue implications.

In general, these categories are presented in rank order of easiest to most difficult to identify and measure or estimate. This suggests a natural priority scheme that may be adapted as appropriate to the objectives and related behaviors of a particular environmental accounting initiative.

After collecting—and thereby making more visible—all available information, if any, on environmental costs that are already attributed directly to the product(s), process(es), or organizational unit(s) of interest, it will be necessary to seek out the additional environmental costs that are not currently well factored into decision making. One can begin by examining overhead pools, looking for costs that arise because of environmental requirements, either directly or indirectly.

Allocate (Reallocate) Costs

Once identified and quantified, all environmentally related costs can be analyzed as to root cause, and allocated (or reallocated) to the process or function that generated them. To the extent possible, such costs should be associated with the responsible product(s), in order to describe more accurately the true cost of production. In this way, key business management decisions regarding product pricing, product mix, and marketing strategy can be made more effectively and generate higher returns. Alternatively, depending on one's objectives and the decision-making structure within the organization, it might be preferable to reallocate costs to a specific function, department, or individual (e.g., purchasing department, process manager, and/or brand manager) who can control these costs.

The term "cost allocation" is often used to refer to the process of breaking environmental costs out of overhead pools and/or better allocating environmental costs to responsible processes or products. In many businesses, environmental costs are treated as one component in a large pool of overhead costs. A common practice in large facilities is to group certain pollution management costs into a "cost center" responsible for operating wastewater treatment plants, incinerators, and/or solid waste management functions. In such cases, pollution management costs are not assigned to the operations responsible for generating them, and corresponding incentives for reducing these costs and reducing the pollution are blunted. As a result, managers who are responsible for and can influence those costs are not held accountable for them as part of their financial performance (e.g., through internal profit and loss reports).

For example, a company seeking to control environmental costs can go only so far to optimize its production waste management system to improve efficiency. Steps taken may include seeking economies of scale in on-site treatment or use of outside waste management vendors, reengineering current waste handling processes to eliminate unnecessary steps, and auditing off-site waste disposal vendors to control potential liabilities. Even greater payoffs can occur, however, from reducing the amount and/or toxicity of waste generated. Although waste minimization and pollution prevention can be accomplished absent financial incentives, assigning waste management costs to specific products or departments can induce a shift from passive acceptance to active encouragement of waste reduction initiatives. When waste generators are allocated their fair share of total waste management costs, they will be more motivated to find less costly process, product, and operational alternatives, which often have better environmental performance characteristics. In this simple example, it is quite possible that, with more complete information, existing incentives to maximize profits or contribution would be sufficient to bring about the desired behavior (reducing cost while achieving source reduction), and that cost reallocation would largely accomplish the objective of the environmental accounting exercise, such that realigning incentives would be unnecessary.

Companies have had success in this arena even when the cost allocations ("charge-backs") have not been complete. This implies that some companies and plants have "fuller" cost accounting than others. Those with more limited environmental accounting might charge back only the costs of treating and disposing of RCRA wastes, wastewater treatment, and sewerage costs, while others might also include expenses for air emissions controls, regulatory compliance, spill cleanup, insurance (if any—many large companies self-insure all or most of their environmental exposure), and so on. The more complete and accurate the charge-backs, the stronger the preexisting incentives. For organizations or departments without clear profit and loss responsibility, such as R&D facilities, even full cost accounting may not be sufficient to create effective incentives. A recent survey found, for example, that one corporation had to internally charge *three times* the out-of-pocket cost of waste disposal before its R&D organization began to practice waste minimization.[7]

Another way of accomplishing the same result may be to take the charge-backs to the procurement department and add environmental costs to the price of the inputs used, be they raw materials, catalysts, paints, cardboard, or solvents. This produces a "true cost" of using a particular material. The goal is the same—to motivate responsible managers to analyze existing materials' use and processes to identify financially and environmentally better alternatives.

Just as assigning environmental costs to responsible processes and products helps to create and strengthen incentives, so does the proper assignment of environmental revenues, such as revenues from the sale of recyclables. Until recently, federal government agencies were required to turn over to the Treasury Department any monies received from recycling; now that a law has been enacted to permit these agencies to keep and use those revenues, more recycling is likely. Similarly, when corporate accounting systems allocate environmental revenues to responsible departments, any existing profit-maximizing incentives are greatly enhanced.

Moving up the operational decisions curve from utilities and waste management/pollution control to supply chain management can produce a wider range of potential improvements, and so can moving up the strategic decisions curve from isolated P2 investment evaluations to the product design stage. Rather than fixing suboptimal materials and processes after they have been employed, a design for environment (DFE) approach can use environmental accounting to evaluate process and product design options prior to operational implementation. While the potential benefits of applying environmental accounting are substantial, at the design stage it currently is far easier to consider environmental factors in a qualitative way than it is to employ environmental accounting to provide the inputs of dollars and cents. Although many companies can readily determine the environmental costs of what they do or have done, they rarely have handy the prospective costs of a menu of alternative ways of doing things. More importantly, because designers do not directly face profit and loss responsibility, cost allocation is less likely to work as a motivational tool for them under most existing incentive structures. Environmental costs and performance can, however, be made a design criterion. To address this problem more directly, managers can ensure that designers both receive tools (and, as needed, training on their use) incorporating relevant information and use those tools to design with the environment and environmental costs in mind.

Examine and Realign Incentives

As a means of "closing the loop" on the various activities comprising an environmental accounting initiative, as well as to promote continuous improvement, we recommend examining existing incentives that guide the behavior of individuals and departments, and making any appropriate adjustments or additions. This may require establishing new patterns of responsibility, accountability, and authority so that all of the desired behaviors and events actually occur, and the organization obtains maximum value for its investment in environmental accounting. Realigning incentives may pose actual or perceived threats to the autonomy and status of diverse individuals within the organization and must, therefore, be approached carefully and on a clear and reasoned basis. Fortunately, by quantifying the costs of environmentally related overhead and determining openly and explicitly how they should be allocated, realigning incentives and decision-making authority will be made easier. Environmental accounting and its results and implications should be transparent and self-supporting, so that they are viewed as fair and in the best interests of the organization, rather than simply the latest in a series of corporate reorganization, reengineering, or downsizing initiatives.

Because incentives are inextricably linked with objectives and behaviors, we recommend starting with a review of what you want environmental accounting to achieve, how, and by whom. At the same time, the objectives of and desired behaviors arising from the environmental accounting initiative should flow from (or at least be consistent with) the overall mission of the organization. Similarly, the objectives and the manner in which they will be achieved should be reflected in the incentive structure and in explicitly defined lines of responsibility, accountability, authority, and communication. Once these issues have been addressed, the expected behaviors of all affected parties can be articulated in an open and unambiguous manner. The final step is simply to ensure that the expected behaviors are reinforced by the appropriate mix of positive incentives and threatened sanctions for undesirable behavior.

Imposing a significant change in work and communication patterns, as suggested above, requires managerial skill and effort, poses risks, and may engender opposition. In our view, the key to overcoming potential suspicion and resistance is to operate an open process with strong multilateral communication. In this way, everyone affected has opportunities for input and can develop a clear understanding of the mission and objectives of the organization, as well as his or her personal role in its future success. This role can and should be expanded to include, specifically, helping to incorporate environmental activities and their costs into daily business management activities, i.e., to "mainstream" environmental management. Examining and, as necessary, realigning incentives is simply the necessary process of ensuring that the organization and its human resources have congruent interests. Through incentives, an organization can translate growing environmental consciousness into consistent, productive action that will lead to improvement in the environmental, financial, and competitive performance of the organization.

Conclusion

There are many entry points and paths for developing and instilling environmental accounting within an organization. These include both strategic and operational levels. Companies may choose to enter these realms at any point but will generally find that starting small and with noncore business issues will produce the highest likelihood of success, in part because addressing the more complex issues requires an environmental accounting infrastructure and commitment that do not yet exist in most organizations.

Applying environmental accounting to core business processes greatly increases business risk (as well as potential benefit), and therefore requires higher levels of management involvement, cross-functional participation, and information intensity. These characteristics make such central business issues as production technology and supply chain management poor choices as subjects of an environmental accounting project unless there is strong management support and organizational buy-in.

It may be advisable to resist the temptation simply to wade into the numbers in an attempt to identify, quantify, and reallocate all of your environmental costs. A more appropriate place to begin is to define the behaviors that are needed to reach your objectives; the complementary step is to ensure that your incentives actually promote and reward those behaviors. While they may be the most apparent focus of "green accounting," quantifying and allocating costs are largely mechanical exercises that require proper orientation to help reach the desired ends (which, for most organizations, center around making more/spending less money).

Implementing environmental accounting is not fundamentally different from any other paradigm shift in an organization. For it to become a self-sustaining, permanent change in the way the organization conducts its business, many different players in diverse roles need to participate because they *want* to, not because they have to. Articulating clear objectives, instituting appropriate incentives, providing useful tools, and communicating effectively are key activities needed to catalyze this transformation.

Notes

1. *Pollution Prevention Benefits Manual,* prepared for U.S. Environmental Protection Agency by ICF Inc. (October 1989).

2. General Motors, *Environmental Report* (1994).

3. Robert Kainz, Manager, Life Cycle Management, Chrysler Corporation. Personal communication (March 1996).

4. Paul E. Bailey and Peter A. Soyka, "Making Sense of Environmental Accounting," 5 *Total Quality* Environmental *Management* (Spring 1996), pp. 1–15.

5. U.S. EPA, *Green Accounting at AT&T,* EPA 742-R-95-003 (September 1995).

6. *Full Cost Accounting for Decision-Making at Ontario Hydro* (1996).

7. Los Alamos National Laboratory report on research waste management costs and practices at 12 companies in the chemical and petrochemical industries, reported in *Weapons Complex Monitor* (December 13, 1995).

Paul E. Bailey is a senior vice president with the Environmental Consulting Group of ICF Kaiser International, Inc., headquartered in Fairfax, Virginia, where he leads work in environmental accounting, life-cycle costing/management, and the monetization of environmental liabilities. His work involves the development of decision aids for prioritization of environmental issues, selection of environmental management strategies, and financial evaluation of pollution prevention/waste minimization actions. **Peter A. Soyka** is a vice president with the Environmental Consulting Group of ICF Kaiser. He provides environmental management consulting services to private and public sector clients, focusing on improved, cost-effective environmental performance through better use of technology, pollution prevention and environmental accounting concepts, and quality management techniques.

22

Design for Environment:
A New Framework for Strategic Decisions

Michael Lenox and John R. Ehrenfeld

Design for environment (DFE) is emerging as a systematic approach to addressing the entire system of environmental impacts across the whole product life cycle. To this point, "design for environment" has been used in reference to a variety of practices and concepts. It has been defined both narrowly and broadly. In order to provide a foundation for discussion it is important that we establish a concise definition of DFE. As stated by EPA, "if used in a broad and simplistic way, DFE can be used to justify almost any efforts, even those that are not in the best interests of environmental preservation."[1] Conversely, if used too narrowly, DFE can fail to fully capture environmental improvement opportunities. In this chapter and in the studies out of which this chapter comes, the following definition is used:

> Design for environment is the systematic process by which firms design products and processes in an environmentally conscious way based on industrial ecology principles across the entire product life cycle.

There are three critical points in this definition of design for environment:

- Environmental impacts across the entire product life cycle are considered.
- Impacts are addressed during the product development cycle.
- Decision making is guided by a set of principles based on industrial ecology or some set of system-configured, integrative principles.

Further, "environmentally conscious" means that the design process, and all who participate in it, consider potential environmental impacts explicitly alongside and in the same manner as all other factors that influence the design process. Such consciousness should reveal environmental impacts and problems to be addressed over the entire life cycle of the product, but it does not mean or refer to any specific set of design criteria that must be met.[2]

Product Life Cycle

Design for environment considers the entire product life cycle. While other practices address particular flows or phases of the product life cycle, DFE, in its most robust form, considers all environmental impacts. Figure 22.1 provides a schema summarizing the areas of potential environmental impact across the entire product life cycle. Each of the arrows in the exhibit represents a material flow, be it a gas, liquid, or solid. Not depicted is the energy use during each phase and flow. The production of by-products and the use of secondary inputs within each phase are also included with the "product" streams. These materials may come directly from the environment or go through various production sequences and represent other product life cycles, demonstrating the interconnectedness of economic activity. Pollution represents any output that is not used as an input to another product life cycle. The pollutants' materials may be treated or released directly into the environment.

The product life cycle is a representation of the flows of materials and energy that accompany a product from the primary production of materials used in its construction to its ultimate end-of-life disposal, including its potential reincarnation as recovered parts or materials. Life-cycle analysis (LCA), as further elaborated below, is a systematic framework to identify and account for (inventory) all of these material and energy flows and their embodied environmental impact. As the discussion below will show, the relation of this set of

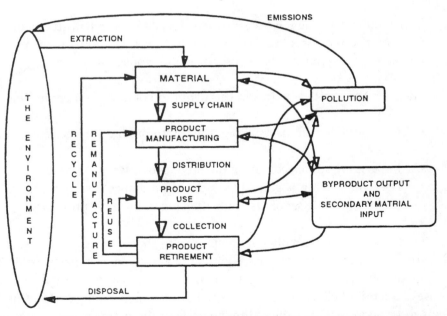

Figure 22.1 Potential Environmental Impacts across the Entire Product Life Cycle

inventory and impact assessments is only tenuously related to the design process. One of the critical elements in any DFE or environmentally conscious manufacturing (ECM) system is how well the LCA base is tied to and informs the designers.

Industrial Ecology

Design for environment guides decisions based on a set of normative objectives related to prevention of toxic impacts, resource conservation, avoidance of dysfunction in the natural system, and so on. There is no consensus on what this set of norms should be, nor is it likely that such a set will appear soon. This absence suggests that one of the key parts of any DFE procedure must be the selection of the environmental norms to guide the design. Our group has been working with one such set called "industrial ecology." Industrial ecology is a "holistic framework for guiding the transformation of the industrial system."[3] It provides the context in which decisions and designs concerning human economy can be made in an environmentally conscious manner. Industrial ecology frames "manufacturing and other activity as part of a larger ecological whole. In doing so, it takes a systems view of design and manufacturing activities in order to reduce or, more desirably, eliminate the environmental impacts of manufacturing processes, technologies and products across their life-cycles, including use and disposal."[4]

The fundamental normative premise behind industrial ecology is that industrial systems should perform like natural ecosystems, which frequently (but not always) exhibit dynamic stability over a wide range of perturbing forces. One key characteristic of natural ecosystems is that there is no such thing as "waste." Natural ecosystems do not produce materials, in any significant amounts, that are not used by some organism within the system. Materials flow through the system in closed-loop patterns. In this way, natural ecosystems behave in a sustainable fashion.

Fundamental to industrial ecology is that environmental impacts across the entire life cycle of products, from cradle to grave, be considered in decision making. It is in this way that industrial ecology is a *holistic* framework. Industrial ecology provides principles by which to guide actions that affect the entire product life cycle. For example, the principles can be organized as follows:[5]

- *Loop closing*—circulating material flows within the system.
- *Dematerialization*—reducing the material intensity in products that produce equivalent functions as those they replace.
- *Protecting the natural metabolism*—restricting the flow of substances that are harmful to natural systems and living organisms.

- *Systematizing energy use*—conserving energy and extracting as much of the available energy content from that which is used or, conversely, minimizing the flow of waste heat back to the environment.

Many of these principles are embodied in current environmental practices, such as:

- *Pollution control*—the treatment of pollutants in order to reduce their environmental impact on emissions.
- *Pollution prevention*—the reduction of pollutants across the entire life cycle. This may include the transfer of "pollutants" as inputs to other product life cycles.
- *Toxic use reduction*—the reduction of toxic materials throughout all flows, especially those that enter the environment or may affect humans.
- *Waste reduction or minimization*—the reduction of materials used in products to minimize "waste" during disposal.
- *Energy conservation*—the reduction of energy required during all phases of the life cycle.
- *Product use extension*—the reduction of the temporal flow of materials from extraction to disposal by extending the user life of products.
- *Recycling, remanufacturing, and reuse*—at the end of consumer use, the recycling, remanufacturing, and reuse of materials and components in an attempt to close the product life-cycle loop.
- *Environmentally conscious manufacturing*—the reduction of environmental impacts during the manufacturing/production phase of products. This embodies many of the notions above, such as pollution prevention and energy conservation as applied to the manufacturing phase.
- *Industrial symbiosis*—the "interaction among companies so that the residuals of one become the feedstock of another."[6] Converting pollutant, disposal, and energy flows into inputs to other product life cycles.

To this point, these practices have been primarily pursued in singular fashion. The strength of industrial ecology is in their joint application over the entire product life cycle. DFE, in its most robust form, systematically combines these practices.

The Product Development Cycle

Design for environment deals with the design of products and processes. For most firms, the creation and distribution of products and services are their primary functions. The process of design is critical to these endeavors. The design phase is where the dominant characteristics of a product are determined, and thus, the part of the product life cycle where the greatest environmental improvements can be introduced.

We may envision product development as a cycle running in conjunction with the product life cycle. The product development cycle is the process by which products and manufacturing processes are designed. In practice, numerous configurations of the product development cycle exist. Figure 22.2 provides a generic product development cycle.

This cycle is loosely based on the life-cycle design framework developed by the University of Michigan Pollution Prevention Program (sponsored by EPA). For our purposes, life-cycle design is equivalent to design for environment. Three main phases of a life-cycle design are the needs analysis, requirements specification, and design product solution.[7]

- *Needs analysis*—In this phase, the general product characteristics are shaped by identifying the particular consumer needs to be met.
- *Requirements specification*—During this phase, a product development team will design checklists, specify requirements, and rank and weigh the requirements.
- *Design product solution*—In this phase, the actual product design is conceived conceptually and, through an iterative process, developed into a detailed design.

We have added a fourth phase—manufacturing or process design. This category includes the design of the processes that convert the primary materials and component parts into the market-ready product. While, conceptually, product and manufacturing design may be considered to be one continuous function, typical industry practice is to separate the two. Manufacturing practices are typically characterized by innovations that become the standard practice for a relatively long period. These innovations often come from research and development efforts or through joint ventures and licensing agreements. New technologies and practices become the state of the art for a whole industrial sector through a diffusion process. Classic innovation/diffusion theory

| Needs Analysis |
| Requirements Specification |
| Design Product Solution |
| Design Manufacturing Solution |

Figure 22.2   The Product Development Cycle

applies most directly to manufacturing or process devices, including medical and other technologies.[8] Product design is a very different process: It is a continuous process to meet consumer needs. In large consumer goods firms, the consumer need is often established well before the product development cycle is begun. Product design can then be characterized as an evolutionary process of periodic changes to existing products, punctuated by the introduction of entirely new products on consumer technologies. A good example of this is the yearly update of automobile makes and models and the rapid succession of new personal computer models.

In practice, product development typically does not follow such a concise, linear process. In reality, the product development cycle can be characterized as follows. Once the decision to design a new product has been established, a management team, such as a business unit, determines the requirements of a particular design. These requirements are usually based on marketing concerns, but are also influenced by players such as the industrial designers. The requirements are given to an industrial design team, which comes up with a conceptual image. These teams are the "creative" force. They do not seek to optimize design, but, rather, to satisfy a series of constraints imposed by management, which, in turn, integrates the objectives coming from both the market and the company. The conceptual design is handed to engineering design groups, which provide a technical, detailed design. The whole process is interspersed with feedback and negotiation among industrial designers, engineers, and marketers. The overall negotiation is mediated and overseen by the business level management that usually has the final say in the design outcome. Eventually, a detailed product design is generated, which is then given to manufacturing. The "throw it over the wall" analogy often is used to describe the interface between these two groups. After the product design group has finished its work, the design is thrown over the wall to manufacturing, with limited subsequent interaction. Typically, this event initiates a second negotiation process between manufacturing and design, once again mediated by some management group. Each of the different groups within this process tend to have different educational backgrounds and cultures. Efforts toward concurrent engineering (i.e., an explicit structure to avoid over-the-wall practice and create integration of manufacturing concerns early on) are often hindered by these differences.

Current Status

The development and application of DFE practice is still in its infancy. An MIT group has been characterizing DFE practices in industrial settings. In our early research, the group has observed a variety of tools that have been developed or are being developed, but virtually none that have been adopted widely by industrial firms at this point. This may be attributed to two factors. First, the tools developed, to this point, have failed to provide for a transparent, detailed approach to design that is easily implemented. The tools so far have focused on the analytic and informational aspects of environmental impacts but have lacked elements reflecting the transformation to design features. Many point to specific practices and materials that should or must be avoided but do not, as yet, include positive guides for what constitutes environmentally sound practice.

The second is a lack of understanding on how DFE can be successfully implemented within the organizational context. By this, we mean that the tools fail to incorporate a sense of design as it is actually done by designers in an organization. While much research is under way into designing better tools, little work has been done to examine effective environmental management systems for design for environment. The importance of DFE tools is directly linked to how corporations manage environmental and other concerns in design. Tools may be necessary, but not sufficient, in an effective DFE program. It is important not only that tools exist, but also that they are used effectively in the organizational context. For this reason, it is important to examine what kinds of tools exist and how various firms are incorporating design for environment, including the use of these tools, into their practices.

Trends in Environmental Design Tools

Tools are available and being developed to aid in designing environmentally conscious processes and products. These tools represent a wide array of approaches to DFE. Among the tools, we have observed three general schools, or spheres of influence: life-cycle analysis, environmentally conscious manufacturing, and design for environment. While each school has its own actors, concepts, and tools, it is important to recognize there is much cross communication and exchange among these schools.

Life-Cycle Analysis Tools

Life-cycle analysis as a concept has been around for decades. The earliest reference to its use in the United States is a study, done around 1967, of alternatives for beverage containers. LCA systems attempt to gather information on environmental flows (emissions and resource consumption) and their consequent impacts across the entire product life cycle. Historic LCA use has exhibited wide variations in the scope of the set of life-cycle stages and of the flows (Figure 22.1). The Society of Environmental Toxicologists and Chemists (SETAC) helped standardize practice with the publication of its LCA guidelines.[9] The approach, championed by SETAC, is divided into three distinct and sequential phases: inventory, impact, and improvement. Inventory analysis is the collecting and organizing of environmental data across the entire product life cycle. Impact analysis is the conversion and aggregation of inventory data into various environmental impacts. Finally, improvement analysis is the identification and consideration of alternative means to reduce and eliminate the impacts identified in the middle stage.

LCA has been used predominantly in one of three capacities: comparison of alternative designs, general understanding of the environmental implications of a given design, and reporting or communicating the results of an analysis. The early uses of LCAs were typically to compare two products to determine which was more environmentally benign. Examples include the numerous studies comparing cloth to disposable diapers and paper to plastic cups. Increasingly, LCAs are being used to reflect on the environmental impact of current products in or being developed for the marketplace. This information is used to identify areas for improvement and provide a baseline for future designs. With the advent of eco-labeling, practices as well as standards for practice (such as the ISO 14000 series of environmental management standards), LCA is being used increasingly as a reporting mechanism.

Several software tools have been developed in the last few years, based on the SETAC methodology. Almost all are tools for the inventory step only. They typically contain and organize vast amounts of environmental data. Using some form of product structure module, a summary of the materials and energy used in each phase of the product life cycle is provided. This information can then be used by designers to assess the environmental performance of a particular design. The vast amounts of data necessary just to create a tool for a single industry or class of products complicates the development of general-purpose LCA inventory tools. Tools appear to be developing fast with attempts being made to move beyond inventory to consider impact. One example, SimaPro, a tool developed by PRé Consultants, has the functional capacity to aggregate inventory data into impacts.[10]

Environmentally Conscious Manufacturing

Environmentally conscious manufacturing (ECM) is largely distinct from activities being called design for environment, although the two names are often used interchangeably. ECM is a collection of tools and practices that seek to minimize the environmental impact of production. ECM has arisen within the manufacturing community, not the product design arena. This is not surprising, given the cultural and organizational divisions between product and process design teams. Interest in ECM seems to be primarily concentrated in the chemical and continuous process industries where design is typically more concerned with process than product.

Most of the tools being developed to this point have been industry-specific. Attempts are being made to create more general ECM software that crosses industries. In some respects, ECM has been practiced within some industries for decades. The design of manufacturing processes has often sought to minimize "waste." Discharges are typically treated or recycled directly back into process systems to minimize material flow out of the system.

Design for Environment

The DFE community is the newest of the three identified so far. Many of the people interested in design for environment come from an LCA or ECM background. The tools being developed represent a wide array of techniques. These tools can be distinguished from LCA and ECM in that they are not as comprehensive as a life-cycle analysis and are concerned with product more than with manufacturing.

To this point, only a few tools have been developed that concentrate on providing top-level qualitative analysis. One novel approach, which moves beyond the traditional notions of product design is Ottman's "Getting to Zero" process.[11] Rather than refining a product, this method seeks to "reinvent" the product in a more environmentally conscious manner. Such a method is well suited for the needs analysis of product development. Various other approaches exist that rely on the use of preestablished guidelines and checklists to aid design. These tools are best for facilitating requirements specification. Using expert knowledge, constraints and processes are imposed on design to achieve desired environmental performance. The MILION method is one such approach to environmentally conscious design, which utilizes checklists and guidelines.[12] Another approach is the use of milestone questions to be answered by project managers, which are in turn used to guide design.[13]

Given the complexity of environmental concerns, it may be that a qualitative approach, which facilitates a comparative analysis between potential environmental impacts, is of the greatest value. Along these lines, semiquantitative methods have been developed. One of the most accepted of these methods is the matrix approach.[14] The matrix approach provides a means to assemble environmental data about the impacts of products and processes across their entire life cycle. While the matrix method does not normally provide a prescriptive for action, it does aid in illuminating the environmental consequences of design alternatives.

One of the dominant premises of industrial ecology is the need to "close the loop" of the product life cycle. This is most often realized in the reuse, remanufacturing, and recycling of materials at the end of consumer use. It has been recognized that it is during the design phase when "retirement impacts and tradeoffs with other objectives can be addressed most effectively."[15] Material selection and the ease and cost of disassembly factor into design teams' consideration of product retirement. Along these lines, software has been developed that facilitates design for retirement. Foremost among these is ReStar, originally developed at Carnegie-Mellon University.[16] ReStar calculates an optimal retirement plan based on a product's design. A product disassembly diagram is used to determine the cost associated with retirement options such as disassembly, reuse, recycling, and disposal. While other objectives may be chosen, the primary goal of ReStar is to identify a cost-effective retirement program.

Few attempts have been made to provide a *comprehensive* quantitative DFE tool that facilitates comparative analysis between design alternatives. Completed tools that provide a comprehensive DFE approach have yet to be identified.

Trends in Environmental Management Systems

Design for environment works within the larger corporate environmental management system. "A corporation's environmental management system supports environmental improvement through a number of key components including environmental policy and goals, performance measures, and a strategic plan."[17] The importance of DFE tools is directly linked to how corporations manage environmental concerns in design. It is important that not only do tools exist, but also that they are used effectively in the organizational context.

Through our research, we have identified the following three ways by which firms are managing their environmentally conscious design function:

1. Designing products and processes that address a specific environmental impact of concern.
2. Providing continuous feedback to product design groups through a corporate or central environmental group that provides expertise on environmental design.
3. Integrating environmental considerations directly into product design groups.

Addressing Specific Environmental Concerns

Often, external events force firms to address specific environmental impacts. Regulation or heightened consumer awareness may require immediate changes in corporate practices. Many firms design products and processes that avoid a specific environmental impact when the need arises. One example is the elimination of CFCs in products and processes in light of concerns about ozone depletion. Typically, such an approach to DFE is ad hoc, coming from teams organized to address the specific problem at hand. Many companies are now developing systems to alert designers and operations staff to chemicals that are regulated or are to be regulated under the Clean Air Act of 1990 and other regulations, along with accompanying policies for the avoidance of their use. Often the administrative efforts to develop these systems are augmented by research and development groups.

Receiving Consultation from Corporate Environmental Group

Many firms address environmental concerns through a corporate or central environmental group. Design teams and product development teams may, but do not have to, consult with this group on environmental matters. The central environmental group behaves as experts on environmental design. They keep track of latest developments and practices and may perform functions from implementing a full life-cycle analysis on a design to suggesting what are environmentally friendly practices.

Incorporation of DFE into Design Groups

Some firms are beginning to incorporate environmental guidelines and objectives directly within the family of constraints to be addressed by product development groups. Typically, this is accomplished in one of two fashions. In one, environmental concerns are addressed only after an initial design has been created. A design team will fully design a product or process; then, this design will be assessed against environmental performance metrics and necessary changes made. In the other, environmental concerns are considered concurrently with other design parameters. From the initial design process, designers are aware of environmental constraints and objectives. For these few firms, DFE is not an add-on consideration, but a fully integrated aspect of design.

A Taxonomy of Tools

In an attempt to better characterize design for environment tools, we have developed the taxonomy shown in Figure 22.3. The purpose of this taxonomy is to move beyond the somewhat artificial distinctions described above and to categorize tools more on functionality. There are three dimensions along which we characterize existing tools. The four phases of product development outlined above represent our first dimension. The second dimension is the particular stage or stages of the product life cycle that the tools address. The final dimension is the degree of decision-making support, using the three steps in the SETAC system as metrics, provided by a tool. The three are further detailed below.

Applicability to various product development cycle phases: Based on our observations, it appears that many tools developed to this point have not considered the product development cycle phase in which they are to be implemented. Often, the tools may have value in each of the product development phases, although there is one phase in which their benefit is greatest. In most cases, the developers of the tools do not appear to have considered the development cycle explicitly. It is important to note that the effectiveness of a tool will be greatly affected by how and where in the product development process a tool is used.

Applicability to various product life-cycle stages: While ideally a design for environment tool will consider impacts across the entire life cycle, most cur-

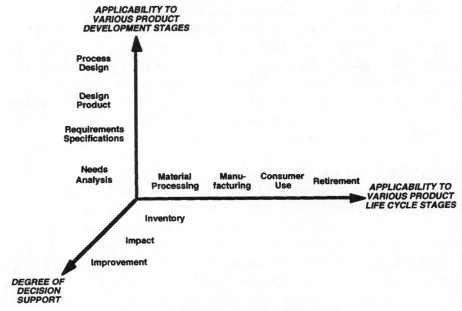

Figure 22.3   A Classification of DFE Tools

rently existing tools address only a few stages. To this point, most tools have addressed one of two phases: the manufacturing and retirement phases.

Degree of decision support: The degree and the manner in which tools provide decision support varies greatly. Borrowing from SETAC's guidelines for life-cycle assessment, we have identified three levels of support: inventory, impact, and improvement. While SETAC and others have developed specific methods associated with each of these levels, we use them simply as broad categories to classify tools. Inventory tools provide data on environmental attributes of a design. Impact tools aggregate data into various environmental impacts. Finally, improvement tools facilitate the selection of alternative design characteristics.

While not included in our taxonomy, we may consider a fourth dimension as well—that is, the type of product or industry. Many of the current tools have been designed to be applicable only to a narrow collection of industries or product forms.

Future Needs and Observations

In light of continued realizations about the environmental limits of our world, corporations will need to be increasingly proactive in addressing environmental concerns in order to remain competitive. Current and pending regulations, as well as potential liability and consumer demand, pose significant financial and competitive hardships on firms that fail to manage environmental impacts. These issues are increasingly important, given the expanding global economy. Environmental regulations will not only affect domestic activity, but will also be important in international trade. Furthermore, the growing acceptance of voluntary codes of conduct, such as Responsible Care® and the upcoming ISO 14000 standards, will place even greater pressure on firms to account systematically for the whole life-cycle set of environmental impacts and take steps to avoid or minimize them. Increasingly, firms that eliminate negative environmental impacts from their activities most effectively will be the most competitive in the global market. For these firms, the acceptance and diffusion of DFE practices will be critical to their success.

The incorporation of DFE practices into firms poses some interesting and unique challenges. Environmental issues are usually characterized by dynamic and uncertain behavior. Knowledge of potential environmental impacts is not always available during the design phase and, if it is, resides in places other than the designers' corporate homes or may be missing from the firm as a whole. Typically, the time and cost of collecting sufficient data to address environmental concerns are unacceptable, relative to the resources available for any given project. The difficulty in aggregating environmental impacts into meaningful measures of environmental performance complicates matters further. Finally, in the real world, environmental objectives will always be compared to and traded off with other objectives, particularly cost and performance. These last two are certainly dominant in the design and development of products competing in consumer markets.

With this background on the current state of tools to support DFE activities and other complicating factors, we finish with some general ideas of how to go about developing such tools and placing them in an organization in an effective manner. The following are four key elements necessary for an effective design for environment approach:

- Design metrics to support objective assessments (preferably quantitative) of environmental quality;
- Design guidelines or rules to assure that environmental concerns are introduced early in the design process;
- Design verification methods to review and assess proposed designs with respect to the above metrics; and
- Design decision frameworks to support system-level tradeoffs between environmental quality and the many interrelated quality metrics.[18]

While these items are useful in suggesting the analytic component of any general system, they are insufficient in terms of producing a new consciousness described earlier. The tools must wake up designers to these new aspects of the objects they create. They are new and unfamiliar at present. The focus on quantitation is appealing, but the developers of DFE systems may shy away from the more critical current need to change the context and cultural structures that create the transparency and routinization of environmental concerns in the product development cycle. Having extensive data on the impacts and their consequences is essential, but the information does not tell designers what features they should introduce into the products and processes to avoid these impacts, except for some of the more obvious cases of substitutes for or minimizing the use of harmful pollutants.

The first step is to begin to use whatever tools are emerging. They are as yet embryonic and incomplete, but contain the means to begin the process of consciousness raising and already capture new normative concerns. They will improve with practice, as will the skills of those who use them. If designed well, they will ultimately facilitate the conversion of what must be analytical and theoretical skills to the same kind of deep-seated competence of master designers, skills that are observed in practice but that cannot be put into words by their masters.

Notes

1. Jean Parker and Beverly Boyd, "An Introduction to EPA's Design for the Environment Program," *IEEE Symposium on Electronics and the Environment,* Washington, DC, May 1993.

2. Consciousness is an important part of design. The primary meaning referred to in this article comes from Anthony Giddens (*The Constitution of Society,* University of California Press, 1984) and other sociologists in the structuration school. Giddens distinguished two forms of consciousness, which he called practical consciousness and discursive consciousness. He added a third category, unconsciousness. Practical consciousness includes the deeply embedded structures, rules, norms, and so on that people use in routine activities. Discursive consciousness is the set of explanations, as theory or other rules of action, that actors give if asked how they have a particular act. Giddens and others argue that discursive precedes practical consciousness. At this early time in the history of environmental design, little or no mastery exists, so we may say that environmental consciousness in the designer community exists only at the level of discursive (explicit) consciousness. Thus, our present criterion that environmental consciousness be explicit comes with the expectation that, over time and routinization of the design functions, practical (implicit) consciousness will develop, and the design process will become more and more seamless and transparent, as is the case for well-established design studios.

3. Ernest Lowe, "Industrial Ecology: a Context for Design and Decision," *Design for Environment: Principles and Practices,* New York: Fiksel, McGraw-Hill, Inc., 1996.

4. Braden Allenby, "Industrial Ecology Gets Down to Earth," 10 *IEEE Circuits and Devices* 1, 1994.

5. John R. Ehrenfeld, "Industrial Ecology: A Strategic Framework for Product Policy and Other Sustainable Practices," Prepared for *Green Goods, The Second International Conference on Product Oriented Policy,* September 1994.

6. Lowe (cited in note 3).

7. Gregory Keoleian and Dan Menerey, "Sustainable Development by Design: Review of Life Cycle Design and Related Approaches," 44 *Air and Waste* 5, May 1994, pp. 645–668.

8. James M. Utterback, "Innovation in Industry and the Diffusion of Technology," 183 *Science* 4125, 1974, pp. 620–626.

9. James Fava, "Life Cycle Thinking: Application to Product Design," *IEEE Symposium on Electronics and the Environment,* Washington, DC, May 1993.

10. PRé Consultants, Bergstraat 6, 3811NH Amersfoot, The Netherlands.

11. "Design for Environment: Gaining Ground, but not in the Mainstream Yet," *Business and the Environment,* July 1994.

12. Ger Duijf and Harry Verkooyen, "Product Design Becomes Life Cycle Design," Contribution to *TERMIE Workshop "Recycling of Materials,"* March 1994.

13. Troels Keldmann and Jesper Olesen, "Managing the Environmental Issue in Product Development: The Environmentally Oriented Milestone Questions and Techniques," *Design for Manufacturability,* DE—Vol. 67. ASME 1994.

14. Braden Allenby, "Design for Environment: A Tool Whose Time Has Come," *Semiconductor Safety Association Journal,* September 1991.

15. Carol Troy, J.C. Fu, and Kazuo Mori, "Ecologically Conscious Manufacturing: Analysis of Current Trends in Design for Product Retirement Software," Presented at the Japan-U.S. Symposium on Flexible Automation, Kobe, Japan, July 1994.

16. Carol Troy, J.C. Fu, Stephen Wong, and Fritz Eubanks, "Design for Product Retirement Software: A Primer and a Comparative Survey," Presented at the 8th Conference with Industry: Partnering for Competitive Manufacturing Processes, Lehigh University, Bethlehem, Pennsylvania, May, 1994.

17. Keoleian and Menerey (cited in note 7).

18. Joseph Fiksel, "Design for Environment: An Integrated Systems Approach," *IEEE Symposium on Electronics and the Environment,* May 1993.

Michael Lenox is a graduate research assistant in the MIT Program on Technology, Business, and Environment, an interdisciplinary educational, research, and policy program. His research interests involve the way businesses manage environmental concerns. **John R. Ehrenfeld** is senior research associate in the MIT Center for Technology, Policy, and Industrial Development and has additional appointments as senior lecturer in the interdepartmental Technology and Policy Program and in the Departments of Chemical Engineering and Civil and Environmental Engineering. He directs the MIT Program on Technology, Business, and Environment, an interdisciplinary educational, research, and policy program.

23

Industry Cases and Practices: Implementing Design for Environment at AT&T

Barry F. Dambach and Braden R. Allenby

AT&T, as a worldwide manufacturer and service provider, now has operations in all corners of the globe that must continue to address environmental concerns to reduce their environmental impact on the surrounding community. We recognize that, as responsible corporate citizens and a leader in environmental activities, AT&T has a responsibility to minimize wastes and emissions, develop clean technologies and environmentally responsible products, and share this information with its neighbors.

Many of today's environmental problems, such as ozone depletion, global climate change, acid rain, groundwater contamination, and increasing volumes of solid waste, affect the air, land, and water we all need to survive. Through TQEM, AT&T now recognizes that reducing the wastes and emissions generated today and in the future must be addressed through a multimedia approach in the initial product/process design. This is the only way to ensure a suitable and sustainable quality of life for future generations worldwide.

Like most companies, AT&T began by looking at the wastes and emissions it was generating; in fact, waste reduction and prevention have always been a part of any successful enterprise. Historically, as within AT&T, it was part of cost-reduction programs to increase efficiencies and maintain competitiveness for manufacturing products. With the onset of more restrictive waste management regulations, and skyrocketing waste management, treatment, and disposal costs, waste reduction and prevention were, and still are, seen as playing a greater role in remaining competitive worldwide.

AT&T saw its customers begin to demand that products be built with a minimum of impact on the environment. They were trying to influence manufacturers through the direct purchase of products they perceive to be better for the environment and through their political backing of "green" representatives and programs. Legislation at all political levels was being written that mandated the reduction of use of toxics; process emission and waste minimization; product waste minimization, through recycling; and product life extension.

We believed that the key to maintaining and enhancing a leadership position in environmental activities, as recognized by customers, local citizens, industry, regulatory bodies, and private environmental groups, would be the utilization and deployment of quality principles in this area. Management has made a total and enduring commitment to quality to guarantee continued long- and short-term business success, as well. It was through the deployment of quality principles that AT&T successfully reduced and prevented waste and emissions from manufacturing operations.

Programs to protect the environment and improve quality from manufacturing operations were not new. What was new was the use of total quality management to specifically address multimedia waste prevention and reduction.

Total Quality Management

TQM consists of continuous process improvement activities involving everyone in an organization, managers and workers, in a totally integrated effort toward improving performance at every level. This improved performance is directed toward satisfying such cross-functional goals as quality, cost schedules, mission, need, and suitability. TQM integrates fundamental management techniques, existing improvement efforts, and technical tools under a disciplined approach focused on continuous improvement. The activities are ultimately focused on increased customer/user satisfaction.

The management process that is being used to engage all AT&T employees in the achievement of corporate goals is policy deployment. This is the executive deployment of selected policy-driven priorities and the necessary resources to achieve performance breakthroughs. It is a management framework based on facts, data, and customer satisfaction that creates a powerful structure for communicating corporate goals and then implementing them through specific projects and plans.

Successful implementation of policy deployment depends on paying constant attention to the ways in which each employee's daily work is clearly connected to achieving corporate goals and exceeding customer expectations. This connection, the "golden thread," helps everyone in the company focus on how they can add to the success of the business and encourages participation in teams. Individual project teams, many of them cross-functional, use standard quality improvement processes to reduce gaps between corporate goals and corporate performance.

AT&T Policy for Environmental Protection

In 1973, AT&T's manufacturing subsidiary, Western Electric, first issued a corporate environmental policy that laid the foundation for a waste minimization program. With divestiture and a restructuring of the company, an AT&T

Policy for Environmental Protection was issued, recommitting the company to the concepts of the original policy. Policy deployment is the process being used to implement this environmental policy throughout the company.

AT&T's policy for environmental protection goes beyond just meeting regulatory compliance. It commits the company to develop and use nonpolluting technologies, minimize wastes, increase recycling, design products and processes with environmental impact as a critical factor, and to instill in all employees an awareness of environmental responsibilities and practices. Most fundamentally, the recently updated policy commits the company to the life-cycle approach and the use of DFE practices throughout the organization. AT&T will deploy this policy as part of its overall quality policy, and it will be an integrated part of business plans.

Corporate Environmental Goals

This policy has initiated several corporate environmental goals that apply to AT&T's operations worldwide. Achieving these goals results in multimedia waste prevention and reduction. These goals were endorsed by the company's chief executive officer and board of directors, and included the following:

1. CFC emissions phaseout from manufacturing
2. Toxic air emissions elimination (SARA)
   Striving for 100 percent by 2000
3. Decrease total manufacturing process
4. Increase recycling of paper to 60 percent
5. Decrease paper use 15 percent

These were intentionally set as "stretch" goals. Striving to achieve far-reaching goals forces you to look for breakthrough technologies, which are needed to attain the highest levels of quality. These goals were, and continue to be, benchmarked against the best companies in the class so that we can continue to strive to be the best.

Deployment Process

The quality policy deployment process, by definition, has overcome many of the perceived impediments to multimedia waste prevention and reduction. A companywide awareness program was implemented so all employees would recognize that top-level management is committed to environmental protection. AT&T realizes that wastes and emissions are quality defects and, to remain competitive from a business standpoint, these must be minimized. This requires us, for example, to review all processes on an ongoing basis, develop data of quantities of waste generated and management/disposition costs, and invest in research for alternate processes and materials that will allow the company to continue to supply quality products while minimizing wastes.

Through policy deployment, the environmental goals are elevated to a similar level with other customer requirements, such as product performance, reliability, and price. The strategic planning organizations for the business units and divisions are developing the programs needed to attain the environmental goals in their short- and long-term plans and budgets. As many of the "easy" or "housekeeping" actions have already been done in the plants, resources for capital equipment and new technologies must be identified and appropriated early in the fiscal budget process.

Pollution Prevention

TQM tells us that preventing defects is more cost-effective, and provides more opportunities for improvement, than dealing with them after the fact. Hence, pollution prevention became the next focused effort to meet environmental challenges. To this end, AT&T participated in two major benchmarking studies. The first, with Intel, was intended to help understand the critical elements needed for a successful corporate-level pollution prevention program. The next, with the Business Roundtable, was to determine the similarities and differences of the critical elements at the facility level.

This information was utilized to develop the basic level program and to provide some tools and structure for the company's individual manufacturing facilities. One important finding was that each company or facility with a successful program had the critical factors, which are basically TQM principles, but had adapted them to fit into their existing culture. There is no one-size-fits-all program that will work for everyone. The program champions also had to determine the best method within their existing culture to make the changes necessary to change that culture and thinking toward pollution prevention and away from the end of the pipe. This also required the engagement of an expanded set of people within the firm to address the issues. Product and process engineers, production staff, facility services, research and development, and others as appropriate were asked to join teams to work with the environmental staff to find solutions.

Getting to Design for Environment (DFE)

TQM trains us to continually focus more upstream to get to the root causes of issues. Therefore, TQEM points us to the design stage and the decisions that are made during a product or process design. Once we recognize that more than 80 percent of the materials, processes, and, therefore, wastes are locked in by the initial design, it becomes clear that this is the place to focus more effort to obtain the most cost-effective solutions over the long run. The progress made through the implementation of TQEM and the pollution prevention efforts has led to the cultural and mind-set changes that enable AT&T to look even further upstream to the design process. Hence the linkages between TQEM and DFE.

To begin to really understand the concepts and reasons for DFE, we must first recognize the still-evolving, larger intellectual framework within which global environmental issues are being addressed. This framework, shown in Figure 23.1, is anchored by a multidisciplinary field known as industrial ecology.[1]

Sustainable Development is both the goal and the vision that supports the framework. Defined as development that meets the needs of the present generation without compromising the ability of future generations to meet theirs,[2] the concept is inherently ambiguous. It is also for some people ideologically charged, in that, in many formulations, it implies a need for some form of population stabilization and a redistribution of wealth from developed to developing countries. It is thus both contentious and difficult to operationalize (what does it mean, for example, to design a "sustainable" widget?). Nonetheless, the concept is quite powerful as a goal and, in fact, is being used as such by the government of the Netherlands, which has the most sophisticated government programs in this area.[3] Sustainability, in some form, is therefore an appropriate goal—in fact, the only appropriate systems-based goal—for the integration of science, technology, economic activity, and environment.

Industrial Ecology is the developing multidisciplinary field focusing on the system that consists of the linkages between the economic (artifactual) and natural systems. It has been defined in the first textbook on the subject:[4]

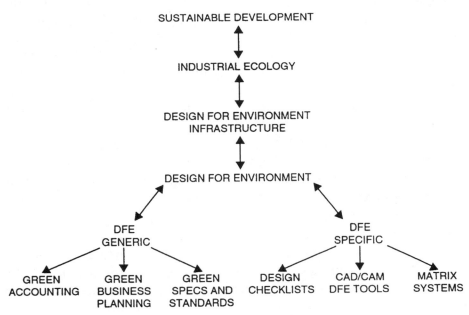

Figure 23.1 Industrial Ecology Framework

Industrial ecology is the means by which humanity can deliberately and rationally approach and maintain a desirable carrying capacity, given continued economic, cultural, and technological evolution.

The concept requires that an industrial system be viewed not in isolation from its surrounding systems, but in concert with them.

It is a systems view in which one seeks to optimize the total materials cycle from virgin material, to finished material, to component, to product, to obsolete product, and to ultimate disposal. Factors to be optimized include resources, energy, and capital.

Industrial ecology will form the objective basis on which choices leading to more sustainable economic activity can be based; it is, to oversimplify, the science of sustainability. Although it is still nascent, it offers a number of operational principles, including that which is most fundamental for our purposes: the need to focus on the rapid evolution of environmentally appropriate technological systems if regional and global environmental perturbations are to be mitigated.

Design for Environment (DFE), the driving of environmental concerns, objectives, and constraints into product and process design, is the means by which industrial ecology can begin to be implemented in the real world today. DFE begins to address these issues up front, where the life-cycle impact of products and processes is being determined through the selection of raw materials and manufacturing processes to be utilized. The economic and social systems within which these products are used must also be redesigned to integrate these environmental considerations. It is also recognized that new, environmentally appropriate, technology will be a key to reaching and maintaining a sustainable state. In particular, electronics and telecommunications will allow the substitution of intellectual and information capital for traditional physical capital, energy, and material inputs.

DFE that will be implemented within most firms will consist of two components: generic DFE and specific DFE. Generic DFE includes programs implemented across the firm that make its operations more environmentally preferable. Examples include standard components lists that have been developed with their environmental life cycle considered, and "green" accounting systems that allocate the environmental activities at the plant back to the individual product and process line to assure that the environmental issues are managed and DFE implemented. Another critical aspect is the inclusion of provisions for the use of environmentally preferable technologies and materials in contracts and specifications. An example is writing product specifications to allow the use of recycled materials.

Specific DFE gets down to the individual product and process level. It is included as another of the many "design for X" items that make up the product realization process. Other examples of "X" include assembly, reliability, testability, and manufacturability. Specific DFE includes computer-aided design (CAD) tools, software, and checklists to assist in the decision-making process. This also includes the implementation of "green" manufacturing processes, such as no-clean technologies.

Implementing DFE will require some organizational changes as the environment is integrated into the firm's technologies. This is a complex task, as it is not just about technology but also about cultural change, not just for the firm but also for its customers and suppliers as well. As the focus moves beyond compliance, it will require the development of new tools, competencies, and new skill sets among numerous personnel. In addition, much of the information that will be needed to conduct, for example, full life-cycle analyses will have to be developed and maintained in databases that are available to all.

Many of the same issues that arise when implementing any new quality initiative are also present when trying to implement TQEM and DFE. Experience in industry to date indicates that organizational and psychological barriers to the introduction of DFE are frequently far more significant than lack of appropriate technology. It is therefore necessary to initiate all of the activities usually involved in culture change in complex organizations: Champions must be identified and supported; reasons for resisting change must be identified and managed; methods of introducing DFE so that it is least threatening and closely resembles existing practices must be developed. Strong rationales for the program, specific to the firm's activities, should be developed and socialized throughout the firm. More subtle, but equally important, the tendency to treat organizational culture issues (which are difficult and complex, and require time to manage) as technological or R&D issues (which can be handled with rational, relatively rapid solutions) must be avoided. Initially, in fact, it is probably more important to concern oneself with changing corporate attitudes and thinking, getting the process started, and raising awareness, rather than worrying too much about the accuracy of the life-cycle analysis methodologies used. These will have to be adapted and updated as the program matures. Sophisticated methodologies will not do any good if they are not utilized.

DFE is not, and in most firms never will be, a traditional environment and safety (E&S) function. This is partly a matter of tactics: Financial personnel will put a lot more credence in a green accounting module that comes from the CFO's office than one coming from E&S. Similarly, engineering and technical managers are more likely to trust and use design tools coming from their R&D

organizations and product development laboratories, rather than those coming from the E&S organization. In these cases, as in others, this is simply a recognition that the E&S group may be competent in environmental issues, but not in financial methodologies or CAD/CAM tools.

The role of the E&S organization will be to provide technical support to the design community as it evaluates decisions, and E&S may be called on to initiate, facilitate, and drive the implementation of DFE, as is the case within AT&T. It should be noted that while DFE programs can, and, if properly implemented, will reduce the exposure of a firm to regulations over time, and thus reduce resources required for compliance activities, firms should not reduce their support of compliance programs and resources. It will require time, even under the best of circumstances, to enact the culture changes needed for DFE to significantly reduce the compliance burden, especially with the continuing trend in the increase in quantity and complexity of environmental regulations globally.

Implementing DFE

To step up to these challenges, AT&T has taken a number of concrete steps to utilize TQEM principles and implement DFE. It has established a DFE organization because experience has demonstrated that trying to support DFE activities as simply an adjunct to existing operations—"additional responsibilities as assigned"—is inadequate, given the magnitude of the necessary culture and organizational changes required for DFE implementation. AT&T has chosen to locate this in the E&S organization to jump-start the process as pending international standards and regulations requiring DFE-type approaches are being followed by this organization. There is, however, a strong argument to be made for centering DFE operations in an R&D or product development organization, rather than in the E&S group. In many cases, this seems to facilitate presenting environment as strategic, rather than as overhead. Your firm's culture must, as always, be considered and the DFE organization located where you feel it has the most opportunity to implement the changes needed.

Next, AT&T established a system of teams to guide the implementation of DFE (and also to facilitate the socialization of the concept within the firm). This includes the AT&T DFE Coordinating Team, with broad, cross-functional, representation from business units and support organizations. Under this umbrella team, there is a series of subteams to address specific programs: the Green Accounting Subteam, the DFE Technical Methods Subteam, the Energy Subteam, the Product Takeback Subteam, to name a few.

Next, the AT&T environmental policy was updated to reflect the change in direction and the recognition that customers are making greater demands on companies from an environmental viewpoint. Two key additions include the following:

[We will] utilize design for environment principles to design, develop, manufacture, and market products and services worldwide with environmentally preferable and energy-efficient life-cycle properties, and support our customers' and suppliers' efforts to do the same.

[We will] promote achievement of environmental excellence by designing new generations of processes, products, and services to be environmentally preferable to the ones they replace.

The company is currently formalizing a training program. A course has been delivered to several design groups for some of its major product lines. This consists of a two- to four-hour program that covers the drivers for DFE, some fundamental DFE principles, and use of the internally developed assessment matrices, and can be coupled with a working session with the designers to answer some specific design questions. The next step is the development of a more formal training program to be held periodically through the company's technical education system. These courses should be aimed at product and process designers, engineers, and managers to get the most impact. These people all have to be brought around to the realization that the environment has become strategic to business and not just an overhead item.

The integration of technology and environment within the firm will raise many questions and functional issues as it goes forward. Such questions will frequently raise issues of law and regulation (globally), product positioning, marketing, product and process design, and environmental science. Moreover, in many cases, the methodologies and data necessary for solutions to issues will be nonexistent or highly uncertain. Accordingly, it is important to establish a capability to rapidly access the most sophisticated resources within the firm to respond to such questions quickly and professionally. AT&T, for example, has established a DFE Rapid Response Team, which responds to queries from concurrent engineering teams, manufacturing engineers, product managers, and others within a time frame to meet the customers' needs. These issues can be very complex and have technical, political, economic, cultural, as well as environmental components. This team should expect to get the tough questions because the design teams will be able to answer many of the more routine items. An additional duty of the team is to distribute their response broadly throughout the company, so that uniform policies can be established and followed.

You will need to establish the capability to review and adapt the best DFE methodologies for your firm's purposes. Many life-cycle assessment methodologies available today, for example, are extremely complex and resource-intensive, and are not appropriate for complex manufactured articles such as electronics products. Use of the wrong tool can waste significant amounts of money and time, and provide much useless data but little information. Accordingly, AT&T has developed a set of matrix tools that permit it to evaluate the life-cycle impacts of complex items such as facilities, computers and telephones.[5] Obviously, some detail is lost in such global assessments—but they can be performed in one or two days by a DFE professional, capture most major life-cycle environmental impacts, target major areas for improvement and research, and are practical in considering the other design criteria and a real business environment. Over time, AT&T will develop a much more sophisticated and targeted set of tools; for now, the emphasis is on getting started and learning as we go.

When beginning a new process or direction, it is always important to choose targets of opportunity. TQM encourages building on successes so that a few successes, whether they involve product redesign or process improvement, can not only help educate the internal DFE teams and fine-tune the methodologies, but can also be used to help encourage further improvement throughout the firm. Accordingly, it is useful to select a few "showcase projects" as initial efforts, but be careful not to choose projects that are too complex or problematic.

We feel it is important to establish a DFE outreach or external affairs program. In such a cutting-edge area, where advances are being made in widely diverse locations and entities, it is important to establish a network of relationships that allows one to keep up with the field and integrate the latest thinking into the firm's programs. Relationships with other firms, academic institutions, national laboratories and governments at all levels (local, state, national, and global) should be established as part of this activity. Particular attention should be paid to jurisdictions, such as the Netherlands, Germany, or Sweden, that tend to be leaders in their thinking about product-oriented environmental management systems.

It is becoming more apparent that an accurate cost accounting (or "green accounting") system for waste management and environmental activities is essential not only to give the environmental projects an equal chance of receiving needed resources, but also to get an accurate description of the true environmental costs associated with the manufacture of each product. It will also be necessary to track the full life-cycle environmental cost for a product. This information will be used to drive the desired behaviors needed for DFE to be successful. It is also believed that when these costs are identified, the more environmentally preferable solutions will also be the best business decisions. AT&T has selected activity-based costing as the means to implement this, as it drives the costs to the cost drivers or root causes. Most environmental costs are still included in the overhead accounts for the facility and are allocated using methods that may have been appropriate for labor-intensive operations, but that will not be so in today's high-tech electronics industry, where labor is continually becoming a smaller portion of the total product cost.

Conclusion

Implementation of DFE within the firm is quickly becoming a necessity, especially for companies looking to compete globally. Customer demands, government regulations, international standards, constrained natural resources, and other forces are combining to make the environment strategic instead of just overhead. TQEM provides many of the basic tools, methodologies, and principles needed to implement the necessary changes within a company in a systematic, cost-effective, and customer-focused manner. In the wave of successful quality implementation programs throughout companies, it is critical if change is to be implemented to show the linkages between DFE and the other quality improvement programs.

Some other key thoughts and lessons learned for getting started:

- Dedicate people to the effort; don't just add it to the responsibilities of already overloaded individuals.
- Keep it simple in the beginning so you can get started now, and learn as you go.
- DFE will be a little different for everyone and, as it is still in its earliest stages of development, there are very few definitive answers.
- As with all quality improvement processes, focus on continuous improvement, and begin now instead of waiting to start when you think you have the ultimate solution.
- Solutions are not going to come easily, because we continue to see the definition of "environmentally preferable" as a moving target as the technology in this area advances.

When are you successful? When DFE is embedded in the product realization process and routinely considered by designers, and the verifiable result is that each new generation of product, service, or offering you provide is being more environmentally preferable than the one it replaces.

Notes

1. B.R. Allenby, *Design for Environment: Managing for The Future,* Facility Paper, 1995.

2. WCED (World Commission on Environment and Development, also known as the Brundtland Commission), *Our Common Future* (Oxford, Great Britain: Oxford University Press, 1987).

3. National Environmental Policy Plan, 1989; National Environmental Policy Plan Plus, 1990; National Environmental Policy Plan 2, 1994. Ministry of Housing, Physical Planning and Environment, The Netherlands.

4. T.S. Graedel and B.R. Allenby, *Industrial Ecology* (Englewood Cliffs, NJ: Prentice-Hall, 1994); see also B.R. Allenby, "Design for Environment: Implementing Industrial Ecology." Ph.D. dissertation, Rutgers University, 1992; B.R. Allenby, "Industrial Ecology: the Materials Scientist in an Environmentally Constrained World," *MRS Bulletin,* 17(3) 1993: 46–51; B.R. Allenby and

D.J. Richards, eds. *The Greening of Industrial Ecosystems* (Washington, DC: National Academy Press, 1994).

5.   B.R. Allenby and T.S. Graedel, Facility paper, 1994. See also Graedel and Allenby (cited in note 4).

Barry F. Dambach is a Distinguished Member of Technical Staff, Technology and Environment Lucent Technologies, NJ. **Braden R. Allenby,** J.D., Ph.D., is currently the Director for Energy and Environmental Systems at Lawrence Livermore National Laboratory (LLNL), on temporary assignment from his position as Research Vice President, Technology and Environment, for AT&T.

24

Using Life-Cycle Assessments in Large Corporations: A Survey of Current Practices

Ellen A. Huang and David J. Hunkeler

One may reasonably claim that any human activity has an environmental impact. For example, products such as soda cans, bottles, and bulk mail all originate with the extraction of natural resources and are typically returned to the earth either by disposal in landfills or through incineration. The by-products of industrial activity in our water, air, and solid waste streams have contributed significantly to the degradation and depletion of natural resources. Traditional "end-of-pipe" solutions of dealing with pollution have been an inadequate means of protecting the environment. Centuries of industrial activity have resulted in vast amounts of water pollution, air contamination, solid waste generation, and noise pollution. Regulating the amount of releases from industry has been viewed as a solution to environmental problems. Today, there is a growing interest in industry to practice environmentally conscious design and manufacturing (ECDM).

The initial great surge of environmental concern in the late 1960s and early 1970s dealt with localized and site-specific problems. Currently, industries are more aware and responsive to consumers' demands and expectations and are developing and utilizing technologies to manufacture environmentally "friendly" products. Research and experience have shown that industry cannot continue to merely treat the symptoms of environmental problems. Instead, a more comprehensive means to reduce pollution is believed by many to be through prevention, by attacking the source of pollution throughout every stage of the product life cycle: raw material extraction, transportation, manufacturing, product use, recycling, and disposal. Corporate environmental strategies have also evolved to include decision-making tools such as life-cycle analysis (LCA), design for environment (DFE), and ECDM. Researchers in Japan have also developed an "Ecofactory" concept as the ultimate 21st-century Ecologically Conscious Factory.

LCA is an evolving tool to assist with management decision-making processes to reduce environmental burdens from industrial activity. It is a holis-

239

tic approach for evaluating the environmental implications of products and processes from "cradle to grave."[1] LCA provides industry with a means for identifying and evaluating opportunities to minimize adverse environmental impacts. Cradle to grave describes the stages of a product life cycle (Figure 24.1) beginning with raw material acquisition, through the manufacturing process, transportation and distribution, product use and reuse, and, finally, recycling and disposal. By identifying the sources of pollution throughout a product's life cycle from conception to disposal, one can determine the opportunities for minimizing environmental damage. LCA does not attempt to be the single solution to all environmental problems. It is being developed as a management and design tool to help guide environmentally preferable practices. Nevertheless, its goals are ambitious and the issues complex. Thus, accepted methods for comprehensive LCAs do not currently exist.

The increasing worldwide recognition of life-cycle concepts as decision-making tools for minimizing environmental burdens has captured significant research attention. The objective of this research was to determine the current degree of development, acceptance, applicability, streamlining, and use of life-cycle concepts in U.S. industry. A mail survey was sent to 386 executives at 175 companies based on 1994's Fortune 500 ranking. Questionnaires were sent to at

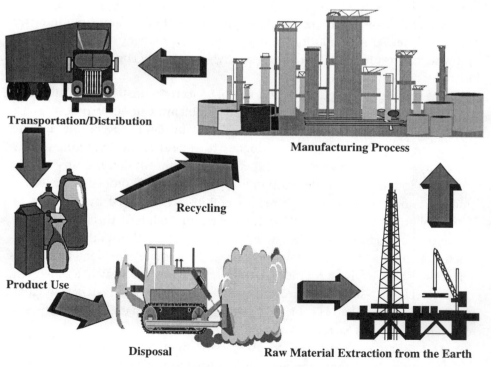

Figure 24.1   Life-Cycle Stages

least 10 executives and five firms in each industry. In most industries, surveys were administered to more than 10 companies. Mail surveys were sent to firms with contact information available in accessible databases, such as the American Business Disk.[2] At the outset, it was decided not to sample government laboratories or consulting firms. The companies contacted were grouped as follows:

- The *high-tech* sector included the aerospace, computer and office equipment, electronic and electrical equipment, motor vehicle and parts, scientific, photographic, and control equipment industries.
- The *intermediates* included the chemical, forest and paper product, metal, mining and crude oil production, petroleum refining, and rubber and plastic industries. Due to the large number of responses from the chemical industry, its results were separated from the Intermediate sector, and called the *chemical* sector.
- The *personal care* sector included the beverage, food, pharmaceutical, and soap and cosmetics industries.

Several potential respondent biases were recognized regarding our chosen sample. We assumed that large firms represent most of the U.S. products sold throughout the world and, therefore, would generate the majority of the waste. Thus, small and medium enterprises (SMEs), which are less likely to be involved with LCA work, were not sampled because they contribute less to the total volume of waste generated. By choosing the sample from the Fortune 500 list, we selected companies that have the financial and personnel resources available to conduct LCAs. As a result, the findings may indicate a greater involvement in LCA activities, expressed as a percentage of U.S. companies, than is actually the case. Furthermore, the surveys were primarily addressed to the CEOs and the vice presidents of health, environment, and safety, whose views regarding corporate environmental strategy may be biased. Most of the respondents were executives responsible for corporate health, environment, and safety issues. The respondents' perspectives primarily pertained to the company overall, although nine of the responses received applied to specific facilities or business units. Only two of the responses received were product-specific. It was assumed that the facility-specific and product-specific responses represent the majority of life-cycle work at the parent company and, thus, all responses were considered equally significant for statistic calculations.

Past surveys have served as precedents for the Vanderbilt survey including the MIT survey,[3] Habersatter survey,[4] Vigon and Jensen survey,[5] and the Tufts Capstone survey.[6] Overall, the results show that there is a wide acceptance of life-cycle concepts in industry, with many companies using some form of a life-cycle framework. However, impact assessment methods are not well developed, and inconsistencies exist. Moreover, environmental protection has not been integrated across the functions of many companies.

Survey Response Analysis

The Vanderbilt survey responses were grouped into industrial sectors in order to statistically analyze trends from each category. The survey revealed that few companies are actually considering the environmental impacts of their products and processes from "cradle to grave" (Figure 24.2). As expected, most firms are looking for opportunities to minimize environmental impacts in the manufacturing stage. This is the area over which companies have the most direct control. The companies that are evaluating environmental impacts during the raw material extraction stage are typically producers of intermediates, including mining, metal, and crude oil producers. It should be noted here that raw material extraction from the earth is actually the manufacturing stage for most of the intermediate firms.

The chemical and personal care sectors consider transportation and distribution impacts more than the other industrial sectors. In the chemical sector, this is likely to be initiated by hazardous spill concerns and potential liability issues. The chemical sector is also more concerned with the impacts of product use than any other sector. All of the high-tech and personal care sectors consider recycling and disposal impacts in their decision-making process. This is possibly due to the short product life cycle and the large volume of packaging materials and plastics used in these sectors. In addition, the high-tech and per-

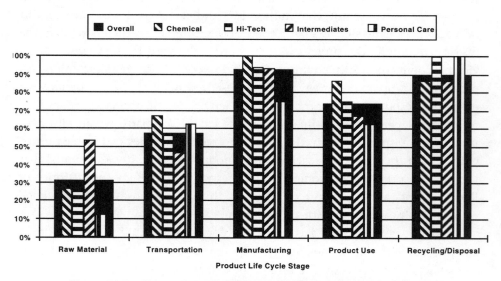

Figure 24.2   Stages Considered in Evaluating Environmental Impacts

sonal care sectors primarily consist of the manufacturers of visible consumer products. Across all industrial sectors, the largest involvement in environmental impact valuation is in the manufacturing and recycling/disposal stages. The former likely represents predominantly cost considerations and the latter is a liability, image, and cost concern.

Figure 24.3 shows that, overall, the respondents are equally concerned about water, solid, and air pollution. The high-tech and personal care sectors are much more concerned with solid waste than the chemicals and intermediates. This is consistent with the previous finding that a primary environmental motivation for high-tech and personal care sectors is the high visibility of their products and the volume of plastics components and packaging generated. The high-tech sector is also twice as likely to report air emissions as a major pollution concern than the other sectors. In addition to wastewater effluent, solid waste, and air emissions, other major pollution concerns were reported, such as hazardous waste, remediation of existing sites, and energy consumption during product use.

Survey participants were asked to list all the motivating factors that influence their current efforts in environmental protection. The top 10 motivators, in order of frequency reported, were:

1. Minimize costs
2. Avoid future liability/remediation
3. Be in compliance with current regulations
4. Enhance image/marketing strategy

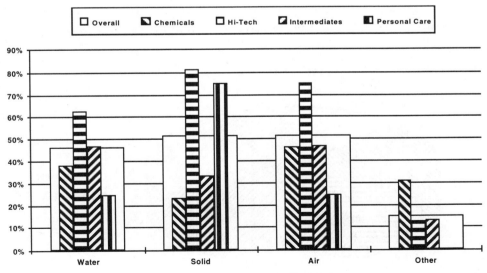

Figure 24.3   Major Corporate Pollution Concerns

5. Preempt regulatory changes
6. Meet customer requests
7. Identify improvement opportunities
8. Capitalize on strategic opportunities
9. Educate internally on environmental issues
10. Aid in the selection of process or material.

Similar to the findings in the MIT survey, most companies responded that the primary reason for corporate environmental efforts was the desire to capitalize on strategic opportunities. Responses were classified into market/cost, regulation, improvement, and stewardship. Figure 24.4 shows that the respondents' environmental efforts were overwhelmingly driven by market/cost issues.

The results indicate that while most companies seek to minimize environmental impacts, they are not motivated strongly by pollution prevention, stewardship, or product and material comparisons, which are the goals of an LCA-based approach. The less popular motivation factors are to avoid being precluded from international markets, understand customers' concerns, stimulate product innovations, educate the public, justify a selected process or material, compare products and/or materials, influence internal research priorities, provide marketing information, understand suppliers' concerns, assist in developing LCA methodology, "be good stewards of the environment," and influence sustainable use.

One question addressed LCA activity in terms of the three components defined by the Society of Environmental Toxicology and Chemistry (SETAC): life-cycle inventory, life-cycle impact assessment, and life-cycle improvement assessment.[7] A short definition of each was stated in the question for those

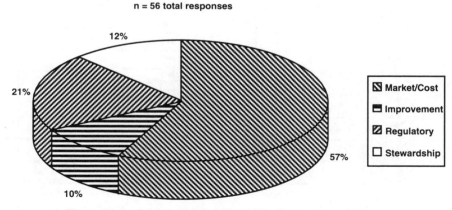

Figure 24.4 Primary Driving Forces for Environmental Efforts

who might have been unfamiliar with SETAC's terminology but might have been implementing similar practices. Figure 24.5 summarizes the status of current LCA activity in industry with respect to the three components. The trend across all industries regarding LCA activity was similar for all three of the SETAC components.

The results indicate that most companies are partially implementing LCA activities. This is inconsistent with the previous response that most companies were not considering environmental impacts from cradle to grave. The findings indicate that most of the LCA-related activities are streamlined approaches. There is a larger percentage of respondents conducting improvement activities than impact assessment in the "partially implemented" and "fully implemented" choices. This shows that companies are making improvement decisions based on inventory data collected, without adequately conducting an impact assessment. The lack of a standardized value system required for impact assessments is likely a contributing factor. Also, the lack of documented quantitative assessment methods implies that most of the LCA-related activities are based on qualitative valuations of environmental impacts.

Approximately 50 percent of companies are implementing life-cycle-based inventory concepts (e.g., mass and energy balances) and improvement assessments. Most of the companies engaged in LCA activities are in the high-tech and personal care sectors, where short product life cycles and high packaging

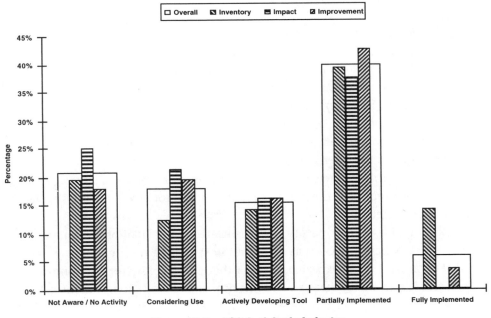

Figure 24.5   LCA Activity in Industry

levels characterize the products. The short product life cycle will result in a large research and development effort and will facilitate data collection. Packaging volumes arouse the interest of public awareness groups and prompt environmental actions from firms. Certainly, green marketing and public relations are implicit motivating factors for some companies.

Perhaps not surprisingly, none of the companies has fully implemented life-cycle impact assessments (LCIA). Only a small percentage of the chemical and intermediate sectors have begun implementing LCIA. The chemical and intermediate manufacturing processes are the most data-intensive, and these industries maintain more extensive databases for environmental evaluation. The response for this question is inconsistent, however, with a later finding regarding methods and tools to evaluate environmental impacts; the chemical and intermediate sectors show the highest activity with respect to developing tools and maintaining databases.

As previously mentioned, respondents indicated that approximately 50 percent of corporations have begun implementing improvement assessments. This is somewhat surprising, considering that the improvement assessment component of LCA has not been clearly defined by SETAC or EPA. In addition, methods to perform trade-off analysis are currently controversial.

Most of the companies utilizing the published guidelines are in the chemical and high-tech sectors. A large percentage of intermediates are not aware of the guidelines, and many of the personal care firms have chosen not to utilize the guidelines available.

ISO 14000 Awareness and Response

Thirty-five percent of those surveyed were not familiar with the role of LCA in the ISO 14000 series (Figure 24.6). More than half of the intermediates and personal care firms responding were not familiar with the upcoming international standards. However, 25 percent reported that their current environmental assessment practices are similar to the requirements of the proposed guidelines. Other comments questioned the need for such guidelines, due to programs such as the Chemical Manufacturers Association's Responsible Care™ program. In contrast, others replied that guidelines are used as a starting point and, therefore, represent the minimum requirement for environmental protection at their facilities.

Although life-cycle concepts have permeated almost half of the companies surveyed, they have not been as successful in spreading throughout each individual organization. As expected, most of the responsibility for environmental assessments falls in the hands of the health, safety, and environment group. The manufacturing and the research and development groups are also fairly extensively involved with environmental concerns. The level of top manage-

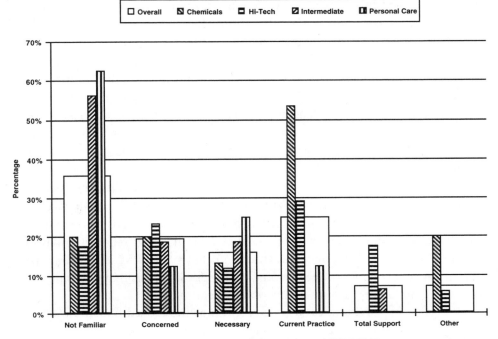

Figure 24.6   Industrial Perspective on ISO 14000

ment involvement is also encouraging, because it has increased over the levels reported from the 1992 MIT survey. However, the accounting and legal groups have not integrated environmental assessments into their routine responsibilities. This is unfortunate, because accountants and lawyers are well experienced to assign cost values to intangibles such as environmental burdens or liabilities. There is also a low percentage of "quality engineering" involvement reported. We are led to believe that many corporations may not have quality engineering groups per se, because there are several documented examples of firms integrating environmental affairs into corporate quality programs.

Most firms with task groups addressing environmental issues have begun their programs within the past five years. Many companies started environmental affairs groups during the first wave of environmental protection efforts in the 1970s. However, most cross-functional groups responsible for activities such as LCA began in the 1990s. Although some companies have LCA-focused task groups, most of the programs address general environment, health, and safety issues.

Many companies do not have a formal name for their environmental improvement program; pollution prevention concepts are the most popular names. The most often cited program in the "other" response was Responsible Care™. "Design for environment" was popular among the high-tech sectors.

"Product stewardship" was used by 15 percent of the companies responding, and "life-cycle assessment" represented almost 10 percent of the respondents.

Despite the increasing attention on environmental concerns, product quality remains the top priority for most companies (Figure 24.7). The increasing popularity of total quality management, ISO 9000, and other quality management programs in U.S. companies is likely to have influenced corporate priorities. Thus, environmental management may be next in line. Already, ISO 14000 is following in ISO 9000's footsteps. Moreover, initial corporate resistance to international standards has been largely reduced by ISO 9000's certification program.

Overall, the average values rank industrial priorities as quality, cost, performance, and environmental concerns, in that order. Slight variations exist among industry sectors. Except in the chemical sector, where cost and environmental considerations were approximately equal and both relatively high in priority, the average ranking value was significantly lower for environmental impacts. A value of 3.88 in the personal care sector indicates that environmental impacts are of low priority in their daily operations.

In evaluating environmental concerns, companies ranked human health as the most important. Ecological issues were next in priority, followed by concerns for resource depletion and social welfare. The average values indicate that human health and ecological issues are of much higher priority than resource depletion and social welfare. In fact, a value of 3.88 in the personal care sector revealed a higher lack of concern for resource depletion than in any of the other sectors.

Industrial respondents reported incomplete data as the number one obstacle for conducting environmental assessments, followed by inconsistent and unavailable data. Other problems and limitations encountered by industry in performing environmental assessments were high costs and time consumption, immeasurable data, data inaccuracy, poor data quality, and outdated information.

More than half of the companies reported using tools and databases for the valuation of environmental impacts. Some companies are developing tools internally; others use published assessment methods and software models or

Overall	Chemicals	High-Tech	Intermediate	Personal Care
Quality (1.63)	Quality (1.85)	Quality (1.64)	Quality (1.50)	Quality (1.50)
Cost (2.02)	Performance (2.15)	Cost (1.93)	Cost (1.88)	Cost (2.13)
Performance (2.35)	Cost (2.23)	Performance (2.07)	Performance (2.69)	Performance (2.50)
Environment (3.20)	Environment (2.69)	Environment (3.36)	Environment (3.13)	Environment (3.88)

Minimum value (highest priority) = 1.0; maximum value (lowest priority) = 4.0

Figure 24.7   Sector Priority Ranking

hire consultants. More than half of the responding companies also maintain a database of information. Intermediates are the most active in using tools and maintaining databases for environmental assessment. Interestingly, this correlates with a low fraction of firms in the intermediate sector that reported being engaged in life-cycle inventory. Because these are also the firms most affected by legislated emissions requirements (such as the Clean Air Act, Clean Water Act, and Toxic Release Inventory requirements), the use of tools and databases are likely motivated by compliance rather than responsible stewardship factors.

Most companies reported evaluating environmental impacts both quantitatively and qualitatively. A few companies in the chemical sector reported that they conduct quantitative assessments. These are likely to be direct comparisons of materials with the same measurable units rather than the trade-off analysis between media (i.e., 5 liters of toluene versus 10 liters of benzene, rather than 5 liters of toluene versus 20 pounds of lead).

In prioritizing environmental impacts, most companies use a ranking method. Although some firms used published methods, most respondents ranked impacts based on priorities set within each department or business unit. Many firms do not perform tradeoff analysis. These firms, predominantly in the personal care sector, prioritize environmental impacts according to the level of regulatory pressure present. A possible explanation is that the personal care sector is the most sensitive to regulatory pressure, possibly due to stringent regulations governing food, pharmaceuticals, and beverages.

Companies were asked how environmental improvement decisions were made without perfect or complete data. Several key words that were repeated in the responses include "subjectively," best engineering and management "judgment," cost/benefit analysis, sensitivity analysis, and "experience."

Important Survey Findings

Only 12 out of 56 companies (21 percent) perform life-cycle cost analysis, and none of these analyses account for impacts from cradle to grave. The chemical and high-tech sectors are the most active in using life-cycle cost analyses. The boundaries of these cost analyses reported ranges from a single manufacturing process to "cradle to shipping door." Therefore, most of the LCA activity used in industry consists of streamlined approaches.

Although several companies have begun integrating life-cycle concepts into their business practices, many barriers impede its application in industry. The main obstacles of LCA as perceived by industry today are time and cost issues, defining boundaries, getting approval to start evaluations, getting business units to see the value of LCA, value system diversity in impact assessment, tangible value in product marketing, need for good screening and streamlining methods, and questionable value in light of other programs in place. These obstacles are not listed in order of the frequency responded, because the issues were presented in the survey as an open-ended question. There are many other issues of concern and controversy regarding LCA. Data availability, data quality, and method for assessing environmental impacts still require further research attention.[8] This attitude is also prevalent among many nonindustrial practitioners and developers of LCA. Nevertheless, recent research by the University of Michigan found that "most companies could slash emissions by as much as 70 percent before hitting a point of diminishing returns."[9]

In light of Europe's eco-labeling initiatives and other environmental legislation, it was postulated that companies with representation and market in Europe are more likely to be involved in LCA. Among our chosen sample of large U.S. corporations, most respondents have overseas interests. Calculations revealed that geographic representation does influence an organization's involvement in LCA-related activities.

The survey responses were also grouped into classes of major pollution concern. The expected response was that either water, solid, or air pollution would be of greater concern to industry. It was evident that companies concerned with air pollution are more likely to implement LCA. The survey responses show that 67 percent of the companies that are concerned with air pollution are implementing LCA, versus 19 percent that are not implementing LCA. Likewise, of the companies that are concerned about solid waste, 63 percent are implementing LCA and 11 percent are not. Of all the companies concerned with water pollution, 63 percent have already implemented LCA, versus 17 percent that have not and 21 percent that are considering implementation. Among the companies that are considering implementation of LCA, 44 percent are concerned about solid waste, 31 percent are concerned about water pollution, and 25 percent are concerned about air pollution.

A comparison was made between LCA activity and industrial use of published guidelines. The results show that the two variables are directly related. Thus, the firms that are not adopting published LCA guidelines are, indeed, not likely to be involved in LCA. This indicates that most LCA practitioners do rely on published methods for guiding their LCA activities. Of all the companies that reported LCA implementation, 60 percent are using published guidelines, versus 38 percent that are not using the guidelines.

Conclusion

The results of the survey show that more than half of the 56 respondents are using LCA for environmental assessments, with market/cost issues as the primary motivation factors. High-tech and personal care sectors are more active in LCA implementation, whereas the chemical and intermediate sectors are more involved with maintaining databases and utilizing LCA tools. From an organizational perspective, life-cycle thinking has not been adequately integrated throughout corporate organizations, and most environmental efforts are initiated by the health, environment, and safety department. However, the percentage of top management involvement has increased since 1992, and is now at moderate levels. Unfortunately, almost none of the companies' accounting departments are involved with environmental activities. Despite LCA's rapid development, companies are skeptical that a standardized method for impact assessments will be accepted in the next few years. Overall, industries are concerned about the costs and inaccuracy associated with LCA. LCA methods need to be further developed in order to expand their industrial acceptability.

Notes

1. U.S. Environmental Protection Agency EPA/742-R-93-003, September 1993.

2. *The American Business Disk,* 1994 Edition (c).

3. M.S. Sullivan and J.R. Ehrenfeld, "Reducing Life-Cycle Environmental Impacts: An Industry Survey of Emerging Tools and Programs," *Total Quality Environmental Management,* Winter 1992/1993, pp. 143–157.

4. K. Habersatter, "Environmental Management: An Expert's Survey Realized at the SETAC LCA Data Quality Workshop," ETH, Swiss Federal Institute of Technology, Zurich, 1993.

5. B.W. Vigon and A.A. Jensen, "Life Cycle Assessment: Data Quality and Databases Practitioner Survey," *Journal of Cleaner Productions,* in press.

6. T. Gloria, T. Saad, M. Breville, and M. O'Connell, "Life-Cycle Assessment: A Survey of Current Implementation," *Total Quality Environmental Management,* Spring 1995.

7. The Society of Environmental Toxicology and Chemistry, *Guidelines for Life-Cycle Assessment: A Code of Practice,* 1993.

8. ISO/TC 207/SC5.

9. "Maybe It Is Easy Being Green," *Business Week,* February 13, 1995, p. 80.

Ellen A. Huang is an associate research engineer at United Technologies Research Center. Her research interests include recycling technologies, environmental management, LCA, DFE, and global green engineering. **David J. Hunkeler** is an Assistant Professor of Chemical Engineering, Management of Technology, and Materials Science and Engineering at Vanderbilt University in Nashville, Tennessee. His research interests include technology and environmental assessments, recycling, and water soluble polymers for environmental applications. He also teaches LCA and DFE topics at the undergraduate and graduate levels.

25

LCA in Japan: Corporate Practices and Trends Relative to the United States

David J. Hunkeler and Ellen A. Huang

In November 1993, Vanderbilt University's U.S.-Japan Center for Technology Management (UJ-Center) sponsored a workshop "Towards Clean and Intelligent Manufacturing." One of the principal recommendations centered on the need for metrics related to environmentally conscious design and manufacturing practices. Life-cycle analysis (LCA) was discussed as a potential tool to measure the greenness of products and processes.

In January 1995, the UJ-Center administered a mail survey to executives from 175 corporations on the Fortune 500 list. The findings indicated that more than half of the 56 responding firms are using LCA as a tool for environmental assessments. Table 25.1 summarizes the other major findings of the survey. The large response encouraged the UJ-Center to conduct a comparative analysis of the use of life cycle concepts in the United States, Japan, Western Europe and a newly industrialized country (Brazil). This chapter details the U.S.-Japan component of this comparison.

Introduction

LCA is an evolving tool to assist with management decision-making processes by estimating the environmental burdens due to industrial activity. It is a holistic approach for evaluating the environmental implications of products and processes from "cradle to grave." LCA provides industry with a means for identifying and evaluating opportunities to minimize adverse environmental impacts. Cradle to grave describes the stages of a product life cycle. Beginning with raw material acquisition, through the manufacturing process, transportation and distribution, product use and reuse, and, finally, recycling and disposal. By identifying the sources of pollution throughout a product's life cycle from conception to disposal, one can determine the opportunities for minimizing environmental damage. LCA does not attempt to be the single solution to all environmental problems. It is being developed as a management and design tool to help guide environmentally preferable practices. Neverthe-

Table 25.1 Summary of the Findings of the Executive LCA Survey of U.S. Fortune 500 Companies

1. Environmental valuations concentrate on the manufacturing, use, and disposal stages of the product life cycle. Few companies consider raw material acquisition or transportation.

2. For 57 percent of companies, the primary driver in their environmental efforts was either market or cost.

3. Companies reported relatively uniform concern for atmospheric, aqueous, and solid waste-based pollutants.

4. More than 50 percent of firms have either developed or partially implemented LCAs.

5. 42 percent of companies were adopting policies equal to or more stringent then the proposed ISO 14000 guidelines. However, 38 percent of respondents indicated that they were unaware of the environmental management component of ISO 14000.

6. LCA activities are not well integrated across corporate functions. In particular, the accounting and legal departments, which can considerably contribute to life-cycle costing, were excluded. Top management involvement was low (30 percent) but increased over previous surveys in 1992.

7. In terms of environmental priorities, human health was valued above ecological health, resources, and social welfare. The later three are reported in descending order of importance.

8. Data-related problems, such as incomplete data, data quality, and outdated information, were the main drawbacks reported for environmental assessments.

9. Most firms use both quantitative and qualitative metrics to evaluate environmental impacts. In the latter category, ranking and clustering are the most commonly reported methods.

10. More than 40 percent of companies are engaged in life-cycle costing.

11. Obstacles to LCA include the cost, difficulty to define boundaries, and resistance to initiating LCA activities within a firm.

12. The major recommendations included focusing on impact assessment and incorporating costs into LCA.

less, its goals are ambitious and the issues complex. Thus, accepted methodologies for comprehensive LCAs do not currently exist.

Most of the United States' effort in LCA development has been led by the U.S. EPA and the Society of Environmental Toxicology and Chemistry (SETAC). According to the SETAC guidelines, LCA is defined as:

> A process to evaluate the environmental burdens associated with a product, process, or activity by identifying and quantifying energy and material used and wastes released to the environment; to assess the impact of those energy and material uses and releases to the environment; and to identify and evaluate opportunities to affect environmental improvements. LCA addresses environmental impacts under study in the areas of ecological health, human health, and resource

depletion. It does not address economic considerations or social effects. Additionally, like all other scientific models, LCA is a simplification of the physical system and cannot claim to provide an absolute and complete representation of every environmental interaction[1]

LCA in Japan

The results of a recent conference[2] have indicated that Japanese companies have three LCA-related interests: (1) applying LCA to ecodesign, (2) Type I eco-labeling as a certification criterion in a program such as the Blue Angel, and (3) Type III eco-labeling, which basically involves an environmental report card similar to the one in place in the United States. The Type III eco-labeling will require the performance of a life-cycle inventory, and a task group has been developed within the newly established Life Cycle Assessment Society of Japan (JLCA). The Japan Environmental Management Association for Industry (JEMAI) will assume the education and training of eco-auditors. JEMAI has an annual budget of 2 billion yen and has 1,400 member companies across industrial sectors such as electrical power, steel, chemicals, automotive, electrical products, paper, and cement. It initiated an ISO committee on LCA in 1993. With regard to eco-design, an interview with Professor Ryoichi Yamamoto, director of the JLCA, stated that Japan will face a critical resource situation within the next 20 years in the areas of food, energy, and environmental disasters. This is largely due to the anticipated rapid economic growth rate forecast for the People's Republic of China and India. Therefore, Japanese governmental agencies, such as MITI, are trying to push the ideas of sustainable development.

The specific Japanese plan for LCA includes a general survey, discussion on how to use LCA, and a third phase, which evaluates alternatives for the development of extensive Japanese-based inventory databases and impact assessment methodologies. The latter, according to the JLCA chair, is the key issue. At present the Japanese award the Eco Mark "to products that contribute to environmental protection"[3]. The basic requirements for Eco Mark certification are defined as reducing the environmental impacts and burdens at the various stages of the product life cycle. The product certification steps are conducted by the Japan Environmental Association under the direction of the Japanese EPA. As of 1993, 3,599 products had been certified. These include freonless sprays and magazines made from recycled papers. This program began in February 1989, considerably later than Germany's Blue Angel program, which began in 1978. However, it predates North American initiatives, such as the Canadian Environmental Choice program, which was inagurated in 1989, and the U.S. Green Seal program, which began in 1993. The JLCA will prepare a final report for the Japanese government on all industrial sectors in March 1997 and propose a national project to develop LCI databases and methodologies. The Japan

Academy of Engineering also has an LCA working group, which will prepare a summary report on the status of LCA in Japan with specific recommendations to the government.

The Ecomaterials Forum, founded in 1993, conducted a study on the state of LCA research in Japan.[4] It concluded that the first LCA in Japan dates from studies in the mid-1980s on energy consumption carried out by the Chemical Research Institute. Other notable LCA studies in Japan have included research on plastics products carried out by the Plastic Waste Management Institute, conducted in 1991. In 1992 the Japan Eco-Life Center was entrusted with the responsibility to investigate the environmental burden of products, by the Japan Environmental Agency. The following year the Science and Technology Agency began the Ecomaterials Research Project, in which the LCA of materials was considered.

LCA Case Studies in Japan

Two noteworthy LCA case studies have recently been conducted. The first involved a refrigerator and was directed by Dr. Inaba of the National Institute of Resources and the Environment. This included the evaluation of alternatives to freon used in the cooling system. Two alternatives were identified. The first involved the use of an explosive fluid which did not require a redesign, while the second required a nonhazardous chemical which necessitated a redesign of the circulation and compression systems.[5] This survey has been coupled with some innovative research at the University of Tokyo. Professor Takashi Kiriyama's Green Browser approach involves the use of strategy models that map the relationships between components such as greenness, cost, safety, and ease of product use.[6] It is intended as an on-line means to facilitate collaboration between designers and consumers. The strategy model will eventually be linked to tools including LCA and DFE-based calculations.

A second LCA involved the application of the inverse-matrix method to the energy analysis of an automobile. This was carried out by the Tokyo Electric Car Research Institute and focused on CO_2 emissions. LCAs are also in progress on the washing machine, portable telephone and personal computer. The Japanese are also interested in fluorescent bulbs, specifically the evaluation and alternatives for mercury containing sources of illumination.

The NEDO branch of MITI sponsors these LCA case studies. Since the foundation of the LCA Society of Japan on October 25, 1995, a 1-½ year program on training and consensus building has been initiated. The JLCA also works on facilitating the exchange of LCA information, the application of LCAs to environmental performance evaluations (EPE), and the construction of LCI data bases. Table 25.2 is a list of LCAs performed to date in Japan.

Table 25.2   Summary of Selected Recent Japanese LCA Case Studies

Case	Comments
Aluminum Cans	Japan LCA Forum
Automobile (Production and Use)	National Institute for Environmental Studies (1992)
Automobile (Energy analysis focusing on CO_2 emissions)	Tokyo Electric Car Research Institute
Automobile (New and Old Models)	Society of Non-Traditional Technology (Science and Technology Agency) (1994)
Automobile (Electric)	Research Institute of Innovative Technology for the Earth
Automobile (Goal is to minimize total energy consumption)	Pending, Toyo Ultimate Car Project (TULC)
Beverage Containers	The National Institute for Environmental Studies (NIES)
Building (Office)	Shimizu Corporation (1993)
Building Facilities/Urban Development	Nikken Sekkei (1992)
Beer Bottles	
Carton Boxes for Oranges	Japan LCA Forum
Daily Necessities (Dishcloths/Tissue Paper, Paper/Cloth Diapers, Batteries)	Kyoto University (1991) Systems Engineering Institute (1993)
Drink Receptacles	Plastics Waste Management Institute, Japanese Consumers Co-operation Union, Chemical Economy Research Institute, Tray Research Center (1993)
Electric Power Plants	Central Research Institute of Electric Power Industry (1993), Society of Non-Traditional Technology (1994), Research Institute of Innovative Technology for the Earth
Packaging (Plastic, Wood, Paper)	Plastics Waste Management Institute (1993)
Personal Computer	In Progress, Sponsored by NEDO (MITI)
Plastic and Paper Trays/Packs	Plastics Waste Management Institute, Kyoto University (1993)
Portable Telephone	In Progress, Sponsored by NEDO (MITI)
Production of Chemicals	Research Institute of Innovative Technology for the Earth
Production of Hydrogen	Research Institute of Innovative Technology for the Earth

Table 25.2   (Continued).

Case	Comments
Recycling and Final Disposal	Kansai University
Refrigerator	National Institute of Resources and the Environment
Social Infrastructure	Kyusyu University (1993)
Solar Cell Generator	Society of Chemical Engineers Japan
Solid Waste Management (Glass, PET, Paper, Cans)	Hokkaido University
Superconducting Power Generator	Science and Technology Agency, National Institute of Resources (1987)
Tray (Waste Management and Recycling)	Kansai University (1993)
Toner Cartridge	Canon (1993)
Vending Machines	The National Institute for Environmental Studies (NIES)
Waste Incineration	The National Institute for Environmental Studies (NIES)
Washing Machine	Society of Non-Traditional Technology Sponsored by NEDO (MITI)
Steel and Other Alloys	National Research Institute of Metals, Science and Technology Agency

The majority of LCA efforts in Japan have been initiated by either governmental or industry associations. However, corporations are actively following global progress in LCA developments in anticipation of the international standards. While U.S. corporations tend to view LCA results as a means to justify their products and processes (with few companies using LCA or related tools in design), Japanese firms are looking to use LCA in order to avoid being precluded from international markets. The approaches to LCA development also differ in the United States and Japan, with the Americans continuing to debate the validity of LCA and examining means to streamline the assessments. In contrast, the Japanese are spending their resources on developing and evaluating tools and methodologies. For example, Sony Corporation's Center for Environmental Technologies has begun to develop software that incorporates design for disassembly and streamlined LCA concepts.

Japanese LCA Survey Results

In terms of environmental burdens, a recent Fortune 500 survey found U.S. firms equally interested in air, water, and solid waste streams. When a similar question was posed to Japanese experts in environmental management, they clearly stated that solid waste was the most significant current problem and concern in Japan. This is particularly true for construction companies, which generate 100 million tons of solid waste per year. This U.S.-Japan difference is likely due to two effects. First, Japan has a limited number of landfill sites and 80 percent of the solid waste is burned (3 percent goes for energy recovery). Second, existing Japanese legislation has already forced companies to address their atmospheric and aqueous discharges. Figures 25.1 and 25.2 show the trend in municipal solid waste generated in Japan as well as the fate of the 50 million tons per year of municipal solid waste. In the same U.S. survey, companies reported that pollution prevention, product stewardship, and design for environment were the three motivations for performing an LCA.

In an informal and nonsystematic survey of Japanese companies, consultants, and university professors, the main Japanese concern was design for environment. An example of the Japanese wanting to use LCA in design is the Toyo Ultimate Can Project (TULC). In this, the total energy consumption is minimized. Typical comparisons include steel versus aluminum and glass versus PET.

U.S. government agencies and industry are also involved in the LCA of automobiles, as is evidenced by a recent EPA/Saturn co-funded project through the Center for Clean Products and Clean Technologies at the University of Tennessee. There was also a workshop, "Environmentally Responsive Technologies

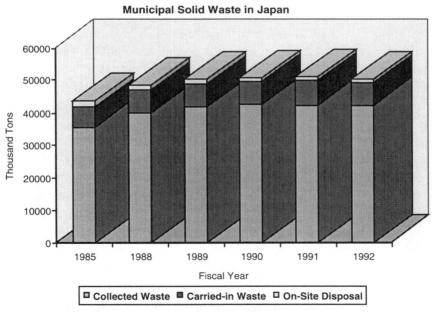

Figure 25.1 Municipal solid waste in Japan

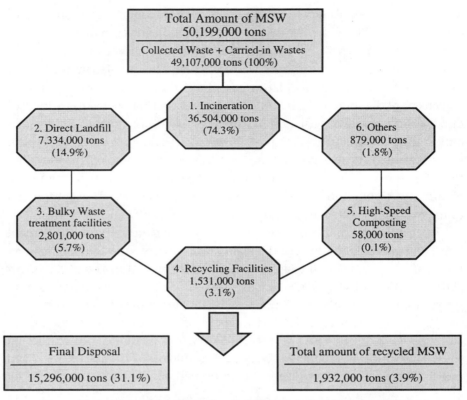

Figure 25.2   Flow chart of the disposal of municipal solid waste in Japan

for the Future," sponsored by the National Science Foundation in January 1996, which included panel discussions on LCA and the automobile. The automobile serves as a good example to illustrate that both the United States and Japan are, however, behind Europe with respect to the implementation of life-cycle thinking and evaluation of life cycle concepts. A recent conference in Vienna focused exclusively on LCA of the automobile; this attracted experts including Ian Boustead, who has developed and markets an LCI database that focuses on the resource extraction and processing stages of the product life cycle.

Other comparative results from the U.S. Fortune 500 survey and the informal Japanese interviews indicated that, in both countries, the use of interdisciplinary teams for conducting LCAs is still limited. The legal and accounting departments of large firms are not yet included in the LCA process, with the exception of a few companies. This result is somewhat surprising, since legal professionals are experts at assigning costs to intangibles, and the whole area of life-cycle costing has overlaps with cost accounting and activity-based accounting principles. However, it likely reflects firms' reluctance to cost environmental impacts as a precautionary measure in the event of future lawsuits. Both the U.S. and Japanese governments do not plan to use LCA as a legislative tool. Fifty-seven percent of U.S. companies reported that cost or market were the driving forces for their LCA efforts, and they ranked quality above cost, performance, and environmental concerns. The informal Japanese survey had cost and price consciousness above quality. Another difference was the top-down nature of U.S. companies, compared with the bottom-up approach practiced to a greater extent in Japan. The LCA practices of multinational firms located in Japan tended to follow the environmental lead taken by the head design center in the home country. Many large companies, both in Japan and in the United States, cited that they have had good publicity from their environmental products. This principally included the introduction of recycled components and energy conservation. Table 25.3 summarizes the results of the informal Japanese LCA survey.

Future LCA Efforts in Japan

The Japanese efforts for the near future include a "Green Procurement Network," which will be supported by the Japanese EPA and will begin in 1996. The Japanese are also planning the distribution of an environmental directory for ecoproducts. As a note of contrast, the U.S. EPA has produced a list of seven guiding principals for the acquisition of environmentally preferable products. The University of Tokyo has also recently formed an Alliance for Global Sustainability with the Swiss Federal Institutes of Technology (ETH) and MIT.[7] The main needs of Japanese companies with respect to LCA are in the area of validating databases generated for non-Japanese processes and the establishment of Japanese databases.

Table 25.3 Summary of Japanese LCA Survey Findings

LCA-related interests include eco-design and eco-labeling.

Solid waste was identified as the most significant current environmental problem in Japan.

Japanese environmental efforts are focused on DFE.

The Japanese EPA does not plan to use LCA as a legislative tool.

Japanese companies ranked cost above quality, whereas U.S. firms gave the opposite ranking.

Interdisciplinary teams are not yet used to address LCA related problems in either Japan or the United States.

LCA practices of multinationals follow the lead taken by the design center in the home country (Japan or U.S.).

Companies have reported good publicity from their environmental efforts.

Japanese Societies with LCA-Related Interests

In addition to the LCA Society, Japan has two other, more established, programs related to LCA. The four-year-old Japan LCA Forum, chaired by Professor Itaru Yasui of the University of Tokyo Institute for Industrial Science, was funded exclusively by approximately 20 companies to define LCA and its potential role in Japan. The LCA Forum has planned to construct an umbrella structure in order to extract information, aggregate it, and establish a database. Various case studies have been conducted and others are in progress, including one for beer bottles, which is now under review and should be published in February 1996.[8] The data include aggregated data from beer manufacturers, such as Kirin, as well as glass producers, including Toya Glass. An LCA project on aluminum cans is proceeding, and a new initiative to evaluate cartons for oranges has just commenced.

Another project that includes LCA components is the Man and Earth System, which is funded by the Ministry of Education and directed by Professor Yasui. This contains 120 individual projects, some of which involve LCA. Evidence of the current popularity of environmental issues in Japan can be seen in the January 1996 issue of the magazine Nikkei Trendy, which presents a general survey of available ecoproducts. As a case study of corporate interest in environmentally conscious products, Sony has developed a lithium battery that can be recycled 1,200 times. Sony is also initiating a life-cycle study on a recycling concept for foamed polystyrene, which is based on the dissolution of the polymer in a naturally occurring citrus extract.

The Clean Japan Center was established in 1975 and is sponsored by MITI. Its role is to introduce new technologies into the private sector and to local governments either from indigenous sources or, if necessary, from abroad. The center conducts seminars, constructs test plants, and leads the public relations efforts toward recycling. It also spent 3 billion yen in 1995 to assist companies in their environmental efforts. It is a member of JEMAI; its off-line database includes environmental information and legislation worldwide.

The National Institute for Environmental Studies (NIES), a government laboratory, is an arm of the Japan Environment Agency. Lead by Dr. Sukehiro Gotoh, NIES is divided into two divisions: Social and Environmental Systems, and Natural Resource Management. NIES includes four researchers working on LCA-related projects. LCA research conducted at this facility includes specific case studies and an investigation of general LCA approaches. To date, comprehensive case studies have been completed on two products and one process: beverage containers, vending machines, and waste incineration. The Japanese reports can be obtained from NIES. Research on general LCA approaches includes data collected from over 500 industrial sectors. Studies include the interactions between industrial sectors, product stewardship practices, stipulations in the recycling law, "design for X" approaches, and standardized environmental assessment methodology issues.

The Resource Recycling Center (RRC) is a group consisting of approximately 40 private companies. The RRC will draft guidance regarding the environmental management systems component of the ISO 14000 standards. The center will draft guidance policies in six areas, including pollution, energy, and resource conservation. Currently, the Ministry of International Trade and Industry (MITI) is also drafting environmental standards for Japan in conjunction with ISO 14000. Companies that have developed EMSs can be certified by the Japan Accreditation Board for Quality Systems Registration (JAB). Table 25.4 lists the Japanese organizations that have significant LCA-related interests.

Related Japanese Legislation

The 1995 packaging law, which is similar to the German take-back legislation, will force a new level of compliance on Japanese companies. Starting in 1997, firms will be responsible for the collection of their products at their own expense, although this legislation is delayed until the years 1999 or 2000 for some products, such as plastics. Japan also passed a recycling law that became effective in October 1991. The aim of this law was to promote recycling; specific roles are assigned to government, municipalities, industry, and consumers. The 1993 amendments to this law include the promotion of waste minimization and the imposition of strict regulations on waste handling agents and treat-

Table 25.4   Japanese Organizations with LCA-Related Interests

Japan LCA Forum (founded in 1991 by 20 private firms)

LCA Society of Japan (founded October 25, 1995, MITI)

Japan Environmental Management Association for Industry (1400 member companies)

Man and Earth Systems Project (Ministry of Education)

Clean Japan Center (founded in 1975, MITI)

Resource Recycling Center (40 private firms)

Ecomaterials Forum

Japan Eco-life Center

Japan Accreditation Board for Quality System Registration (MITI)

Japanese EPA

National Institute of Resources and the Environment

NEDO Branch of MITI

Science and Technology Agency

Plastic Waste Management Institute

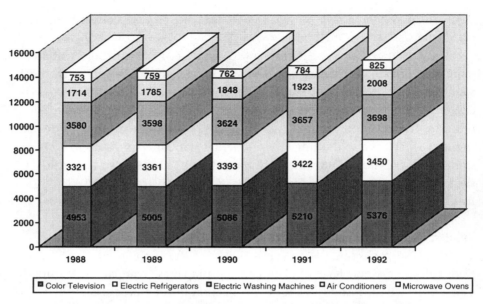

Figure 25.3   The trend in the annual disposal of electric appliances in Japan

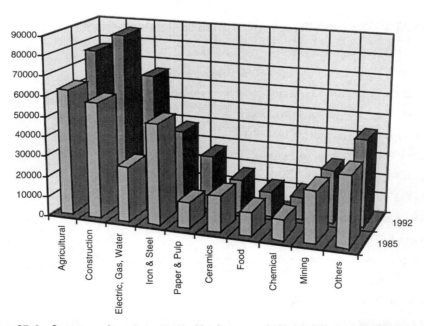

Figure 25.4   Summary of waste generated by Japanese industrial sectors in 1985 and 1992

Table 25.5   Japanese Legislation with LCA Implications

Legislation (Year Passed)	Requirements
Recycling Law (1991)	• Assigned specific roles to government, municipalities, industry, and consumers in the effort to promote recycling.
	• 1993 amendments included the promotion of waste minimization and strict regulations on waste handling agents and treatment facilities.
	• As of March 1995, rubber auto tires, television sets with screens of 25" or larger, electric refrigerators with capacities of 250 liters or more, and spring mattresses were designated as "specifically controlled wastes."
Packaging Law (1995)	• Similar to the German take-back legislation.
	• Starting in 1997, firms will be responsible for the collection of their products at their own expense. The legislation is delayed until 1999 or 2000 for some products, such as plastics.

ment facilities. As of March 1995, rubber automobile tires, television sets with screens of 25 inches or larger, electric refrigerators with capacities of 250 liters or more, and spring mattresses were designated as "specially controlled wastes."[9] Figure 25.3 itemizes the disposal of electric appliances in Japan. The moderately increasing trend is perhaps not as alarming as the numbers of appliances disposed of. Several large Japanese electronics manufacturers are engaged in design for disassembly programs—for example, to recycle the picture tube from discarded televisions. Figure 25.4 classifies the waste generated in Japan by industry. As is the norm for most industrialized countries, construction and agriculture account for the majority of solid waste generation. Figure 25.2 shows that even with Japan's massive incineration programs, the ratio of recycled resources to discarded material is approximately 1:10. Table 25.5 summarizes recent Japanese legislation that has LCA-related implications.

Notes

1. Society of Environmental Toxicology and Chemistry, Guidelines for Life-Cycle Assessment: A "Code of Practice," 1993.
2. International Conference on Ecobalance, October 25–27, 1994, Tsukuba, Japan.
3. Network News from Japan, The Environmental Network Newsletter by the Working Group of the Japan ECP Committee, 95–7, page 18.
4. Ecomaterials Forum, "Present State and Further Subjects of LCA Research in Japan," The Society of Non-Traditional Technology (1994).
5. LCA on Refrigerator: Options for Freon as a Coolant, Dr. Inaba, of the National Institute of Resources and the Environment, Director.
6. Green Browser: Professor T. Kiriyama, University of Tokyo, RACE, personal communication.

7. Japanese Alliance Director: Professor T. Matsuo, Department of Urban Engineering.

8. Japan LCA Forum, LCA Case Study of Beer Bottles, Journal of Environmental Toxicology and Chemistry.

9. Clean Japan Center, "Recycling Factbook," September 1995.

10. Clean Japan Center, "Recycle Japan," March 1995.

David J. Hunkeler is an Assistant Professor of Chemical Engineering, Management of Technology, and Materials Science and Engineering at Vanderbilt University in Nashville, Tennessee. His research interests include technology and environmental assessments, recycling, and water soluble polymers for environmental applications. He also teaches LCA and DFE topics at the undergraduate and graduate levels. **Ellen A. Huang** is an associate research engineer at United Technologies Research Center. Her research interests include recycling technologies, environmental management, LCA, DFE, and global green engineering.

26

Putting Life-Cycle Assessment to Work in the Marketplace: Modern Environmental Labeling Applications*

Stanley P. Rhodes and Linda G. Brown

The decision by industry and policy makers to standardize environmental management, auditing, and labeling practices through the ISO 14000 process demonstrates the increasingly important role that sound environmental practices and business reputation are playing in the world economy. For instance, in the United States, seven out of ten people say that a company's environmental reputation or a product's environmental attributes can affect their decision to purchase a particular product, and believe that environmental protection and economic development should go hand in hand.[1] Equally significant, environmental performance requirements are being woven into the fabric of government, institutional, and corporate procurement policies, and are influencing technology developments in fields as diverse as the building and construction industry, the office equipment and supplies sector, and the fashion world. In Europe, these trends are even more pronounced.

One of the principal objectives of the ISO 14000 process has been to establish uniform guidance for companies wishing to make public claims of environmental achievement. These guidelines are intended to protect consumers by preventing a proliferation of misleading or deceptive claims, while simultaneously ensuring that appropriate scientific documentation exists to support claims which are made. In addition, the guidelines are intended to help guarantee a level playing field among competing companies, and to ensure that environmental labeling programs do not impede fair competition in international commerce. In all, nine general principles for environmental labels and declarations are outlined in ISO 14020. (See Table 26.1.)

Increasing sophistication in our understanding of the environmental performance characteristics of industrial systems and products has led to corresponding developments in the field of environmental labeling. This growing

Table 26.1 Principles for All Environmental Labels and Declarations

Principle 1: Environmental labels/declarations shall be accurate, verifiable, relevant, and non-deceptive.

Principle 2: Procedures and requirements for environmental labels/declarations shall not be prepared, adopted, or applied with a view to, or with the effect of, creating unnecessary obstacles to international trade.

Principle 3: Environmental labels/declarations shall be based on scientific methodology that is sufficiently thorough and comprehensive to support the claim and that produces results that are accurate and reproducible.

Principle 4: The development of environmental labels/declarations should, wherever appropriate, take into consideration the life cycle of the product or service.

Principle 5: Environmental labels/declarations shall not inhibit innovation that maintains or has the potential to improve environmental performance.

Principle 6: Any administrative requirements or information demands related to environmental labels/declarations shall be limited to those necessary to establish conformance with applicable criteria and standards of the labels/declarations.

Principle 7: The process of developing environmental labels/declarations should include an open, participatory consultation with interested parties. Reasonable efforts should be made to achieve a consensus throughout the process.

Principle 8: Information on the environmental aspects of products and services relevant to an environmental label/declarations shall be available to purchasers from the party making the environmental label/declaration.

Principle 9: Information concerning the procedure, methodology and any criteria used to support environmental labels/declarations shall be available and provided upon requires to all interested parties.

Source: ISO 14020 Working Draft

understanding is reflected in the ISO process itself, which has become a forum for discussion and debate of ideas with implications that reach far beyond the labels themselves.

The Role of Life-Cycle Assessment

Among the most important of these debates is the appropriate role of life-cycle assessment (LCA) in labeling, and, particularly, in comparative marketing claims. Labelers have long recognized the value of incorporating a comprehensive cradle-to-grave perspective into environmental product labels—i.e., a perspective that considers each phase of a product's life, from raw material extraction and processing through product manufacturing, distribution, sale, use, and, ultimately, disposal. However, there have been a number of obstacles to fulfilling this goal:

1. *Most eco-labeling systems predate the science.* Industry and policy makers have understood the opportunities presented by environmental label-

ing for decades. The first of the modern eco-labeling schemes, the German Blue Angel, was launched in 1978, long before LCA practices were standardized for widespread use. The Blue Angel and other similar programs relied on expert panels to develop "green" product criteria based on a subjective review of available research. Such approaches have become deeply entrenched, despite the inconsistencies in product criteria that have resulted from one eco-labeling scheme to another, and despite subsequent life-cycle evidence indicating that products that qualify for the label are not always better for the environment than products that do not qualify.

2. *Environmental tradeoffs*. One of the hallmarks of life-cycle science is its ability to uncover environmental "tradeoffs" between various product or technology options. For instance, while recycling may be a highly valued method of reducing solid waste, a recycled paper product may account for higher levels of emissions and greater energy consumption than its standard virgin paper counterpart. In other words, products that intuitively seem "preferable" may in fact offer as many disadvantages as benefits for the environment. Labeling schemes geared toward determining environmental preferability have not easily contended with such tradeoffs.

3. *Complexity and costs*. The strength of LCA—its comprehensive reach—has also been its limitation. In order to conduct an LCA, one requires access to a very large database and a computer model capable of tracking inputs and outputs associated with upstream and downstream industrial processes. Historically, there have only been a few such models and databases, built over decades and licensed at fairly high cost. Equally important are the know-how and patience to conduct a rigorous life-cycle study—to carefully define the system function, the study boundaries, and assumptions, then define the sequence of interconnected "unit processes" comprising the system and collect data accordingly. In the past, few schools have taught these techniques, and the number of qualified LCA practitioners has been quite limited. Finally, LCA, by its very nature, involves the collection of substantial amounts of information. Given the few practitioners, the costs to businesses have been relatively high, and viewed by some manufacturers as prohibitive.

There have also been serious technical challenges related to the science itself. Conceptually, LCA has been defined as containing three phases: (1) an inventory phase, in which inputs (raw materials and energy) and outputs (emissions and wastes) are catalogued for each life-cycle stage of an industrial system; (2) an impact phase, in which the environmental significance of these measured inputs and outputs is determined; and (3) an improvement phase, in which specific environmental improvement strategies are derived from study findings. In actual practice, however, LCA has evolved primarily as an inventory exercise only; inputs and outputs are measured or calculated for each unit process, then aggregated together to describe the overall system. Under this life-cycle inventory (LCI) approach, the basic objective is to balance the mass and energy entering the system against the mass and energy leaving the system.

While this technique has proven quite useful as an engineering tool for describing material and energy flows in industrial systems, it offers little assistance in linking the measured inputs and outputs to actual environmental effects—the very information that could often be of greatest benefit to companies and policy makers. For instance, the sulfur dioxide emissions from one manufacturing facility may be connected to acid rain effects downwind, whereas equivalent emissions from another location may have no observable acid rain effects. Wood may be harvested from one forest that is managed for sustainability, whereas the same amount of wood may be harvested from another forest in which few precautions are taken for long-term sustainability. Water effluents may surpass toxic thresholds in one river system, while causing no effects in another. Inventory procedures do not ferret out these differences, and simply lump the emissions together into a sum total. From a labeling standpoint, and particularly in terms of comparative assertions, the usefulness of life-cycle inventory (LCI) has therefore been limited. Indeed, the LCA subcommittee has stated that comparative assertions should not be made based on LCI alone.[2]

Some people have argued that, in light of these complications, LCA should not be used as the basis for environmental labeling. However, this argument has proven difficult to defend on two grounds.

First, while those who oppose LCA's use in the marketplace cite its shortcomings, none has put forward a superior—or even viable—alternative methodology capable of providing the same cradle-to-grave breadth of assessment. To date, LCA is the one internationally recognized scientific approach that "is sufficiently thorough and comprehensive," "produces results that are accurate and reproducible," and "take[s] into consideration the life cycle of the product or service," consistent with Principles 3 and 4 of ISO 14020.

Second, from a practical standpoint, the horse has already left the barn. Published life-cycle studies are already being used to support a wide variety of public marketing claims, and to drive policy decisions. Some of the most widely publicized of these studies have compared plastic bags to paper bags, disposable diapers to cloth diapers, plastic drinking cups to paper cups, and beverage containers made from glass, aluminum, and plastic. Less publicized, but far more numerous, are the life-cycle studies being conducted ostensibly for internal use only, but which are driving industry and government agency decision making in terms of material selection and product design, and thus are having a direct affect on upstream material suppliers as well as downstream customers and stakeholders.

Rather than deny LCA's inevitable role in the marketplace, the international community has come to recognize the need to provide a standardized framework for presenting LCA findings, developed within an open, consensus forum such as ISO.

Overcoming the Obstacles

One by one, the logistical, political, and technical hurdles are being overcome. LCA has become more accessible, and the costs of analysis have dropped considerably. As LCA has moved into wider practice, there has been a growing appreciation for the value of supporting environmental label systems based on an objective, reproducible methodology. And, as discussed in more detail below, new, environmental performance-based labeling approaches have been developed specifically with LCA in mind, and are now undergoing standardization within ISO.

In terms of the science, LCA is now progressing far beyond its basic inventory roots squarely into the impact assessment arena. Particularly useful is a new branch of life-cycle impact assessment that has emerged specifically to address the needs of environmental performance evaluation and environmental labeling by defining with quantitative certainty the environmental effects of an industrial system. This approach, referred to as life-cycle stressor-effects assessment (LCSEA), is described in ISO draft documents being standardized within the LCA subcommittee's Working Group in Impact Assessment.

LCSEA is the first LCA methodology to merge the cradle-to-grave *breadth* of traditional life-cycle inventory (LCI) with the *depth* of traditional environmental impact and ecological risk assessment disciplines. While LCI involves a basic material and energy balance accounting of the input and output streams of an identified system, LCSEA expands on this information by analyzing the *relative contribution, significance,* and *uncertainty* of environmental effects attributable to the system. The essence of the methodology is to bring an increased sophistication to the classification and characterization of life-cycle impacts.

As the name implies, the LCSEA approach revolves around the identification of "stressor-effects networks," which can be defined as the interlocking physical, biological and chemical events which connect a specific system input, output, or activity (i.e., the "stressor") to an observed effect or related group of effects (Figure 26.1). Early identification of the stressor-effects networks associated with a given system (1) helps ensure that the right data are collected from which to draw meaningful conclusions; and (2) heads off the needless and costly analysis of excessive inventory data that have no environmental relevance.

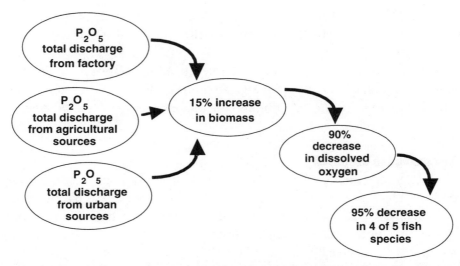

Figure 26.1 Simplified schematic of a eutrophication stressor-effects network. In this example, factory discharges combine from other sources in receiving waters, leading to a pronounced decline in fish population of four species.

Whereas it is generally difficult to draw any conclusions about the environmental significance of emissions data collected under LCI, the LCSEA data are specifically characterized in terms of their regional, local, and global effects. Through this characterization process, the voluminous quantity of raw, uninterpreted LCA data can be consolidated into a more manageable group number of 15 to 20 effects indicators, each representing a major category of global, regional, or local environmental impact. This consolidation makes the findings accessible to industry users and customers alike. At the same time, these effects indicators represent the limit to which reliable consolidation of LCA data can take place. There is no objective method available for *valuation*—that is, equating dissimilar effects such as global warming, ozone layer depletion, acid rain, and human toxicity, on a uniform value scale (Figure 26.2).

With its emphasis on analyzing the actual environmental effects of industrial systems and the products they produce, and its ability to narrow LCA data down to a more manageable amount of information, the LCSEA approach bridges the important gaps needed to make LCA suitable for advanced environmental performance evaluation, management, and labeling.

The Emergence of Environmental Performance-Based Labeling

Recent developments in the field of LCA have been paralleled by advances in the area of environmental labeling. Within ISO, a new labeling option—

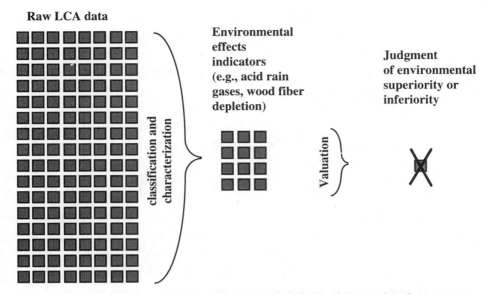

Raw LCA data

Environmental
effects
indicators
(e.g., acid rain
gases, wood fiber
depletion)

Judgment
of environmental
superiority or
inferiority

classification and
characterization

Valuation

Figure 26.2 The LCSEA methodology translates hundreds of data points into manageable information sets while maintaining a high quantifiable certainty between a system's stressors and environmental effects. As indicated by the schematic, there is currently no proven scientific method for further consolidation through valuation.

"Type III" labeling—has been recognized and is now undergoing standardization.[3] Type III labels are independently certified declarations of a product's or process's environmental impacts, based on LCA. The Type III standard is the first standard within the ISO 14000 series to build directly on the foundation of the LCA guidelines being finalized within SC5, the Subcommittee on Life-Cycle Assessment.

Type III Labeling Definition
(ISO 14025 Draft Document N-3)

A quantified declaration of a product's environmental performance under a group of pre-set environmental indicators based on the findings of a life-cycle assessment (LCA).

The Type III designation distinguishes this type of labeling approach from "Type I" environmental seals of approval issued on the basis of subjective product criteria, and "Type II" claims related to specific product attributes, such as recycled content or biodegradability. Type III environmental labeling embodies the nine principles for environmental labeling set forth in 14020, and has four major goals:

1. *Translate LCA findings into a declaration of key environmental information about products and processes.* Type III environmental labeling was developed specifically for the purpose of identifying and reporting the key findings of LCA studies regarding a product's or process's environmental impacts. For instance, the "Certified Eco-Profile™," developed in the United States as a prototype Type III label, reports LCA findings under 16 preset effect indicator categories[4] that are uniformly applicable to all products and processes (Figure 26.3). These indicators are dictated by the LCSEA methodology.

   This declaration of impacts effectively establishes a product's "environmental profile," a unique fingerprint reflecting the specific features of the particular industrial system examined. For instance, two identical products in the marketplace may have vastly different environmental profiles, reflecting the fact that one company has installed modern pollution prevention technologies while the other company relies on older, more polluting technologies.

   The environmental profile becomes a benchmark against which a company can measure and demonstrate internal improvements. In addition, it establishes a basis for comparisons between products, revealing environmental tradeoffs that may exist.

2. *Labels should be nonexclusive and nonprescriptive.* A second goal of Type III labels is to provide a common basis for examining all products, regardless of the materials used or the technologies employed. There are no prescriptive criteria to exclude certain products within a category, and no product categories deemed unsuitable for labeling. This

Certified Eco-Profile Effects Indicators
Fresh water depletion
Wood and wood fiber depletion
Petroleum resources depletion
Metals depletion
Mineral depletion
Ecosystem depletion
Total energy used
Greenhouse gas emissions
Stratospheric ozone-layer depletion
Acid rain
Smog
Hazardous air emissions
Toxic water emissions
BOD
Hazardous solid waste
Nonhazardous solid waste

Figure 26.3

goal reflects the overriding purpose of Type III labels—to be an informative, impartial declaration of information about a product's environmental profile, rather than act as judge and jury of a product's relative "greenness."

3. *Stimulate continuous environmental improvement.* The third goal of Type III labels is to support the larger ISO objective of stimulating continuous environmental improvement in industrial operations. This goal is consistent with the objectives of Agenda 21, the document produced during the 1992 United Nations Earth Summit, which established a framework for achieving "sustainable development" on a global scale, and which spawned the development of the ISO 14000 series.[5] Type III labels stimulate improvement by keeping the focus on the actual environmental performance levels rather than focusing on means to achieving these levels, thus freeing companies to pursue improvement through any innovative means possible.

4. *Avoid trade barriers.* Finally, Type III labels are intended to address the issue of trade barriers, which have created problems for other labeling approaches. By sticking to a reporting of quantitative environmental profile data generated through an internationally standardized methodology (LCA), Type III labels inherently avoid creating either intended or unintended barriers to trade.

Within this framework, Type III labels can take a variety of forms. In addition to the traditional label appearing on the side of a package, other means of communicating environmental profile information are now being explored. For example, in the United States, the Certified Eco-Profile program is now moving to take advantage of modern information technologies, such as the Internet, and has begun expanding the programs' reach in other ways, such as through the development of an "Environmental Lifestyle Analysis™," designed to integrate environmental impacts from the consumer phase of the product life cycle into the overall environmental profile (Figure 26.5). This personalized environmental profile approach is designed to give individual consumers a greater sense of their own responsibility in creating environmental impacts, and a better understanding of their own role in working in partnership with industry toward environmental solutions.

In addition to its consumer-oriented applications, Type III labeling is the first quantitative environmental performance evaluation (EPE) tool built on LCA. Its universal metrics are designed to assist companies in measuring current performance levels, and monitoring subsequent improvements toward the achievement the performance goals established through their internal ISO

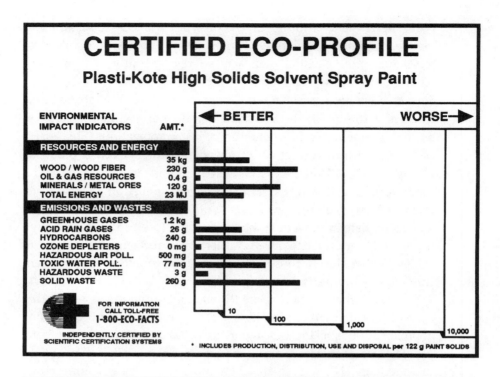

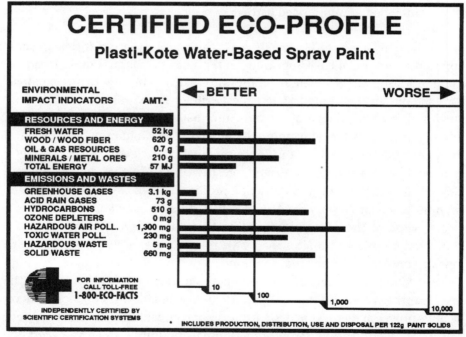

Figure 26.4   Certified Eco-Profile

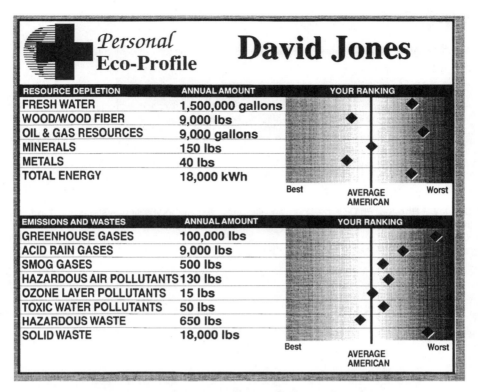

Personal Eco-Profile   **David Jones**

RESOURCE DEPLETION	ANNUAL AMOUNT	YOUR RANKING
FRESH WATER	1,500,000 gallons	
WOOD/WOOD FIBER	9,000 lbs	
OIL & GAS RESOURCES	9,000 gallons	
MINERALS	150 lbs	
METALS	40 lbs	
TOTAL ENERGY	18,000 kWh	

Best   AVERAGE AMERICAN   Worst

EMISSIONS AND WASTES	ANNUAL AMOUNT	YOUR RANKING
GREENHOUSE GASES	100,000 lbs	
ACID RAIN GASES	9,000 lbs	
SMOG GASES	500 lbs	
HAZARDOUS AIR POLLUTANTS	130 lbs	
OZONE LAYER POLLUTANTS	15 lbs	
TOXIC WATER POLLUTANTS	50 lbs	
HAZARDOUS WASTE	650 lbs	
SOLID WASTE	18,000 lbs	

Best   AVERAGE AMERICAN   Worst

Figure 26.5   Examples of Environmental Life Style Analysis

14000 certified environment management systems. Specific EPE applications include:

- Identifying the range of environmental impacts associated with different management, operational, and production decisions, and choosing options that satisfy corporate objectives;
- Establishing priorities that promote the efficient expenditure of resources to achieve the greatest environmental improvements; and
- Optimizing procurement to minimize environmental impact from supplies.

Through these EPE applications, Type III labels help companies pinpoint the most important and logical opportunities for internal improvement, while simultaneously providing a mechanism for communicating their improvements and achievements to customers and stakeholders.

Notes

1. 1992 Advertising Age Survey; 1995 Roper Poll conducted for Times Mirror.
2. ISO 14040, Working Draft 3.
3. Twenty-seven countries have committed delegates to the standardization of Type III labeling.
4. The Certified Eco-Profile was developed by Scientific Certification Systems, Inc., an Oakland-based third-party environmental certification organization.
5. 1992 United Nations Conference on Environmental and Development, Rio de Janeiro, June 1992.

Stanley P. Rhodes, Ph.D., is president and CEO of Scientific Certification Systems, Inc. **Linda G. Brown** is vice president, communications, of Scientific Certification Systems, Oakland, CA, 94612.

27

Industry Cases and Practices: Life-Cycle Management at Chrysler

Robert J. Kainz, Monica H. Prokopyshen, and Susan A. Yester

Companies cannot afford to ignore the impact that the environment, occupational health and safety, and recycling (EHS&R) have on products and the business decision-making process. Nor can industry any longer rely on reactive programs to address these issues. The addition of end-of-pipe controls or personal protective equipment is no longer state-of-the-art management. Waste disposal can no longer be accepted as a cost of doing business.

Worldwide economic and political events over the last decade have hastened the changing business environment for corporate America. These changes are characterized by intense worldwide competition, pressure to reduce costs, increased need for manufacturing flexibility, shortened product development cycles, improved quality, and increasing technological change.[1] These pressures have, predictably, caused firms to seek sustainable advantages in all aspects of business. Companies, in increasing numbers, are changing the focus of procurement to a proactive strategy for competitive advantage.[2]

In this era of growing competition, innovative firms are incorporating EHS&R into their overall business plans. These firms are finding that pollution prevention does pay—in both social and economic ways. EHS&R has become more than a set of tools to evaluate the stewardship of a corporation—it has become a way of gaining competitive advantage.

The key is to make pollution prevention part of business decision making. One way this can be accomplished is through life-cycle management (LCM). The LCM concept can be used to evaluate EHS&R issues in a systematic business-decision framework. In this way, EHS&R becomes a critical part of the overall business plan of the company.

Background

The command-and-control regulations of the 1970s are giving way to more innovative joint regulatory and stakeholder approaches. Chrysler has recently been working with EPA through the Common Sense Initiative (CSI) to share concerns and ideas on how industry can best protect the environment, workers, and the community. The automotive industry, as a participant in the reform process, is seeking to meet the regulatory aims of reducing environmental and community health impacts while satisfying traditional business and shareholder obligations. Regulatory agencies are seeking new ways of protecting the environment, the community, and workers, while encouraging the use of recycled materials through a closer understanding of economic drivers. This new approach does not imply the elimination of regulation—it suggests new ways to regulate.

Chrysler has chosen LCM as the program with which to start the 21st century.[3] LCM stimulates cultural change to produce quality products at the lowest *total* cost while protecting the environment, worker health, and the community. This model provides the opportunity to view EHS&R costs as true product costs. LCM affords managers the chance to address the cost of air, water, and solid waste disposal as non-value-added costs in a business plan. This brings the plant and design, engineering, and other staffs closer together.

Business and Competitive Implications

LCM integrates EHS&R with traditional business variables, and seeks to incorporate EHS&R costs into business decision making. The discussion below outlines some of these costs.

The Cost of Meeting Environmental Regulations

In the United States, environmental regulations impose a range of requirements, including chemical inventory and Toxic Release Inventory reporting, permitting and certification requirements, labeling of parts and vehicles, emission caps, and waste disposal procedures.

Beyond these obvious environmental costs are the more subtle costs to corporations, namely:

- Potential capacity constraints
- Cycle-time reduction constraints
- Decreased operational flexibility
- Increased producer costs
- Inaccurate or negative consumer perceptions

For example, a supplier may have volume production tools and facilities in place to satisfy a manufacturer's contractual obligations, but the supplier's operating permit may restrict allowable emissions to the extent that the volume requirements cannot be met. The operating permit may prohibit or severely limit production, allow production for a short period only, or prescribe alternative materials and processes to meet emission limitations. The process required to modify the permit to allow for greater production may take as long as 18 months. Underestimating permit acquisition time can delay product launch or extend the product development cycle time.

It is difficult to fully anticipate all the U.S. and international environmental initiatives and regulatory requirements that will arise in the coming years. However, trends across many countries are consistent. One trend is the increasing number and complexity of environmental regulations. Another is the targeting of certain heavy metals for elimination from automobiles and other consumer products.

Regulatory and customer requirements must be considered and balanced with producer constraints. Accordingly, a responsive EHS&R management system is key to positioning environmental performance as a competitive advantage.

The Cost of Using Regulated Substances

The use of regulated substances also imposes cost burdens, including:

- Labeling
- Increased operating and maintenance expenses
- Capital cost of controls
- Personal protective equipment
- Screening and testing of materials
- Occupational health costs

When components are imported, significant costs can also be added by *material* restrictions on imports, as well as by required inspections and documentation. For example, tooling purchased overseas may contain substances that are restricted in the United States. In one case, a manufacturer used lead-based paint on tooling and equipment. It was necessary to divert the tooling for painting to meet U.S. standards.

It is equally important to understand the regulations of countries to which products are being exported. Limitations on the use of heavy metal colorants or stabilizers in plastics may prohibit import of after-market components and cause delays in repairs and service, with consequent customer dissatisfaction. This can occur where the allowable level of a regulated substance is higher for the aggregate product than for a component. For example, the amount of cadmium in a vehicle may be capped at 0.001 percent, but it may be capped at 0.0003 percent in a component.

In the case of exports, there may also be interpretational differences depending on which of several departments (including homologation, ministry of the environment, or customs) enforces the regulations. Differences in interpretation could lead to variations in enforcement. These possibilities need to be considered in developing the LCM approach.

The Cost of Lost Sales

Failure to fully consider EHS&R costs may also affect sales. For example, marks of origin or labels may create negative customer perceptions. Specifically, a regulated substance label that is mandated by law to be prominently displayed on the product may impede sales. (See Figure 27.1, which illustrates a cadmium label. This label must be sized to be clearly visible to the customer.)

The presence of regulated substances may also limit the ability to recycle the product and may subject the manufacturer to end-of-life "product take-back" requirements in some countries, thus increasing producer costs.

Additionally, failure to consider recycled materials in product design and sourcing decisions may create a cost disadvantage vis-à-vis competitors that use favorably priced alternatives to virgin materials.

Lastly, customers are beginning to ask about the percentage of recycled material in products. A systematic approach to collecting and providing this information serves both the customer and the producer.

LCM Model

The object of an LCM model is to expose formerly hidden EHS&R costs, and to tie them to specific products and components using an activity-based costing (ABC) methodology. Because 80 percent of potential cost-saving opportunities can be realized during the design phase,[4] the model emphasizes assisting the decision process for future products. In the case of Chrysler, of course, this involves the development of future vehicles.

The LCM model is cost-focused and includes four integrated elements: environment, health, safety, and recycling. Examples of environmental costs include expenses for hazardous material disposal and add-on pollution controls, as well as requirements relating to environmental labels and permits. Health costs include medical monitoring and personal protective equipment costs. Safety

---

WARNING

Contains Cadmium
Cancer Hazard
Avoid Creating Dust
Can Cause Lung and Kidney Disease

Figure 27.1   Cadmium Label

costs include personal protective equipment and ergonomic devices. Recycling includes dismantling costs and salvage value of recovered materials. (The aim here is to create value and profits that encourage further development of an independent recycling infrastructure and associated commodity markets.)

Supplier Involvement

An LCM approach must involve suppliers in order to be effective. This is especially true in the case of manufacturers or other organizations that are highly dependent on their suppliers, and that require supplier participation at the beginning of the decision-making process. With highly outsourced original equipment manufacturers (OEMs), supplier participation is critical to the success of any LCM program. The need for early supplier involvement extends to participation in the development of the raw material strategy that encompasses regulated substance control, material selection and rationalization, and design for recyclability/separability.

The bounds of early supplier involvement have expanded to include product stewardship. In the global marketplace, product stewardship is enhanced through strategic supply base management. Procurement considerations must address the global concerns of EHS&R in concert with traditional quality, performance, cost, and timing objectives. Among the key procurement considerations are reducing or eliminating regulated substances, worldwide material selection and rationalization, and designing for recyclability, separability, and disassembly.

Model Bounds and Scope

Using the LCM model, product stewardship is extended through the value chain tier by tier. "A-B" comparisons are made, using only relevant costs. For instance, if a supplier is able to offer two different designs produced at a given location—such as a lamp assembly with two choices of actuator switch—the LCM model does not enumerate transportation costs. Although transportation has environmental implications from the perspective of total resource consumption, in an A-B comparison, this cost would drop out because it is the same for each alternative. Essentially, only the EHS&R factors that differ for the two choices being examined are evaluated.

Figure 27.2 illustrates the sphere of influence with respect to EHS&R in a value chain segment. The scope extends from acquisition through final disposal and considers a broad range of performance measures to prevent "suboptimizing," or exchanging one undesirable effect for another. Thus, issues such as personal safety are considered concurrently with environmental impacts and other performance measures. For example, in evaluating a com-

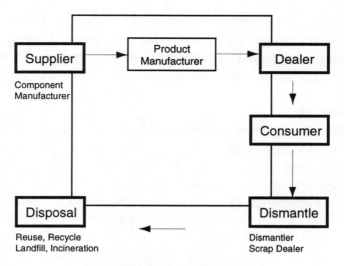

Figure 27.2   Sphere of Influence

posite shift-lever assembly versus a heavier steel alternative with higher recyclability, the outlay for an ergonomic lifting device is viewed as a relevant incremental cost. Similarly, the cost of personal protective equipment (such as dust masks and exhaust hoods) would be relevant where a mechanical fastening system is compared to a welding process.

LCM focuses predominantly on those portions of the product life cycle or value chain in which EHS&R issues can be influenced:

- *Suppliers:* Through the supplier, the OEM can influence material selection, as well as design for recycling, separability, and disassembly.
- *Dealers:* With information about materials available through dealer programs and related material recovery streams, the manufacturer can design products that incorporate competitively priced recycled materials and reusable or remanufactured components.
- *Consumers:* Considering the consumer-use aspect of the life cycle can result in the design of longer-lived products.
- *Dismantling and disposal process:* By considering designs that permit profitable recovery of materials or components during the dismantling and disposal portions of the life cycle, materials can be diverted from landfills. In addition, by eliminating substances of concern (such as mercury or lead) at the design stage, the manufacturer can reduce end-of-life dismantling and disposal costs—while also reducing potential liability from improper disposal or accidental release by third parties.

Moving Ahead with ISO 14000

LCM Model Data Types

Understanding the four elements involved in the LCM model makes clear why certain data are being collected and the potential applications of these data to decision making.

Recycling

Recycling data for the automotive industry are collected from competitive "tear down" reports and supplier material disclosure reports. The U.S. Council for Automotive Research (USCAR) developed the Regulated Substance and Recyclability Certification (RSRC) reporting approach to reduce the substance reporting burden for suppliers. This approach enables early identification of substances of concern, provides a baseline measure of recyclability, and suggests areas for improvement. Data are collected under the following categories:

- Recyclability/Disassembly Detail
- Material Contents of Detail Components
- Substances of Concern

At Chrysler, information regarding recyclability is recorded at each level of assembly during the manufacturing process. Incorporating USCAR's RSRC ratings for recyclability and disassembly at multiple levels permits the isolation of components that adversely affect recyclability or disassembly. In addition, theoretical material recyclabilities (as well as recyclability for purposes of the Federal Trade Commission definition) can be calculated.

Material content data are collected by part number. Pre-consumer and post-consumer recycled contents are tabulated, and materials containing substances of concern are flagged.

"Substances of concern" data are selected from a list based on the main worldwide markets in which Chrysler produces or sells its product.

Environmental

Environmental costs are divided into control, disposal, and administrative costs. Based on materials disclosed for production and nonproduction parts, a forecast of reportable chemicals is compared against the current SARA database, and against reporting and permit thresholds, in order to determine the allocation of control costs to specific components (such as energy, depreciation, occupancy costs, and monitoring). These comparisons suggest priorities for material elimination or reduction.

Through the selection of appropriate cost drivers, documentation costs are assessed against specific parts and OEM processes that cause these costs to occur. For example, a grinding process (which is a potential hazardous air pollutant source) may require a permit specific to the operation. The grinding process may also lead to protection costs or medical monitoring.

Health

Substances that require engineered controls for environmental reasons may also require medical monitoring and personal protection for individuals. For example, foundries are required to implement add-on pollution controls, as well as employee protection and medical monitoring (including periodic lung function, hearing, and X-ray tests). By identifying particular assembly or manufacturing processes (such as brazing, gluing, or sonic welding) that give rise to health concerns early in the product concept stage, appropriate controls and protection can be engineered from the start. In addition, more time will be available to investigate reformulation of products to eliminate or reduce the need for controls.

Safety

Safety costs may include items such as guards, shields, personal protective equipment, and ergonomic lifting devices. Insurance data may be used as a proxy to rank the safety risks of certain processes.

Incorporating DFE, LCI, and LCA

Life-cycle management incorporates aspects of approaches such as design for environment (DFE),[5] life-cycle inventory (LCI), and life-cycle assessment (LCA). However, LCM differs from these approaches in some important ways.

LCM focuses on comparative evaluations of key life-cycle segments. It considers environment, health, safety, recycling, and traditional product metrics as part of an existing business decision-making process. By contrast, LCA focuses predominantly on material and energy balances over the product life cycle. With LCA, fewer variables are analyzed, but, in some cases, the depth of study may be greater.

LCA is one of many tools that can be used to support the LCM decision process. But, because LCA does not consider health and safety factors, using LCA alone to decide between, for instance, an aluminum and a steel car body may result in a suboptimal solution that ignores an occupational health risk. LCM considers the additional toxic respiratory effect of aluminum dust that may be generated during metal finishing of the vehicle skin.

Similarly, LCI is a useful recording tool that identifies the regulated materials contained in a product. LCI is effective for establishing a baseline against which to measure progress.[6] LCM incorporates aspects of LCI, but also goes beyond this to consider "design for recycling." Through recycling, the material chain of events may be shortened, conserving energy, materials, and cost, while reducing waste and protecting workers and the community.

Implementing LCM at Chrysler

At Chrysler, many design and production decisions are made by "platform teams" (i.e., groups working on new vehicle platforms). Interdisciplinary "Green Car Teams" serve as a coordinating structure to disseminate EHS&R information to the platform teams, recommend vehicle targets, establish program milestone dates, and measure performance toward targets.

Green Car Team participants come from many departments within Chrysler, including Finance, Procurement and Supply, Recycling Administration, Product Strategy and Regulatory Affairs, Engineering (Materials, Vehicles, Systems, and Fasteners), Product Planning, Program Management, Serviceability Planning, and the Design Office, among others.

The Green Car Teams obtain much of their information from material and component suppliers, who collect and electronically report information on material content, substances of concern, and disassembly and separability ratings. Suppliers may also suggest design improvements and applications that can incorporate recycled materials.

Improving Coordination and Communication

In order to address emerging EHS&R issues, the Green Car Teams need a tool to improve coordination among the various groups. LCM serves as an integrating tool and provides this communication bridge. The LCM model allows for collection and dissemination of organizational learning by populating a database with information that decision makers formerly had difficulty accessing and sharing.

Before LCM, communication among the different departments within Chrysler was focused on isolated issues. (Some of the pre-LCM communication channels are illustrated in Figure 27.3.) As a result, not all EHS&R aspects were included in the overall design and engineering process.

With LCM, a single focus is developed that brings all parties together to discuss the entire product from all perspectives. All issues are considered concurrently, as illustrated by Figure 27.4.

Providing EHS&R information to the platform teams through the LCM model allows the teams to incorporate EHS&R considerations as part of the decision process. As a result, new "design for" initiatives (such as design for recycling, separability, or disassembly) can readily be incorporated into the existing engineering and decision-making processes.

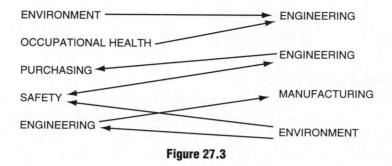

Figure 27.3

Procurement and Product Stewardship

For highly outsourced OEMs, successful product stewardship is grounded in experience, knowledge, and awareness of the supply base. An organization's . procurement operations department can support product stewardship not only through the structure of the organization and the supply base, but also in:

- Identifying cost reduction and value-adding opportunities worldwide.
- Providing data about material availability, supplier performance, and cost to the organization.
- Contributing to emerging technology access through supplier selection strategies.
- Participating in concurrent engineering teams.
- Supporting supplier education through internal and external communication media, conferences, and joint venture training programs with academia.
- Measuring, rating, and rewarding suppliers (through programs such as Chrysler's Supplier Cost Reduction Effort, or "S.C.O.R.E.").
- Reducing the number and types of materials procured (for instance, procuring fewer plastic families or formulations or fewer fastener types) and taking other "complexity reduction" initiatives.

Figure 27.4

Moving Ahead with ISO 14000

An example of how the sourcing process at Chrysler supports environmental initiatives is the company's treatment of regulated and restricted substance reporting. For current suppliers of tooling and equipment, bid packages must contain disclosure of substances of concern to be considered complete. By eliminating substances of concern, a supplier may receive S.C.O.R.E. credit for making a product or component recyclable.

Ensuring Cost-Effective Sourcing Decisions

An emphasis on the total value chain is necessary to assure the most cost-effective sourcing decisions. Secondary cost factors (i.e., factors beyond investment, piece price, and transportation) must also be considered. These indirect costs, coupled with the primary costs, collectively determine total sourcing costs.

To improve the accuracy of overhead cost measurements and to facilitate cost improvement efforts, Chrysler has been using an activity-based costing (ABC) approach and encouraging the same approach among its suppliers. The ABC approach is being extended to managing environmental, health, and safety issues—cost being the common measure to compare alternative designs and to integrate these factors into a dynamic decision process.

Educating Suppliers

Generally, learning about these issues is the supplier's responsibility. But, through OEM training consortia, academic partners are providing training tailored for both OEM and supplier employees.

Two specific courses that have been developed for suppliers to the automotive industry are design for recycling and regulated substance and recyclability certification (RSRC). RSRC is the latest in a series of initiatives under the recycling umbrella of USCAR. For production part suppliers, RSRC is a milestone in the master timing schedule.

Case Study: Designing an Underhood Lamp Assembly

The apparent cost of a material or component—as calculated on the basis of such customary factors as transportation, packaging, and tooling costs—may not represent the true cost to the corporation. Environmental, health, and safety compliance may add significant costs that change the product decision. Chrysler's experience with designing a "convenience lighting package" illustrates how a cost-focused LCM model can bring these hidden costs to light, and thereby influence decision making.

Background: Increasing Restrictions on Mercury

Several states (including Michigan, Minnesota, and Wisconsin) have enacted or proposed legislation restricting the use, and banning landfill and incineration disposal, of mercury. The Great Lakes states have taken the initiative in this area because of mercury's tendency to bioaccumulate in the food chain.

As of August 1995, vehicles became subject to the mercury landfill statute in Minnesota, which states that "[a] person may not crush a motor vehicle unless the person has first made a good faith effort to remove all of the mercury switches in the motor vehicle." (Minnesota Statutes 1994, Section 116.92, subdivision 4.) With regard to this legislation, the Minnesota Pollution Control Agency has suggested, "If manufacturers had to bear the cost of recovering and recycling mercury switches from their automobiles, they might switch to other alternative lighting."[7] In addition, Minnesota has instituted a program to pay dismantlers for each mercury switch removed prior to shredding.

The Michigan Mercury Pollution Prevention Task Force has encouraged the state to "urge U.S. Congress to enact legislation requiring labeling of all products containing intentionally introduced mercury, but enact legislation now providing for such labeling to take effect in 1998 if Congress does not act." In addition, this task force has solicited suggestions from Ford, GM, and Chrysler on voluntary removal, disposal, and recycling of mercury-containing switches.

On the international front, a ban on mercury for vehicles sold in Sweden has been announced.

Impact on Manufacturers

These restrictions and bans on mercury create potential costs for manufacturers, including:

- Costs of identifying products that contain mercury, and accompanying them with instructions for removal and/or disassembly.
- Increased disposal costs resulting from landfill and incineration bans.
- Increased service complexity due to label and content requirements that vary from state to state and from country to country.
- Increased reporting complexity (including mercury tracking and analysis reports).
- Potential permit requirements for mercury use in nonessential applications.
- Potential hazardous material liability for mercury.

LCM Analysis

Although mercury switches were being phased out when Chrysler was making its decision on the underhood lamp assembly, they continued to be specified in carryover assemblies for reliability reasons. Preliminary information indicated that non-mercury substitutes would result in a "piece price" penalty. Figure 27.5 shows how the application of the LCM model (which accounts for EHS&R overhead costs) alters this conclusion.

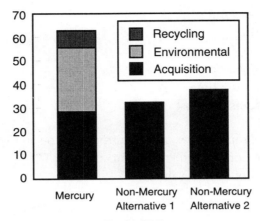

Figure 27.5

Engineers for various vehicle platforms created a team to evaluate a number of different underhood lamp assembly designs. By adopting a design that did not require mercury, Chrysler could avoid the cost of environmental labels, as well as potential disposal costs. Labeling costs would include labor for installation and vehicle build-order software changes, as well as the actual cost of the labels themselves.

In this case, Chrysler also collected information on the cost of maintaining a separate, non-mercury-containing service component, although these data are not reflected in the figure. The label data alone provided sufficient support for a non-mercury switch in this application.

Recyclability calculations were also completed on the lamp assemblies. Based on material content, component recyclability improved from 62 percent (mercury) to 75 percent (non-mercury).

Case Study: Selecting Ethylene Glycol for Use in Antifreeze

Chrysler also used an LCM approach to choose between ethylene glycol (EG) and propylene glycol (PG) for factory fill coolants in vehicles. A team that included personnel from environmental, occupational health and safety, engineering (vehicle, powertrain, aero-thermal, and material), and purchasing, as well as supplier representatives, was formed to identify issues and concerns.

Factors considered in the decision included:

- Regulatory direction
- Customer wants
- Product warranty, liability, and performance
- Concomitant system modifications
- Toxicological effects

- Sources of exposure
- Exposure risk
- Recycling
- Environmental burden
- Implementation time
- Product acquisition cost

Supporting information was obtained from the Poison Control Center, the Centers for Disease Control and Prevention, and EPA. The following alternative antifreeze compositions were evaluated:

Virgin EG
Remanufactured EG
Virgin PG
Remanufactured PG

Regulations

Both PG- and EG-antifreeze are defined as hazardous wastes if they contain more than 5 ppm lead contamination from use.

EG-antifreeze meets Resource Conservation and Recovery Act Section 6002 criteria for materials that can be made with recovered materials:

- Availability
- Contribution to solid waste reduction
- Technical and economic feasibility
- Multiple markets for recovered material

Customer Wants

Customers were requesting longer service intervals and environmentally preferable products. Customers were asking for a "safe" antifreeze.

Product Warranty and Liability

Mixing PG- and EG-antifreeze may destabilize corrosion inhibitors. In addition, if PG-antifreeze is used in engines not designed for it, the result may be localized engine hot spots, seal failure, insufficient boiling point elevation, or freezing point depression.

System Modifications Needed

To achieve the same thermal transfer performance with PG-antifreeze, the specific vehicle evaluated would have required a radiator four inches wider and one inch higher, with a resultant eight-pound weight penalty and concomitant component design changes.

Toxicology, Exposure, and Risk

PG has a lower toxicity than EG, but both are toxic. The issue is not toxicity alone, but more one of exposure. Using a long-life additive package increases the fluid change interval and, therefore, reduces the opportunity for exposure. The oral LD50 levels for propylene glycol and ethylene glycol are 20–30 g/kg and 1.6–15 g/kg, respectively.[8]

Recycling

An established recycling infrastructure exists for EG. Remanufactured EG from polyester production is available. Using recovered or recycled EG reduces the amount produced and discourages indiscriminate disposal, thus reducing the probability of exposure. The market for remanufactured EG has already influenced waste oil collection outlets to offer similar services for used EG. Mixing PG- and EG-antifreeze impedes recycling and is not desirable.

Environmental Burden

EG biodegrades rapidly in aerobic, anaerobic, and aqueous systems.[9] By specifying remanufactured EG in factory fill fluids, the market for used EG is strengthened, reducing waste and further encouraging recycling. Franklin Associates has determined that EG-antifreeze is preferable to PG-antifreeze.[10] Their study found that production of PG-antifreeze used more energy, generated a greater amount of solid waste, and created more atmospheric pollution.

Time Needed to Implement

Because of required modifications to the engine, cooling system, and vehicle designs, conversion to PG-antifreeze would take longer to implement.

Decision Made

Long-life additive ethylene glycol coolant was selected, using recovered EG. This remanufactured EG coolant provides the longer service interval requested by customers. In addition, it provides a price and supply stabilizing influence because a substitute product (remanufactured EG versus virgin EG) is now approved by the OEM. The reduced frequency of coolant change, and the market for recovered EG, reduce the probability of spill and improper disposal, which could lead to accidental exposure in humans or animals. The extra cost of concomitant vehicle design modifications required for PG-antifreeze further supported the decision to use antifreeze made from remanufactured EG.

Figure 27.6 summarizes some of the variables in the ethylene glycol antifreeze decision. It should be noted that when the decision was made to use EG-antifreeze produced from remanufactured ethylene glycol, LCA analysis data were not yet available.

	VIRGIN EG	REMANUFACTURED EG	VIRGIN PG	REMANUFACTURED PG
REGULATION		meets RCRA 6002		
WARRANTY			higher risk	higher risk
TOXICITY	low	low	low	low
EXPOSURE	low risk	low risk	low risk	low risk
RECYCLING INFRASTRUCTURE		YES		
ENVIRONMENT BURDEN (LCA)	low (2)	lowest (1)	highest (4)	medium (3)
TIME TO IMPLEMENT	0-1 yr	1-1.5 yr	3 yr	3 yr
CUSTOMER PERCEPTION			"Safer"	"Safer"

Figure 27.6   Antifreeze Formulation Decision Variables

Case Study: Using Remanufactured Rubber

Chrysler also used LCM analysis in deciding to replace the plastic splash shields and sound deadeners in the fender area of its cars with a single component produced from remanufactured rubber.

An LCM review revealed the presence of regulated substances in the sound deadener material. Other points of contrast between the two alternatives studied (plastic with sound deadener versus remanufactured rubber) include:

Plastic with Sound Deadener

- Three components needed, plus sound deadener
- Two employees needed to install splash shields
- Worker protection needed for sound deadener application ("end-of-pipe" controls)
- No use of recycled materials

Remanufactured Rubber

- Single component required
- Reduced installation labor
- Elimination of regulated substances and the need for associated protection
- Use of post-consumer recycled material

LCM Analysis

Although the splash shield produced from remanufactured rubber had a higher acquisition cost, there was a net system savings (in parts, sound suppressant, personnel protection, and installation labor) of $0.25 per vehicle.

Summary

The LCM decision model uses input from many sources to provide information for better-informed business decisions from the perspective of design, engineering, manufacturing, and procurement. The model is an engineering-based system of evaluation (based on concepts such as "design for recycling" and "design for disassembly"). It provides a systematic, objective framework for assessing either components or entire products and for apportioning EHS&R targets. This approach allows a company to enhance profitability while increasing protection of the environment, workers, and the community.

LCM analysis provides baseline data, identifies environmental improvement opportunities, and allows cross-functional ideas and industry "best practices" to be more easily shared. The use of relevant costs and comparative analyses provides valuable information on which to base business decisions. The LCM approach reduces the burden of data collection and analysis and shortens the decision-making process, as compared with life cycle assessment. By tying EHS&R costs to the activities or products that generate them, costs that do not add value can be identified and eliminated.

As illustrated throughout this article, information provided by the LCM model can make clear the relative merits of competing design proposals. Once the EHS&R issues have been translated into familiar business terms, they can more easily be incorporated into a company's business plan. Preventing pollution with LCM does pay, and it can provide large returns.

Notes

1. J.R. Carter and R. Narasimhan, "Purchasing in the International Marketplace: Implications for Operations," *Journal of Purchasing and Materials Management*, Vol. 26 (Summer 1990), pp. 2–11.

2. R.M. Monczka and R.J. Trent, "Global Sourcing: A Development Approach," *International Journal of Purchasing and Material Management*, Vol. 27 (Spring 1991), pp. 2–8.

3. Chrysler has adopted the LCM approach, rather than design for environment, life-cycle inventory, or life-cycle assessment, for a number of reasons well documented elsewhere. See F.R. Field III, J.A. Isaacs, and J.P. Clark, "Life-Cycle Analysis of Automobiles: A Critical Review of Methodologies," *The Journal of Minerals, Metals and Materials Society*, Vol. 46, No. 6 (April 1994), pp. 12–16; R.J. Kainz, W.C. Moeser, and M.S. Simpson, "Life Cycle Management: A Solution for Decision Making," *Automotive Engineering*, Vol. 103, No. 2 (February 1995), p. 107; K. Shapiro and A.L. White, "Life Cycle Assessment, a Second Opinion," *Environmental Science & Technology*, Vol. 27, No. 6 (1993), p. 1016.

4. R.J. Kainz, W.C. Moeser, and M.S. Simpson, "Life Cycle Management: A Solution for Decision Making," *Automotive Engineering*, Vol. 103, No. 2 (February 1995), p. 107.

5. See K. Saur, M. Schuckert, H. Beddies, and P. Eyerer, "Foundations for Life Cycle Analysis of Automotive Structures—The Potential of Steel, Aluminum and Composites," Technical Paper 951844, SAE (Society of Automotive Engineers) International, Warrendale, Pennsylvania, Total Life Cycle Conference (October 1995).

6. B.W. Vigon, et al., *Life Cycle Assessment: Inventory Guidelines and Principles*, EPA/600/R-92/245 (February 1993), p. 41.

7. M. Rust, M. Rafferty, and J. Ikeda, *Automobile Shredder Residue Report* (Minnesota Pollution Control Agency, St. Paul, June 1995), p. 7.

8. Correspondence with Arco Chemical Company.

9. Comments of the Chemical Manufacturers Association Ethylene Glycol Panel on the Draft Technical Report for Ethylene Glycol/Propylene Glycol (December 29, 1993), p. 19.

10. Franklin Associates, Ltd., *Life Cycle Assessment of Ethylene Glycol and Propylene Glycol Based Antifreeze Final Report* (1994).

Robert J. Kainz, Monica H. Prokopyshen, and **Susan A. Yester** are with Chrysler Corporation.

Exhibits 2 through 6 are reprinted with permission from SAE Technical Paper 960407 © 1996, Society of Automotive Engineers, Inc.

Index

Competition:
    markets and, 9–11
    sustainable development and, 185–191
Compliance:
    business management, industry case
        studies, 88
    sustainable development and, 190
Comprehensive Environmental Response,
    Compensation, and Liability Act
    (CERCLA), 62
Confidentiality, certification/registration
    process, 139–140
Corporate culture, implementation, busi-
    ness implications of, 97–99
Corporate reporting, 177–182
    Coalition for Environmentally Respon-
        sible Economies (CERES), 178–179
    overview, 177–178, 181–182
    Public Environmental Reporting Initia-
        tive (PERI), 179–180
    United Nations Environmental Pro-
        gramme (UNEP), 180–181
Cost/benefit analysis, environmental,
    health, and safety (EH&S) systems,
    52–55
Cost-effectiveness, registration barriers,
    119–121
Costs:
    agency costs, registration barriers, 121
    cost allocation, environmental
        accounting, 205–208
    environmental accounting, 198–200
    environmental costs identification,
        204–205
    implementation, business implications
        of, 108–109
    life-cycle management, 280–282, 289
    sustainable development and, 190–191
Czech Republic, ISO 14000 standards, 7

Decision-making:
    certification/registration process,
        128–130
    design for environment (DFE),
        211–225. See also Design for Envi-
        ronment (DFE)
    environmental accounting, 195–198
    life-cycle management, 289
Design for Environment (DFE), 211–225
    AT&T example, 227–238
    current status, 216–217
    design tools, 217–220

future needs, 222–224
industrial ecology, 213–214
life-cycle management and, 286–287
overview, 211
product development cycle, 214–216
product life cycle, 212–213
tool taxonomy, 221–222
trends in, 220–221
Developing countries, ISO 14000 stan-
    dards, 3, 19
Document and data control, pollution
    prevention practices, ISO 9000/ISO
    14000 synergy, 68–69

Eco-Management and Audit Scheme
    (EMAS):
    ISO 14001 environmental management
        systems (EMS) and, 3, 6–7, 82
    pollution prevention practices, 71
Efficiency, business management, indus-
    try case studies, 88–89
Enforcement, voluntary standards and,
    17–18
Environmental accounting, 193–210
    activities, 200–209
        behavior definition, 201–202
        capability enhancement, 203–204
        cost allocation, 205–208
        diagnostics, 202–203
        environmental costs identification,
            204–205
        incentives, 208–209
    cost management, 198–200
    decision-making, 195–198
    overview, 193–195, 209–210
Environmental Auditors Registration
    Association (EARA), 154–155
Environmental audit training, 153–162
    ISO 14012 guidelines, 155
    overview, 153–155, 161–162
    potential effects, 157–161
    U.S. implementation, 155–157
Environmental corporate reporting. See
    Corporate reporting
Environmental, health, and safety (EH&S)
    systems, 47–59
    assessment process, 51
    assessment protocol, 48–51
        ISO 14001 specifications, 49–50
        OSHA Voluntary Protection Program
            (VPP), 50–51
        U.S. Department of Justice, 50

Safety, life-cycle management, 286
Site assessment, problems with, 61–62
Slovakia, ISO 14000 standards, 7
Small and medium-sized enterprises
    (SMEs), ISO 14000 standards, 25–26
Software. *See* Environmental management
    information system (EMIS)
South America, ISO 14000 standards, 4–5
Stakeholders:
    certification/registration process, 134
    EMIS, 164–165
    pollution prevention practices, 75–76
Strategic decision-making. *See* Decision-
    making
Superfund Amendments and Reauthoriza-
    tion Act (SARA), 68, 74, 149
Suppliers:
    ISO 14000 standards, 24
    life-cycle management, 283, 289
    Survey response analysis, life-cycle
        assessment (LCA), 242–246
    Sustainable development, competition
        and, 185–191

Taiwan, implementation, 96
Technological innovation, business man-
    agement, 79–84
Total Quality Environmental Manage-
    ment (TQEM) approach:
    design for environment (DFE), AT&T
        example, 228
    environmental performance evalua-
        tion, 172–174
    implementation, 111, 112–114. *See also*
        Implementation
Trade. *See* Markets
Trade barriers, registration barriers,
    121–122

Training:
    environmental audit training, 153–154
    ISO 9000/ISO 14000 linkage, 69, 150
Turkey, ISO 14000 standards, 7

United Kingdom:
    ISO 14000 standards, 6
    pollution prevention practices, 70
United Nations Environmental Pro-
    gramme (UNEP), corporate report-
    ing, 180–181
United States:
    certification/registration process,
        134–140
    environmental audits, 155–157
    environmental management standards,
        15–17
    ISO 14000 standards, 4
    technological investment, 80–81
U.S. Department of Energy (DOE), imple-
    mentation, 96
U.S. Department of Justice:
    environmental, health, and safety
        (EH&S) system assessment, 50
    implementation, 96
U.S. Department of Transportation (DOT),
    responsibilities of, 107
U.S. Environmental Protection Agency
    (EPA):
    beyond compliance concept, 16, 17
    enforcement and, 17, 18
    implementation, 96, 111
    NSF International and, 29–30, 75–76
    responsibilities of, 107

Voluntary standards:
    enforcement and, 17–18
    global perspective, 21–23